THE POEMS OF SIR THOMAS WIAT

THE POEMS OF SIR THOMAS WIAT

EDITED
FROM THE MSS. AND EARLY EDITIONS
BY

A. K. FOXWELL, M.A. (Lond.)

VOL. II
INTRODUCTION
COMMENTARY
APPENDIXES

NEW YORK
RUSSELL & RUSSELL · INC
1964

FIRST PUBLISHED IN 1913
REISSUED, 1964, BY RUSSELL & RUSSELL, INC.
IN AN EDITION LIMITED TO 500 SETS
L. C. CATALOG CARD NO: 64—18608

PRINTED IN THE UNITED STATES OF AMERICA

ERRATA

Vol. II

INTRODUCTION—

p. xiv, l. 26, omit words *and again* after foo.
,, l. 27, read *knows* instead of knowes.
p. xix, l. 6, read *though* instead of thought.
,, ll. 6–7, read commas after *triumph* and *better*.
p. xxii, l. 11, read *gayn* (Harl. MS. and T.) instead of *game* (Britwell text).

COMMENTARY—

p. 28, l. 25, read *dentro* instead of deutro.
p. 31, ll. 27–28, read *Je ne souhaite* instead of Te ne sonharte.
p. 34, last line, read *mon* instead of more.
p. 41, l. 2, read *ciascun* instead of ciaseun.
p. 44, l. 2, read *cf.* after found, and omit "see Gavin Douglas, l. 8.
p. 46, l. 6, read *Sannazaro* instead of Sannozaro.
p. 47, l. 25, read *ritrova* instead of retrova.
p. 50, l. 27, read *Off Cartage* instead of Of Catage.
p. 72, last line but one, read *Debat* instead of Debut.
p. 101, l. 20, read *Favori* instead of Favovi.
p. 119, last line but two, read *eguale* instead of equalæ.
p. 125, l. 1, read *pianger* instead of pranger.
p. 171, footnote, read *Venus* instead of Venice.
p. 214, read *Firenze* instead of Finenze.

Poems of Sir Thomas Wiat.

INTRODUCTION

Wiat's position as a poet has not yet been clearly defined. The fact that he has so long remained an isolated figure in literature partly accounts for this want; for he has ever been considered as one who, dissociated from the past, struggled to reform verse without definite knowledge of verse-structure. His connection with Surrey, the younger poet, has served still further to obscure his work; because it has never been sufficiently emphasized that Surrey practically began where Wiat left off,[1] and was able to proceed along a path cleared by Wiat from the literary debris of over a century.

The intention of this Introduction is first to set Wiat in relation with continental writers, and secondly to gather up some of the strands of thought running through his poems. First, a clearer vision of Wiat's aim and work is obtained by regarding him in his relations with the continental writers of his day, instead of viewing him as an isolated English poet, for in this respect he was fifty years before his time. Scholar and diplomatist, his life was either spent amongst books, with great men of the past, or in the stirring times of his day in the company of the most eminent men in Europe. This dual element in Wiat's life helps to the understanding of his poetry. His intellectual side preferred thoughtful retirement and a certain amount of ease, with the recreations of lute-playing and versifying; whereas his

[1] Late criticism has, however, pronounced Wiat to be the pioneer. Cf. Cambridge, *History of Literature*, Vol. III., and Courthope, *History of English Poetry*, Vol. II.

interest in life and humanity, coupled with a keen observation and brilliant wit, made him at home at Courts, where his linguistic gifts allowed him to gain a deeper insight into the literary life of the countries he visited than would have been possible otherwise.

Fortune favoured him in the early years of his diplomatic career by opening out opportunities which brought him into direct contact with the leaders of Europe. Visiting France with Cheney, he was chosen to carry, and deliver personally, messages from Henry VIII to the French King. He could speak French with ease, and "had as much wit to mark and remember everything as any young man in Europe." [1] At Rome with Russell the following year, he was chosen to carry the letters to the Venetian Council on account of a slight accident to the ambassador which prevented him from performing the duty.

The year 1527 marked a serious political crisis in Italy; great diplomatists met at Rome and in Venice. Wiat actually came into contact with Ghiberti, papal datary and patron of letters, and Berni his secretary, who is chiefly remembered for his easy letters in terza-rima, marked by a certain fluency and freedom of style rarely found in this measure. At Venice, amongst other great statesmen, he met Navagero and Baldassaro Castiglione, the two men whose influence was most felt among other nations. At this time Castiglione's famous book, *Il Cortegiano*, had been in manuscript for some years, and was published a few months later at Venice. *Il Cortegiano* immediately became the text-book for courtly manners at every Court in Europe, and was responsible, to a great extent, for the general ideas concerning Neoplatonism, which until then had been reserved for the scholar and thinker.

The book is written with great charm of style, and, in imitation of the Platonic discourses, consists of conversations

[1] State Papers. Sir Thomas Cheyne to Wolsey. May 1, 1526.

carried on by the men and women of the Court of Urbino. The characters are well-known personages; Bembo, for example, as the author of the *Asolani*,[1] utters the discourse on Platonic love. The whole book is a reflection of Plato's thought, and Ficino's Commentary on Plato; and in dealing with love the author sometimes translates Petrarch, as, for example, the passages which describe the power of the lover's glance.

Wiat appears to have derived many hints from *Il Cortegiano* for his translations from Petrarch and for his more ambitious Court poems. His choice of several sonnets on the power of the eye is traceable to this work. For example: "The courtier shows by signs rather than wordes, and the Iyes are the trusty messengers of the heart"; again, "the Iye is a guide to love"; and the mediæval idea of a glance from the eye wounding the heart of the lover reappears in *Il Cortegiano*, and is re-echoed by Wiat in the song "So unwarely." The curious epistolary poem "Greting to you both" is derived from a passage from the same book. The perfect courtier is prohibited from "fayning" or using "jestes." One of the original sonnets begins "To rayle or jest ye know I use it not"; and in his last fragment, the "Song of Iopas," there is considerable resemblance to a passage in *Il Cortegiano* concerning the heavens.

The interest in the book was strengthened for Wiat by his acquaintance with the author. One of the most beautiful characters of that time, he was to Italy what Garcilasso de la Vega was to Spain and Sir Philip Sidney to England. Diplomatist, courtier and idealist, he actually bore out in his own life the ideals he expressed in the *Courtier*.[2] The personality, as well as the work of the author, had a great

[1] The *Asolani*, a little treatise on love in prose and verse, addressed to Lucrezia Borgia, attained very great fame; every person of culture was supposed to have read it.

[2] His discourses on women have special force. His own married life was ideally happy.

effect upon Wiat. Castiglione's ideals corresponded with Wiat's own view of life, and the platonism which is expressed later in the poem "Lo what it is to love" was quickened by his knowledge of the *Courtier*, and developed as he came into contact with the eager spirits of the literary circle at Lyons in later years.

Further, *Il Cortegiano* kept Wiat in actual contact with Italian contemporary thought, for though some of the personages were dead when the book appeared, others, like Bembo, lived for many years later. I emphasize this point, because Wiat's poetry shows [1] that he started with the translation of Petrarch side by side with his following of Chaucer; he continued with the poets of the fifteenth century, and thence to contemporary Italian writers, such as Sannazaro, Ariosto, Alamanni and finally Aretino. The *Courtier* seems to provide a background of ideas throughout his work.

Another personality probably went far to quicken Wiat's ambition for English verse. Navagero, poet and writer of the history of Venice, whose descriptions of the countries he passed through are of inestimable value to-day, was a great patron of letters, and encouraged foreign poets to write in the Italian hendecasyllable. He undoubtedly had some influence on M. Sève, the great Lyons poet, and in 1526 he had encouraged Boscán, the Spanish poet, to substitute the Italian hendecasyllable for the short Castilian measures. This was a few months before Wiat met him at Venice.

Boscán's letter to the Duchess of Soma serves as a prologue to the second book of Boscán's poems, published in 1543, after his death. In it occurs the following famous passage—

"Porque estando un dia en Granada con el Navagero (al qual por haber sido tan celebrado en nuestros días, he querido aquí nombralle á vuestra Señoría), tratando con él en cosas

[1] See lines of poems as they occur in the E. MS., end of Vol. I.

de ingenio y de letras, y especialmente en las variedades de muchas lenguas me dixo por qué no probaba en lengua castellana sonetos y otras artes de trovas usadas por los buenos autores de Italia. . . . Partime pocos días después para mi casa; y con la largueza y soledad del camino discurriendo por diversas cosas, fui á dar muchas veces en lo que el Navagero me habia dicho; y así comencé á tentar este género de verso."

Thus Wiat came under the influence of two eminent Italians at the beginning of his career as a poet, and he was encouraged to formulate definite principles, for English verse, at the time when similar influences were at work in Spain and at Lyons.[1]

The year 1526–7 is, therefore, of the utmost importance, since it marks the beginning of Italian influence in verse in poets of Spain, England and southern France, and this influence runs parallel during Wiat's life. Wiat proceeds from sonnet to ottava-rima, and finally to terza-rima, which he appropriates as his individual verse stanza. Boscán began with the sonnet, proceeded to terza-rima, and finally to ottava-rima, and died in the same year as Wiat. Garcilasso de la Vega ran a shorter and more brilliant course, and died in 1536. His genius prefers the pastoral and eclogue. The Lyons' circle of poets shows Italian influence somewhat later. The beginning of the third decade is probably the earliest date for the *appearance* of Italian influence in poetry, though Maurice Sève came under the influence of Navagero earlier.

The literary activity reached its height at Lyons a few years later; Wiat came into touch with the *École lyonnais* during his residence at the Spanish Court, and the poems written in Spain are contributions to certain phases of thought discussed by the Lyons' circle. The unfinished

[1] In northern France, Italian influence is but slight until after the publication of Alamanni's rime in 1532-3.

poem, the "Song of Iopas," is not only a contribution to a popular subject, but was probably influenced by Maurice Sève's "Microcosme," which was finished in 1538 though not published until 1562.

The share Wiat had in the literary movement in the south of France may be one reason why his verse shows no Spanish influence. Another and more obvious reason is the fact that the brilliant young poet Garcilasso was dead, and Boscán, inconsolable at his loss, was living in retirement preparing his poems for publication.[1] Moreover, Boscán was industrious, but not brilliant, and if Wiat had read examples of Boscán's poems he would merely have found imitations corresponding to his own earlier efforts. De Mendoza probably inspired the Epigram "In dowtfull brest." But Wiat's position was too insecure in Spain, and the hatred shown him on account of his Lutheran tendencies was too intense to allow of any intellectual sympathy springing from his intercourse with learned Spaniards. Looking through Boscán's translations from Petrarch, there is one sonnet, "Pomme en la vida más brava, importuna," of which the English version from the Italian is "Set me whereas," *ascribed by Puttenham to Wiat*, but assigned to Surrey in the MS. and in Tottel. The English version is undeniably from the original source, and if indeed Surrey's, is a later translation than Boscán's version, and shows Wiat's influence in a very marked degree. The interest lies in the fact of the parallel version in English and in Spanish from the Italian original.

Lastly, in connection with Wiat's intercourse with foreign contemporaries, Trissino supplied him with definite principles of construction in verse with copious examples. Wiat was one of the first to follow the teaching of the *Poetica*,[2] and of Dante's treatise which was bound up with it. The

[1] Boscán died in 1542, and his widow published Boscán's poems together with those of Garcilasso de la Vega in 1543.

[2] *La Poetica et de la Volgare Eloquentia tradotte*, 1529.

extraordinary facility which he acquired in verse, and the variety of his stanzas in the lyrical poems, as well as certain characteristic ways of treating his verse,[1] are to be traced to Trissino. Of special interest is the following passage, where Trissino asserts that the *Poetica* is intended chiefly for foreigners—

"I have spared no fatigue. Besides the *Volgare Eloquentia* and the *Regoli di Antonio di Tempo*, I have read almost all the ancient trovatori, Sicilian, Italian, Provençal and Spanish, that I could lay my hands upon; and I shall think nothing of the fatigue if I may thereby have satisfied those *many ingenious foreigners* who are desirous of information on this subject."—Translation of *Poetica*, lib. ii. p. 92.

The clue to Wiat's position is discoverable in Cheney's description of him: "He hath as much wit to mark and remember . . . as any young man in Europe." In France, and Italy, and Spain, his eagerness in life and his fine intellectual qualities gave him a command over circumstances. Since the ambassadors were scholars and poets who were temporarily engaged in the duties of diplomacy, he used his special gift of "marking and remembering" to such purpose that, in his intercourse with continental statesmen, he acquired a literary astuteness, and an acquaintance with the streams of thought which, having their source in Italy, were beginning to flow through the countries of Western Europe. Life and literature were one with Wiat; hence that living element in his poems, that impetuosity in his utterance when he is moved, and the vividness of speech that colours his best work; herein lies his claim to originality, although the greater part of his poetry is translation.

Wiat's Poetry.

One of the oldest myths in classical mythology is the rising of Athene from the brain of Zeus, the god of light,

[1] See Appendix E.

or *bright sky*, as his name denotes. Like all myths, it has profound meaning. All creative power comes from the brain and soul of the creator, and is the effort to express Truth, which in Art is sought after through the channels of Beauty. The ideal of Plato, the mysticism of St. Paul, the teaching of Christ, turns on the quest of Beauty through the light of Truth.

While all life originates in natural processes, mankind is supreme in the world by reason of the divine gift within him that places him "a little lower than the angels" and "crowns him with glory and honour." This divine gift in its narrowest sense is the power to follow truth and discover the Beauty which lies in goodness; in its highest sense it is the power to *produce*, i. e. to express through the medium of colour, or form, or language, new phases of Beauty, new aspects of Truth.

A Madonna of Raphael is the expression of the Beauty of all womanhood and motherhood; it reveals the truth that woman is the centre of the universe, because in and through her lies all the hopes of the race. The countenance of Raphael's Madonna does not reflect the delight and intense passion of motherhood, but the gravity of eternal truth rests upon her brow, the purity of perfect simplicity looks out through the eye, and the calm beauty of possession, and hush of twilight peace, emanates from the whole figure.

In stone, Michelangelo Buonarroti has graven his ceaseless efforts to express Truth through Beauty. His power is greater than Raphael's, because in his creations he has shown the enormous expenditure of labour, and pain, and torture of mind, that is the inheritance of those who seek to penetrate the mysteries of life in order to arrive at Truth.

In the art of words, in the domain of poetry, Wiat is by no means the least among those who, in the sixteenth century, sought to express the Beauty of life through Truth.

The upholding of Truth in life, and the continual war

waged against falseness, are the two dominant notes in Wiat's poetry. True, in his first bitter experience of the falseness that rides so insolently abroad in the very highway of life, he cries—

What vaileth trouth ? Or by it to take payn ?
To be juste and true : and fle from doublenes ?

And in another rondeau he says—

Thou hast no faith :
Eche thing seketh his semblable
And thou hast thyn of thy condition.

And again—

Truth is tryed where craft is in ure.

One of the fine expressions of his code of life for honourable manhood is expressed in the somewhat difficult original Sonnet, No. 13—

. . . no way man may fynde
Thy vertue to let : though that frowerdnes
Of ffortune me holdeth

. . . . . .

Suffice it then that thou be redy there
At all howres : still under the defence
Of tyme, trouth, and love, to save thee from offence.

Again, by contrast, he expresses his allegiance to truth, following the teaching of the *Courtier* to refrain from "Jestes"—

To rayle or jest ye know I use it not
Tho that such cause somtyme in folkes I finde.

But the finest expression (apart from the Psalms) of his adherence to truth in life is expressed in the following stanza—

Within my brest I never thought it gain
Of gentle mynde the fredom for to lose ;
Nor in my hart sanck never such disdain
To be a forger, faultes for to disclose ;
Nor I can not endure the truth to glose :
To set a glosse upon an earnest pain :
Nor I am not in nomber one of those,
That list to blow retrete to every train.

These verses attest Wiat's actual standard of life, and are the outcome of his convictions.

In connection with this ingrained virtue lies the most sombre experience of his life. He was separated from his wife, with no possibility of reconciliation, as far as he was concerned, since Truth had been shattered; various hints in his poems show how deeply he suffered in this connection—

> Though that with pain I do procure
> For to forgett that ons was pure.

The poem—

> What shulde I saye,
> Sins faithe is ded
> And truth awaye
> From you ys fled,

is the cry that proceeds from the deep pain of the heart, and expresses the anguish of lost confidence in one who had been dear to him.

In Wiat is to be found the embodiment of Shakespeare's lines beginning "To thine own self be true."

He not only believes in the old saying, "Know thyself," but his keen power of observation gives him an insight into the characters of others. His faculty of "avysing" unlocks much to him which is closed to the casual-minded, and gives him a knowledge of life in all its phases. Of the double-faced acquaintance, he says--

> None is worse than is a friendly foo, and again
> . . . . .
> Yet knowes it well that in thy bosom crepeth.

In the Satires he ironically writes—

> The frendly ffoo with his dowble face,
> Say he is gentill, and courtois therewithall
> . . . . .
> Say he is rude that cannot lye and fayn
> The Letcher a Lover.

And in the same Satire he says to his friend in a tone of intense earnestness—

> My Poynz, I cannot frame me tune to fayne,
> To cloke the trouthe for praise withoute desart.

In the third Satire he strikes deeper. It is not only the want of truth in the world, but the assumption of truth by the false-hearted in an outward show of morality that does most harm. His satiric advice to Brian is to refrain from truth if he wishes to prosper—

> Thou knowst well first, who so can seke to plese
> Shall pourchase frendes where trowght shall but offend;
> Ffle therefore trueth, it is boeth welth and ese
> For tho that trouth of every man hath prayse
> Full nere that wynd goeth trouth in great misese.

And finally, in the Letter to his Son he implores him to be "honest"; but, failing honesty, he assures him that "to seme to be" is the greater sin.

This deeply rooted love of truth has its origin in the fine character of his parents. Sir Henry Wiat carried out in his life Chaucer's description of the "Knight" who loved—

> Truth and honour, freedom and courtesy.

His mother was a finely intellectual and strong character, managing the estates, rearing her sons, and keeping up a standard of morality within her domain during her husband's frequent absences in the King's service. Wiat, trained under these influences, early learnt the habit of obedience to authority and acquired the love of truth and simple courtesy which distinguished his father. Whole-hearted service to King and country appears in the Epigram "Tagus fare well"—

> My King my Contry alone for whome I lyve.

Truth, inbred in Wiat, gives the clue to his attitude towards love and women. Respect and honour for the sex, belief in the equal distribution of moral right and wrong, and in equal punishment and reward for man and woman, is clearly discernible in his writings. And this is the attitude of his day, which in some respects was even more "modern," as we term it, than our own. Passages in the Utopia of More, the Colloquies of Erasmus, and the *Courtier*, all touch upon the necessity of an equal standard in morality for men and women. For, as nature has decreed that man and woman are the complement of one another, no lasting morality can accrue from unequal burdens.

The women of Wiat's day with whom he came into contact at the Courts of Europe were such as Shakespeare portrays them, intellectual, resourceful, knowing life in all its bearings, and using it for good. Such were Margaret of Navarre, Renée of France, the Duchess of Ferrara, Vittoria Colonna, Catherine of Aragon (to a certain extent), Mary Richmond, the Lady Margaret Howard, and Wiat's mother and sister; all these women held their own by the force of their intellect, the high standard of their morality, and their personal charm.

Occasionally, indeed, Wiat uses the stock phrase that change pleases a woman's mind; he also says—

"Like to like the proverb saieth."

Wiat married early, and the domestic trouble which followed later deprived him of the fulness of joy in happy married life, such as Robert and Elizabeth Browning express in some of the finest love lyrics that the world has produced —enthrallingly beautiful because of their truth. Wiat's lyrics are poems of emotion rather than of love, for the deepest feelings expressed are sorrow at parting, bitter grief at loss of confidence. In this respect Wiat strikes an original note in the lyrical poetry of his day. Nothing could be more beautiful in its profound pathos than the song, "And wylt thow leve me thus."

The dignity of sorrow is expressed in the finely modulated harmony of "Fforget not yet," and the pain of memory is finely expressed in an original manner in the song, "When fyrst myn eyes did view and mark"; the note of pathos is intensified in the stanza beginning—

> And when my handes have handled ought
> That thee hath kept in memory.

One little poem, indeed, "Grudge on who liste," strikes a note of gladness, but it is put in the mouth of a woman, and one wonders whether it were not intended for Mary Richmond. Of all Holbein's portraits, the loveliest in its portrayal of the beauty of youth, combined with strength of character and womanly sweetness, is the portrait of Mary, the child-wife of the King's son, Henry Richmond; a face that fulfilled its promise in the deepened character of later years, and called forth Wiat's single poem on his ideal of womanhood in the Epigram, "A face that shuld content me."

In the Petrarchan sonnets Wiat's selection is guided partly by the rules laid down for the perfect courtier in *Il Cortegiano*, and partly by his preference for conceits rather than for descriptions of nature or of the lady. What appears artificial to-day had a special charm to Wiat's contemporaries, the charm of the "dolce stil nuovo" which had transformed and irradiated Italian verse in the thirteenth century.

The artificiality rests not so much upon the conceit, but in the false conception of the woman. This struck equally upon the minds of thoughtful people in the sixteenth century; passages in *Il Cortegiano* reflect upon the absurdity of regarding a woman as a monster if she refused to accept attention, and of punishing her with everlasting slander if she yielded to the prayers of the lover. Still more artificial is the belief in the inconstancy of women. The irony of the situation reaches its height in the poems of Donne, who continually affirms inconstancy to be the chief attitude of a woman, while he unblushingly affirms that in him "Inconstancy hath begot a constant habit."

The ugliness of passion is clearly distinguished in Wiat's poetry from the love experienced in friendship and in married love. A hard and fast line is drawn between unlawful passion and love. It is clearly expressed in the debate, "Lo, what it is to love," and in the Epigrams "Cruell desire" and "From thes hye hills." The intense note of the Psalms, and the fine poem "If thou wilt myghty be, flee from the rage," utters the last word in his final expression of the Truth of life that cannot rest in baseness of any sort. He expresses on this side what Blake puts so tersely in the proud utterance of the polished pebble of the brook—

Love seeketh only self to please
To bind another to its delight
Joys in another's loss of ease,
And builds a Hell in Heaven's despite.

Wiat, however, refuses to name this aspect of passion as love, but significantly calls it "cruell desire."

Wiat shares with Browning the gift of looking at different sides of a question. There are sundry pairs of poems, following one another, expressing two different points of view—

Cf.	Patience, tho I have not	with	Paciens for my devise,
	Full well yt maye be sene	with	Syns love ys suche,
	Longer to muse	with	Love doth againe.

Single poems may be included in this connection, such as "Most wretched hart," and "Lo, what it is to love." The first poem is a debate on life, contrasting optimism with pessimism; the final word is given to the optimistic point of view. The best poem representing two points of view is the dialogue "It burneth yet." Its supreme beauty lies in the tensity of restrained emotion that throbs through every line. But the greatness of the poem lies in Wiat's portrayal. The "Lady" is the comprehension of the tenderness and sympathy and unselfishness that true love awakens in the woman.

Wiat's power to see different sides brings with it that optimism that Browning possesses. Though of all men Wiat knew the sorrows of life, he never falters in truth—

> Never dreamed thought right were worsted wrong would triumph.
> Held we fall to rise, are baffled to fight better.
> Sleep to wake.

The strength and power of Wiat's verse lies in the terza-rima. Here, with variety of cæsura and overflow, he allows his thought to flow, hardly hampered by rhyme, which just serves for accent and rhythm. Here we find many personal touches. In the Satires are references to his home, to animal life, and to the simple pursuits of a country life. In the Psalms certain reminiscences of his own life run between the lines. For example, the joy of the prisoner who escapes his enemy's ward, the simile of the "seman in his jeoperte," who—

> By soden light perceyvid hath the port,

And of the horse—

> I lo for myn errour
> Ame plongid up, as horse out of the myre,
> With strok of spurr, such is thy hand on me.

Such allusions are vivid recollections of his own experiences. To take one example, he writes, December 1539, from Amboys, "The Emperor having set off for Loches, I followed, with much ado, on *plough horse* in the deepe and foule way. . . ."

There are magnificent passages in the Psalms that soar up in their divine wonder and faith, rising at times to the pure flame of joy of the mystic, whose mind discovers the vision of the eternal beauty of goodness in ecstatic vision (cf. Seventh Prologue). The Jehovah is a Presence with the power of a God and the attributes of a father.

> Within thy lok thus rede I my comfort . . .
> Myn Iye shall tak the charge to be thy guyde.—Ps. xxxii.

In the Psalms Wiat expresses all the radiance of joy which has been denied to him in earthly love.

The following verses might have been written by Blake, where joy, the radiance of emotion, proceeding from the belief in a reality of Divine goodness, is incorporated with the Divine Being as Joy personified—

> Suche Joy as he that skapis his enmys ward
> With losid bondes, hath in his libertie,
> Such Joy, my Joy, thou hast to me prepard.

Wiat's life and work is a song of harmony. The "music of the spheres" is here. It is a vindication of what man can become with lofty aim and set purpose. Faults he has, including those to which an impulsive, hot-tempered, generous nature is prone. In later years a profound calm and impartial manner of viewing life succeeded to the impulsiveness of his early manhood, while the love of truth grew and became centred in a sympathy with humanity which burns with intense radiance through the Psalms.

Wiat's life is the practice of his views. He had many friends; the devotion of John Leland, one of the greatest men of his day in learning and achievement, and the love and respect that Surrey, self-centred and proud to a fault, bore him, are the greatest witnesses. The men and women who gathered round him during the three happy years at Court; Cromwell's affection and the King's partiality for him all attest the worth of his character.

His reputation for scholarship outlived him, and he was to his generation the "chief lantern of light." Puttenham, who prides himself upon writing verse in the reign of Edward VI, constantly draws examples from Wiat's verse in the *Arte of Poesie*, evidently writing from a personal knowledge of the great reputation that outlived him.

Gascoigne, Turberville, and the poets who wrote in the long couplet from 1540 to the Elizabethan age, were well-meaning but dull imitators of a moral view that in Wiat is set off by a rare vitality and a charming style.

In the early Elizabethan sonnets phrase after phrase may be traced to Wiat. In Daniel and Drayton the influence is strong; and in Shakespeare various passages are derived from Wiat's fine lines in the Satires.

Such a passage as that beginning, "All tho thy head were howpt with gold," anticipates the famous speech on ceremony in *Henry V*.

In verse Wiat has influenced poetry down to the present day. The Elizabethans took from him the sonnet, the poets of the seventeenth century used his octave, the eighteenth preferred the couplet of which his poem, "Speke thou and spede," is a perfect example, and in the nineteenth century Shelley was the first to write in terza-rima in the same free style that characterizes Wiat's use of this form, contrary to the Italian rule.

Lastly, the wealth and variety of his lyrical forms and his power to interpret the harmony of language in musical refrains, has gained for him no mean reputation amongst lyrical poets.

Wiat is a poet for all time because he interprets life, in the stress and emotion of the mind; and fearlessly proclaims the high purpose in life which he so strongly believes in himself. His presentment of life is neither mawkish nor bitter, neither over-passionate nor over-severe. He shows by his own convincing faith, by his own rectitude of life, that truth is to be found, that good exists. "All is possyble" for those who believe in truth, for they are endowed with the divine gift of clear vision.

Henry Howard, who loved Wiat as a man, and respected and honoured him as a great master of verse, wrote the following lines, which represent Wiat's personality and ring true. The friend, writing the character of the man who placed "truth above all the rest" had perforce to be true to that friend by drawing his character truthfully.[1]

WIAT resteth here, that quick could neuer rest:
Whose heauenly giftes encreased by disdayn,
And vertue sank the deper in his brest;
Such profit he of enuy could obtain.

A hed, where wisdom misteries did frame:
Whose hammers bet styll in that liuely brayn,
As on a stithe: where that some work of fame
Was dayly wrought, to turne to Britaines game.

A visage, stern, and myld: where bothe did grow,
Vice to contemne, in vertue to reioyce:
Amid great stormes, whom grace assured so,
To lyue vpright, and smile at fortunes choyce.

A hand, that taught, what might be sayd in ryme:
That reft Chaucer the glory of his wit:
A mark, the which (vnparfited, for time)
Some may approche, but neuer none shall hit.

A toung, that serued in forein realmes his king:
Whose courteous talke to vertue did enflame.
Eche noble hart: a worthy guide to bring
Our English youth, by trauail, vnto fame.

An eye, whose iudgement no affect could blinde,
Frendes to allure, and foes to reconcile:
Whose persing loke did represent a mynde
With vertue fraught, reposed, voyd of gyle.

A hart, where drede yet neuer so imprest,
To hyde the thought, that might the trouth auance:
In neyther fortune lyste nor so represt,
To swell in wealth, or yield vnto mischance.

A valiant corps, where force, and beawty met:
Happy, alas, to happy, but for foes:
Liued, and ran the race, that nature set:
Of manhodes shape, where she the molde did lose.

---

[1] The last lines are omitted, which give a rather artificial, tombstone kind of ending.

CONTENTS

			PAGE
INTRODUCTION			v
COMMENTARY			1
APPENDIX	A.	ITALIAN SOURCES	183
,,	B.	LELAND'S "NÆNIÆ" IN MORTEM T. VIATI	231
,,	C.	THE DEVONSHIRE MS.	241
,,	D.	VERSIFICATION OF PYNSON'S "CHAUCER"	247
,,	E.	INFLUENCE OF TRISSINO	250
,,	F.	RELATIONS BETWEEN WIAT AND ANNE BOLEYN	253
,,	G.	EXAMPLES OF WIAT'S PROSE—	
		(i) LETTERS TO HIS SON	257
		(ii) DECLARATION TO THE COUNCIL	265

ILLUSTRATION

To face page

REPRODUCTION OF THE TITLE-PAGE OF LELAND'S "NÆNIÆ" . 231

LIST OF EARLY EDITIONS OF WIAT'S POEMS IN MISCELLANIES

Tottel's *Miscellany*. First Edition, June 5, 1557.

Songes and Sonettes written by the right honorable Lorde Henry Howard, late Earl of Surrey. Sir T. Wyate the Elder and other. (This edition includes ninety poems by Wiat.)

" " Second Edition, July 31, 1557, contains six additional poems by Wiat.

" " Third Edition, 1559.

" " Fourth Edition, 1565.

" " Fifth Edition, 1567.

" " Sixth Edition, 1574.

" " Seventh Edition, 1585. Printed by T. Windet.

" " Eighth Edition, 1587. Printed by R. Robinson.

The *Courte of Venus* (*c*. 1542 ?) Britwell fragment of eight folios in the Britwell Library.

A COMMENTARY ON THE POEMS OF SIR THOMAS WIAT

INTRODUCTORY

A CAREFUL examination of the Egerton manuscript in the light of contemporary events, and of the facts of the poet's life, leads to the conclusion that Wiat did not study verse systematically until after his visit to Italy in 1527.

In 1528 he was appointed Marshall of Calais, and he did not return to England until 1532. He had abundant leisure during these years, in spite of his official duties, to master the difficulties of the five-foot line.

Now apart from the fact that the years spent at Calais represent the only period in Wiat's career when he had opportunities for so great and difficult an undertaking, there are other considerations that point to the same conclusion.

The brief glimpses into his life previous to 1526 reveal a young man addicted to outdoor exercises and knightly accomplishments.[1]

The companion of George Brooke, son of Lord Cobham, married at seventeen,[2] a father at eighteen,[3] at Court with George Brooke at the age of twenty, taking a prominent

[1] Wiat Memoirs.

[2] To the daughter of George Brooke, Lord Cobham, of Cobham Hall, Kent. His estates adjoined those of Sir Henry Wiat, father of the poet.

[3] In 1542 his son is described as "twenty-one and upwards." In 1537 he wrote from Spain to his son, already married and living with his wife.

part in feats of arms and other Court gaieties, he drank deeply of the pleasures of life, gaining a reputation for lute-playing and versifying, and winning the favour of Henry VIII by his fearless bearing, his beauty of person and his ready wit.

These were the heedless days of his career—years affording no opportunity for the meditation and study necessary for the task he achieved later in English verse.

But the pleasant and happy periods of life are not the best for bringing forth the finest results in intellectual productive energy or in character; and Wiat had already experienced misfortune when he turned his attention to the technical side of verse.

In 1526 'Fortune' was his 'fo'[1]; domestic troubles came to him; an intimacy, mutually agreeable, though probably not serious, was summarily broken by the King.[2] Wiat exchanged Court life for diplomatic service, accompanying Sir Thomas Cheney to France the same year, and Sir William Russell to Italy in 1527.

The following year (1528) he was stationed at Calais. He returned to England in 1532 with the reputation of a finished scholar, and he regained a place at Court, not as a gay young reveller, but as a man of the world with a shrewd insight into human nature, and a brilliant wit.[3]

Before 1527 his contributions to verse are in the octosyllabic verse of the light Court lyric; many Early Songs are to be found in the D. MS., and show, from a comparison with the Royal Song-books of the early sixteenth century, not only the use of common material in rhyme and ideas,

[1] Chaucer, *T.* I. 837.

[2] See Appendix, "Relations between Wiat and Anne Boleyn."

[3] According to the prevailing fashion of the day of composing a device from the letters of the name, Wiat's easily became "A Wit." That of Maurice Sève was "Vice Se Muera."

but an adaptation of songs probably composed at a much earlier date and re-set by Wiat.[1]

The first poem in the Egerton MS. shows studied, even laborious, care in the setting; the earlier poems in this MS. give the impression that he was with difficulty evolving a five-foot line by translating, and following to a certain extent the principle of, Italian verse.

Wiat clearly had masters whom he followed in this precise and careful study of prosody. Two facts help in fixing the date: the edition of Pynson's *Chaucer* in 1526, containing the "Canterbury Tales" and numerous poems, several of which are now assigned to other authors; and Giorgio Trissino's *Poetica*, published in 1529, are in themselves evidence of the influences which guided him in the earlier stages of his metrical studies. The first few lines of the Prologue of the 1526 edition contain many of the characteristic rules of Wiat's verse.[2] A precedent for every rule in Wiat's versification is to be found in Pynson's *Chaucer*, the *only* exception being Wiat's peculiar use of a trisyllabic *fifth foot*, found in the earlier poems, and absent from Wiat's mature work.

But Wiat does not only follow the *prosody* of Pynson's *Chaucer*. Several poems show traces of imitation of *poems to be found only* in Pynson's *Chaucer*. This fact sufficiently proves that the earlier editions of *Chaucer* [3] were not used by Wiat.

Again, Thynne's edition of *Chaucer*, published in 1532, was too late for his earlier efforts in prosody.

By the year 1533 Wiat had become, and was recognized

[1] See my *Study of Sir Thomas Wyatt*, Chap. X. p. 104, *et seq.*

[2] This question is fully dealt with in my *Study of Sir Thomas Wyatt*, Chap. VI.

[3] The earlier editions were very elaborate, and no doubt very costly. Pynson's edition is what one might term a popular one—made to be read, with numerous wood-cuts.

as, a skilful poet; he was writing Epigrams in a fluent style[1]—a form of verse adopted very successfully after his earlier studies in the Rondeau and Sonnet.

But there are signs in Wiat's work that Pynson's *Chaucer* was replaced by Thynne's edition from the year 1533 and onwards. The reasons are obvious. Like the preceding edition, it was published specially for the Court.[2] It contained the Boethius as well as many poems which are absent from Pynson's edition. Wiat's original poems, written between 1533–9, show a constant imitation of Chaucer, notably in the "Troilus and Cressida" and the "Knight's Tale." A direct reference to both these poems occurs in the Satires—

> Praise Sir Thopas for a noble tale,
> And scorn the story that the *Knight tolde.*
> Sat. I. ll. 50–51.

And the allusion to Pandarus—

> be not so unwise
> As Pandare was in such a like dede.
> Sat. III. ll. 74–75.

Again, the Boethius is imitated and paraphrased in his later poems.

In estimating their influence upon Wiat, these two editions of Chaucer have a definite and distinctive value.

The use of Pynson's edition lay mainly in its prosodic value; it helped Wiat to eliminate Chaucer's system of versification as he found it there, and to apply it to his own interpretation of the Italian hendecasyllabic form of verse.

1 See "Sometime I fled," an Epigram which refers *to the event of October 1532,* if it has any real significance, and I think this can hardly be doubted.

2 Henry VIII, like Francis I, not only took a keen interest in literary productions, but in the actual printing protession.

A lesser influence is to be traced in the imitation of certain poems found only in Pynson's edition and ascribed to Chaucer,[1] such, for example, "Dido's Prologue" and "Complaynte."

The influence of Thynne's edition of Chaucer upon Wiat is to be seen in his later and more mature style, between the years 1533–9. At this period in particular Wiat's appreciation of Chaucer's masterpieces, "Troilus and Cressida" and the "Knight's Tale," finds an outlet in many similar phrases and thoughts, perhaps unconsciously reproduced, as well as exact references to both poems.

For *definite rules* of prosody and copious examples of the various metres in Provençal and Italian poetry, Wiat had an excellent guide in Giorgio Trissino,[2] the celebrated Italian prosodist. From the opening years of the sixteenth century Trissino had become a prominent figure. Apart from the European renown gained by his tragedy of "Sophonisba," he was a poet, writer of comedies, and translator of Dante's treatise on verse, as well as the compiler of the *Poetica.*[3]

The *Poetica* was published together with the translation into Italian of Dante's Latin treatise in 1529. This was an epoch-marking event and deserves more attention, since the technical part of the poetry of the Pléiade and of the Elizabethans was undoubtedly based upon the text book of Trissino and his translation of Dante's treatise. Definite rules laid down by Trissino are to be found in Wiat's verse; and a certain treatment of terza-rima in the Psalm, "Altho' thow se," as well as his handling of other forms of verse, is explained by passages in the *Poetica.*[4]

[1] See *Study of Sir Thomas Wyatt*, "Chaucerian Influence," p. 53.

[2] He combined literary labour with diplomatic duties, holding office under Leo X and Clement VII.

[3] La Poetica e de la volgare eloquentia tradotte, 1529.

[4] See Appendix E.

During the years 1526–7 Wiat was gaining a wider experience of life by his travels in France and in Italy, and new vistas of poetry opened out before him.[1] But whereas his visit to the French Court merely deepened his interest in light songs and in musical melodies, his experiences in Italy changed him from a mere versifier into an earnest student of verse, with high aspirations for English poetry.

He began his task at Calais in 1528 by translating Petrarch, with Chaucer as a guide; later he was enabled to verify his work in Italian metres, by rules and examples from Trissino's *Poetica*.

Thus, a curious and interesting dual influence is to be found in Wiat's versification, brought about by a close study and following of Italian metres side by side with Chaucerian versification as found in Pynson's edition.[2] The eleven-syllable verse [3] which outweighs the ten-syllable in the first poem, "Behold love," the dominant feature of slurring vowels, which is certainly derived from carefully reading Italian measures, and the metrical experiments, are Italian importations. These features are blended with completely

[1] I differ from Sir Sidney Lee on the question of French influence. See *French Renaissance in England*, viii. 110. Wiat and Surrey are placed together as deriving the same influence from France. What is said in this passage applies, I think, to Surrey, but not to Wiat, "for example, Surrey and Wyat alike spent much time at the French Court. . . . It was in France rather than in Italy that both Wyat and Surrey acquired a substantial measure of the Italian taste and sympathy. . . . Thus in all probability were Wyat and Surrey most effectually brought in Paris under the Italian literary yoke. At every turn of our story Paris presents itself as the chief mission station of renaissance culture." I shall endeavour to prove later that Italian influence came through Italy with Wiat and was paramount, while it was the connection with Lyons, not Paris, that brought him into touch with contemporary French thought at a later time.

[2] See Appendix, "The Metre of Pynson's Chaucer."

[3] The Italian hendecasyllable.

English tendencies, such as inverted stress, absence of weak stress, trisyllabic feet found in Chaucer,[1] but absent from Italian verse.

It may be urged, however, that since examples have been found in Pynson's *Chaucer* for every rule of verse found in Wiat, with the exception of the final trisyllabic foot, it is misleading to mark down certain tendencies in Wiat's verse as Italian, and other tendencies as Chaucerian or English.

However, there were certain tendencies in Wiat's day indissociable from a right understanding of the position. Italy was the fountain-head for all inspiration and all teaching in arts and letters; a movement, consciously undertaken. was afoot to introduce the Italian hendecasyllable into other countries. At the very time Wiat was reconstructing English verse, the Spanish poet, Boscán, following the advice of Navagero, the Venetian Ambassador, was substituting the Italian hendecasyllable for the short Castilian measure, and a year or two later French poets were emulating Italian measures. Wiat was fresh from contact with great leaders of Italian learning.[2] He, therefore, did not merely translate poems, but carefully analyzed the metre at the same time, and his excessive use of slurring

[1] The sixteenth century was an age of discovery, and in France, Italy, Spain, as well as in England, there were to be found poets who were experimenting in verse. Alamanni, for example, experimented in a trisyllabic form of verse, but in a late work which did not appear until after Wiat's death. The most renowned example in France was Baïf's *vers mesurés*, more than twenty years later. But such *English* characteristics in verse as are mentioned above are indigenous to English verse, being part of our Old English heritage.

[2] Wiat had the good fortune to come into personal contact with G. Ghiberti, the Pope's Datary, not only eminent in letters, but in moral character; he was closely connected with such scholars of the time as Bembo, Bibbiena, and other Italian humanists and poets, and his chief secretary was Berni, the literary opponent of Aretino.

is most certainly due to his close attention to Italian models. The knowledge that Chaucer, his English master of style, showed distinct evidence of tendencies derived from the Italian, gave to Wiat himself confidence to proceed.

The first-fruits of his studies in the Italian hendecasyllable were the Rondeaus and Early Sonnets.

THE RONDEAUS

THE Rondeaus and earlier Sonnets were written during the first years at Calais. There are nine Rondeaus in the collection. Of these, seven were written about 1528–9, the eighth, a realistic Rondeau ("Ye Olde Mule"), was written about 1532–3, judging by its mature style and its place in the MS. The last Rondeau, "What no perdy," is in octosyllables, and was probably written earlier, but is placed *among the group of Court poems in light verse*, which occupies the place in the MS. between the Calais period (1528–32) and the Satires (1536–7). All but the last Rondeau show imitation of foreign models and conscious endeavour in metrical style; they must be regarded as experiments in metre. The last is one of the few original poems, struck from the heart, giving us a brief glimpse of Wiat's personality in emotion, not "remembered in tranquillity," but struck red-hot from the brain that formulated the passion of the heart in moments of strong feeling.

The Rondeau group presents a medley of Italian and French imitation. It is quite clear that Petrarch was Wiat's model, but he is haunted at the same time by French refrains and melodies recently heard at the French Court.

No. 1. **Behold love,** is a translation of Petrarch's beautiful madrigal, "Or Vedi Amor.[1] To a musical ear the opening words at once suggest a refrain. Wiat, more familiar with the Rondeau than the Madrigal form of lyric, used his opportunity. He converted his Italian translation

[1] See Appendix A for Italian sources.

into a French mode of lyric, and made a refrain of the opening words which are equally rich in cadence, whether in Italian or in English. The refrain comes after the eighth and thirteenth lines according to the type of Rondeau in vogue with Clement Marot and Mellin de St. Gelais. A slight variation of this Rondeau occurs in the D. MS., the refrain being added after the fifth line.

The Rondeaus were most probably set to music. Musical scores of the sixteenth century[1] extant show elaborate settings of Rondeaus, Madrigals, and even Sonnets, for four voices.

In order to set the proper valuation upon these metrical beginnings in the Egerton MS., it is most important to remember that music and verse were firmly united; what appears harsh or discrepant in reading a Rondeau or Sonnet disappears when sung to music. Again, the constant change from a five-foot to a four-foot line in the Rondeaus is quite natural when a musical accompaniment is understood. In the absence of music the Rondeaus and Sonnets *should be read with modulated voice*, filling out equivalent strong stresses to make up for the absence of weak syllables, and regarding trisyllabic feet as a *triplet* in music, *i. e.* as an equivalent to two ordinary notes, and to be got into the same space of time. In the refrain, "Behold love!" for instance, "love" must be read with the equivalence of *one foot*, as also "payne" in l. 2. The rhythm of the verse is thus marked, and acquires a richness altogether lacking when his editors and correctors have tried to reduce it to a dull and monotonous regularity of Iambic movement;[2] for

[1] Cf. Song-Books, British Museum.

[2] The Iambic line needs force and finish, and has characteristics which Wiat did not aim at attaining; yet no English poet has made a more careful study of form than Wiat, or succeeded better in adjusting his thoughts to a characteristic form.

as he never aimed at achieving correctness as such, his verse must of necessity suffer when made to conform to the standard of regular Iambic verse. Wiat's verse was never intended for a "classic" line, and consequently suffers when it is measured by that standard. A specimen page of this Rondeau is produced from the MS., in order to show corrections by later hands, without Wiat's authority. The spelling corrections are numerous, and there are textual alterations.

Certain characteristics of Wiat's verse are found throughout his MS. from beginning to end,[1] and *Tottel's version obliterated these characteristics*, while the A. version tends to carry out what Tottel achieved. The first few pages of the MS. betrays a "philistine" hand with the same tendency as Tottel; though it is clear that Tottel was *not* the corrector of the MS., because certain poems, *peculiar to the E. MS.*, are not inserted in Tottel's *Miscellany:* such poems are Wiat's finest productions, and could not have been passed over by an intending editor.

Comparing the Rondeau as given in the text with the specimen page from the MS., it will be noted that final "e's" and double vowels have been added, as in "behold*e*," "to*o*," "me*e*," "she*e*"; this alteration is observable from the difference in the shape of the letter and in the colour of the ink. In other places final vowels are crossed out. Since this altered spelling conforms neither to that of Wiat nor his scribes, but represents mid-sixteenth century spelling, the text of this edition is made to conform with the *original spelling*.

l. 7. *her liff*. A typical case of a later correction is seen here in the insertion of "all" before "her." Wiat read "disdaynful" as four syllables here; the line scans :—

[1] See *Study of Sir Thomas Wyatt*, Chaps. III.-IV., for the principles of Wiat's metre.

To thé | disdá | ynfúle || her líff | she léd-eth.

This reading gives a good hendecasyllable, with a well-marked cæsura after the sixth syllable, which is the proper sense pause; for the reading of "-ayn" as two syllables, cf. Sonnet 6, where a rime-ending of the octave is "-ayned," and requires to be pronounced as three syllables.[1]

l. 13. *entreateth*. In both MSS., E. and D., this word is written "entreath." This is possibly merely a shortened form of writing "entreateth"; in Middle English Texts there are constant examples of syncopation of third person singular verbal endings.

A later hand has corrected the MS. to "*her* entreateth." The text follows the spelling "entreateth" to avoid ambiguity. Tottel converted this Rondeau into a Sonnet by filling up the line of the first refrain and omitting the last refrain. Setting aside later corrections and emendations, the original Rondeau is harmonious and well-balanced. A definite purpose in the construction can be made out. It will be seen that ll. 1, 2 (allowing for time equivalence on "love," l. 1, and "payne," l. 2), and ll. 6, 7, are hendecasyllables, concluding with the weak ending "-eth."

All the lines with romance ending "-ure" are decasyllables, as also the lines concluding each part of the Rondeau, *i. e.*, l. 5, l. 8, and l. 13.

In the first two parts, the extra syllable "-eth," and the long vowel-sounds of the refrain, and the Romance rhyme-ending "-ure," all help to produce a slow, sad effect; making sound answer to sense. In the third part, ll. 9–13, the mood changes to indignation; the lover needs redress of his wrongs, the movement is hurried, and the effect is gained by making the rhyme-ending "-eth" on the *tenth* instead of the

[1] This pronunciation is compatible with the Old Teutonic "ai" and also the Romance "ai," which is a compound, not a pure vowel sound.

eleventh syllable. Cf. the difference in sound and sense of l. 1,

Behóld | lóve | thy powér | how shé | dispís(eth)

with l. 9,

I ame | in hold : || if pit | ie the | meveth.

All the vowel syllables are drawn out in the first line, and the sharp, short notes falling in quick succession of l. 5 graphically express the indignant mood of the lover.

And this design, one remembers, is the natural one for an author who is first a musician, accustomed to compose musical accompaniments and trained in the technique of music.

This Rondeau is the best possible object lesson in contrasting Wiat's verse *as he made it*, characterized by its musical stress and vowel melody, with the version of his later correctors *as they desired it to appear*.

Wiat's method of dealing with the original Italian is interesting. Here, as always, he avoids special reference to Nature, and detailed description of the woman;[1] omitting such description, he does not translate the very beautiful ll. 4–5 of the Italian Madrigal.

ella in treccie e'n gonna—
Si siede et scalza in mezzo i fiori et l'erba.

"Or Vedi Amor" is, apparently, the only Madrigal translated by Wiat, and he set it in a Rondeau form, at a time when French refrains and musical melody were influencing him.

Later, however, he used the Madrigal form of "Or Vedi Amor" for a madrigal of his own composition, "My love is

[1] For the one exception see Epigram 28, "A face that shuld content me." But even in this instance it is *character* portrayed, not physiognomy.

lik unto the eternall fyre," which I have placed amongst the Epigrams (see No. 27).

It is curious, however, that *while using the scheme abb, acc, cdd,* as found in the three-tercet combination of "Or Vedi Amor," he *re-arranged his English madrigal*, grouping it as quatrain-tercet-couplet, thus, abba, ccc, dd, instead of in the three-tercet form.

This first Rondeau, this first poem, of Wiat's MS., is a unique example of the dual effect of foreign influences at work in him, resulting in the translation of an *Italian* Madrigal in English hendecasyllables, but set in *Rondeau form*, with refrains after the French manner.

Boileau defines both types in *l'Art Poetique*, Chap. II.—

> Toute poème est brillant, de sa propre beauté
> Le *rondeau* né gaulois, a la naïveté
> Le madrigale plus simple et plus noble en sa tour
> Respire la douceur, la tendresse et l'amour.

In truth Wiat was not skilful enough for the smoothness and harmony, the easy grace and delicate feeling of the Madrigal. He had not yet found the form most suitable to his particular bent; his mastery of the five-foot line, and his discovery of ottava-rima, are simultaneous, and brings us to the end of his apprenticeship.

With maturity came an inclination towards paragraph lengths of line and terza-rima setting.

No. 2. **What vaileth trouth.** The Rondeaus, Nos. 2–6 inclusive, are dominated by French influence, not consciously studied as in the Italian imitations, but re-echoing French thought and French refrains, from songs remembered pleasantly.

The chief feature in the verse is the inclusion of trisyllabic feet: l. 3, "to be juste"; l. 7, "in disdayn"; l. 12, "lo such à," with Wiat's stress mark over "à," showing clearly that a tri-syllabic foot was meant; "à" has the effect of the modern stressed "the" in colloquial speech with a superlative adjective understood. Tottel inserts an adjective after "à," and omits the stress mark.

l. 13. *crueltie*. Wiat's slurring mark occurs here. Such signs are of supreme importance in making clear his principles of verse, adding incontrovertible testimony to what is quite obvious in studying the MS. This occasional guidance under Wiat's authority proves what otherwise could only be construed as probably theory.

This Rondeau begins in a five-foot measure, and continues in four-foot verse. Tottel corrected to a five-foot line throughout, and changed the form from Rondeau to Sonnet (see also Nos. 1 and 7). The poem is a somewhat bitter reflection upon life. The heedless, pleasure-loving days of Wiat's life were in the past, and his recent experiences had obliged him to face the sterner side of life. Domestic troubles, which are veiled in obscurity, with lesser anxieties involved in the fret and worry of official life, and the remembrance of his broken intimacy with Anne, made Wiat despondent—even bitter—at this period.

No. 3. **Ffor to love her.** This and the two following Rondeaus give the impression that Wiat was struggling with a desire to write five-foot verse while the genii of four-foot verse compelled his pen; ll. 1, 2, 6, and 7 easily scan as four-foot lines with double weak endings, though they are probably meant to scan as decasyllabic, with lapses into four-foot time in l. 3 (with slurred foot, "to have had"), and in l. 5 (with double slurred first foot, "and hath geven").

ll. 8, 10, are octasyllabic; *e. g.* contain an extra weak ending.

l. 11. *retorn* has the value of three syllables: "retoren."

Poetical licence was generally allowed, and is intimated by the explanation of Gascoigne, *Notes of Instruction*, § 12.[1] "This poetical licence is a shrewde fellow and covereth many faults in a verse, it maketh wordes *longer*, shorter, of *mo sillables*, of fewer . . . for example ydone for done, adowne for down, orecome for overcome, tane for taken, *power* for powre, heaven for heavn—and a number of other whiche were but tedious and needelesse to rehearse since your owne judgment and readyng will soone make you espie such advantages."

l. 12 contains an example followed from Pynson's *Chaucer* of a strong accent after the cæsura.

The refrain and idea is a reminiscence of C. Marot's Rondeau No. X.: "D'Estre Amoureux."[2]

Cf. Wiat's Rondeau, ll. 4, 7, with ll. 2–5 of the French version below; and cf. l. 8 with Rondeau LXXXI. "S'il est ainsy," ll. 2 and 3, on page 18.

Rondeau X. (1525).[3]

D'estre amoureux n'ay plus intention
C'est maintenant ma moindre affection ;
Car celle là de qui je cuydois estre

Le bien aymé m'a bien faict apparoistre
Qu'au faict d'amour n'y a que fiction

Je la pensais sans imperfection
Mais d'autre amy a prins possession
Et pource, plus je ne veulx entremettre
D'estre amoureux.

---

[1] Gascoigne, *Works*, ed. John W. Cunliffe, I. 470. 1907.

[2] C. Marot, *Œuvres Complètes*, M. P. Jannet. 1884.

[3] Sir Sidney Lee's *French Renaissance in England* was published after the chapters were written on French Influence in my *Study of Sir Thomas Wyatt*. A long study of Wiat compels me to differ from him in much that he says of French influence in regard to Wiat.

Au temps present par toute nation
Les dames sont comme un petit sion
Qui toujours ploye à dextre et à senestre.
Bref les plus fins n'y sçaivent nen congnoistre
Parquoy concludz que c'est abusion
D'estre amoureux.

See also Rondeau LXXXI., given below, printed by M. Jannet (*œuvres complètes de C. Marot*).

No. 4. **Helpe me to seke.** The measure is in five-foot verse by combining two-syllable with three-syllable feet.

The idea of a heart leaving the body is found in Provençal poets and doubtless has an older history. The twelfth-century French poet Chrestien de Troyes introduces the conceit very effectively in the Cligès.

Marot's Rondeau, "tant seulement," expresses the idea in an artificial manner without the humour of Wiat or the delicacy of sentiment found in the older poets, such as in Chrestien de Troyes' "Cligès" for example.

Of the lover's heart Marot writes—

Si tu le veux metz la soubz ta commande
Si tu le prens, las ! je te recommande
Le triste corps : *ne le laisse sans cueur*
Mais loges y le tien, qui est vainqueur
De l'humble serf qui son vouloir te mande
Tant seulement.

The rhythm of this Rondeau takes us back to the more regular type of Skelton's tumbling verse. Wiat was possibly recalled to this kind of verse by thoughts of Skelton, who died in 1529. About the same time Wiat undertook a more ambitious task—translating the Canzone, "Quel antiquo mio dolce" ("Myne olde dere enmy"). He chose for his setting *not* the Chaucerian Troilus measure, but the Skeltonic type, the fifteenth-century travesty of this beautiful form. Since Skelton's longer poems are in this measure it may be that Wiat imitated the style as a tribute to the late court poet.

The Rondeau is brisk and humorous. Notice the play upon words in the last line, "It was myn hert, I pray you hertely." Wiat treats the idea with grace and humour; his characteristic simplicity of speech gives a charm to an otherwise threadbare topic in love-songs. This personal language of Wiat imparts a touch of sincerity and quaintness to all his best poems. It is characteristic of his letters and dispatches.[1]

No. 5. **Yf it be so.** This Rondeau is another instance of the dual influence (French and Italian) upon Wiat. "Yf it be so" is a free rendering of a sonnet attributed to Serafino, which I came across quite recently in the Bologna edition (*Collezione di opere inedite o rari*, p. 163, vii. G.). The refrain and setting, however, is influenced by C. Marot's Rondeau, "S'il est ainsy." This Rondeau was first printed by M. Jannet from the MS. FF. 2335, f. 65. Bib. Nat. Paris. ll. 2 and 3 should be compared with l. 8, Rondeau 3. It runs as follows, ll. 1–8 :—

S'il est ainsy que ce corp te habandonne
Amour commande et la raison ordonne
Que je te laisse en charge de ma foy ;
Le cueur ja tien, car par honneste loy
Aulcun ne doit reprendre ce qu'il donne
Ne pense que alieurs jamais s'adonne,
Plustost la mort sans que Dieu luy pardonne
Le puisse prendre et meurdrir devant toy
Sil est ainsy.

---

[1] Surely there never was, before or since, an ambassador who wrote his dispatches in the conversational and piquante manner peculiar to Wiat! One feels that he made amends with both Cromwell and the King for his apparent failure in his embassy, the fault of circumstance and not of the servant.

The Italian source is given here, in order to compare the French with the Italian, and both with Wiat.

Se questo miser corpo t'abandona
  Inclita mia madonna, el cor ti resta
  In cambio di mia gé, che è cosa onesta
  De non ritar quel ch'un tratto se dona.
Amor mi tien, necessite mi sprona,
  Lo star mi piace, el parti mi molesta,
  Ma sia che vuol, se'l ciel vita mi presta
  Lontan da te non amero persona.
I'me ne vo se tu m' amastai mai
  Te raccomando el cor, che rimar teco
  Forse che'l corpo piu non revedrai :
E s'alcun te dicesse : l'amor cieco
  Se ha fatto in altro amar, risponderai
  "Come amar puo che non ha el cor non seco ?"

Although the above sonnet lacks the subtle charm of Petrarch it is pleasing, and if, indeed, it be the work of Serafino, it is less ornate, less conceited than his usual style.

Wiat's rondeau has sdrucciola [1] rhyme in ll. 4 and 5: affétion," "perféctïon"; in ll. 6 and 7, "opínïon," "inténtïon"; and in ll. 9 and 10, "fasshïon," "posséssïon."

Slurred feet occur, l. 3: "yet my hert"; and l. 8, "then may I."

"As thou lyst," l. 5, scans as a trisyllabic foot.

Lines rhyming in "-ion" are in five-foot, those in "y," "e," in four-foot verse.

1 *Sdrucciola rime.* Sir Phil. Sidney, *Apologie for Poetrie*, p. 67. "Lastly, even the verse-rhyme itself the Italian cannot put it on the last syllable of the French-named masculine rime, but still the next to the last which the French call the Female, or *the next before* that which the Italian [call] sdrucciola; the English hath all three kinds as Dúe, Trúe; Fáther, Ráther; Pótion, Mótion." The ending '-tion' in sixteenth-century verse is generally two syllables as in French; while spirit, heaven, is invariably monosyllabic. The exigency of the verse leads to variety in pronunciation.

l. 1 is difficult to scan.

It may be taken as a five-foot line,

"Yf it | be so | that I | forsáke | thé

with a monosyllable for the last foot, or as four-foot trochaic, with initial dactyl—

Yf it be | só that | Í for | sáke the.

The former rendering is more in keeping with the whole rondeau, the latter is not in Wiat's style.

The idea of the exchange of hearts has its origin in the Provençal writers, and doubtless has an older history still. A French poet, for example, Chrestien de Troyes, presents it with perfect simplicity and beauty in "Cligès," in one of the most beautiful love scenes in romantic literature.

"Cligès," l. 5086. "But he [Cligès] longs to reach her whom he loves and desires, and he hastens o'er sea and land and the way seems very long to him, so eagerly does he yearn *to see her who takes away and purloins his heart from him.*[1]

"But she [Fenice] yields him a fair return . . . for she in her turn gives her own heart in payment to him whom she loves no less. . . ."

And Cligès returns again to Fenice, but fears to tell his love lest she reprove him, l. 5153,[2] "for every day he can see her and sit *alone by her side* without any one gainsaying or forbidding, for nobody imagines or thinks evil of it."

[1] l. 5090. . . . celi voie
Qui son cuer li fortret et tot.

[2] l. 5153. Que tote jor la puet veoir
Et seul a seul lez li seoir
Sanz contredit et sanz nefonse
Que nul mal n'i autant reponse.

The last line (5156) contains one of those glorious touches for which we admire and render homage to Chrestien to-day.

At length Fenice summons up courage to ask him if he found a lady to love in the course of his wanderings. l. 5178. "Quickly was he able to explain all to her as soon as she challenged him on that point. '*Lady,*'[1] *quoth he,* '*I was in love while yonder but I loved none who was of yonder land.* In Britain *my body was without a heart* like bark without timber. When I left Germany I knew not what became of my heart save that it went away after you. *Here was my heart and there my body.*[2]'

"I was not absent from Greece, for my heart had gone thither *and to reclaim it I come back here* . . . and yet I seek it not and cannot do so. . . ."

Thirty more lines follow before the avowal—

"*Of a surety lady it came to you.*"[3] "To me! then it came not into exile for *mine also went to you.*"[4]

For sheer beauty of thought and delicacy of handling it would be difficult to match this passage. It is a far cry from Chrestien de Troyes, with all his freshness and grace, to the artificial and elaborated sentiments of the Petrarchists. Yet the very simplicity of Chrestien and his consummate knowledge of human nature betoken the perfection of art.

[1] l. 5178.
"*Dame,*" *fet il* "*j'amai de la*
Mes n'amai rien qui de la fust
Aussi com escorce sanz fust
Fu mes cois sans cuer au Bretagne."
. . . .

[2] l. 5185. Ca fu mes cuers et la mes cors,

[3] l. 5227.
"Dame certes a vos vint il a."
"A moi ? Ne vint pas en essil
Qu'aussi ala li miens a vos."
"Cligès," ed. by W. Foerster, from the Old French Romanische Bibliothek.

[4] "Cligès." Translated from the Old French by L. J. Gardiner, 1912.

The most charming version of the exchange of hearts in sixteenth-century lyric is Sir Philip Sidney's song. It is inserted here from Puttenham's version, *Arte of English Poesy*, III. 233, because of the lyrical form and the refrain. Elsewhere it is found as a sonnet.

My true love hath my hert and I have his
By just exchange, one for another geven
I holde his deare and mine he cannot misse
There never was a better bargaine driven
My true love hath my hert and I have his.

My heart in me keepes him and me in one
My heart in him his thoughts and senses guides:
He loves my heart, for once it was his owne
I cherish his because in me it bides
My true love hath my heart and I have his.

No. 6. **Thou hast no faith.** For the strong-stressed syllable in l. 1, fifth foot, cf. l. 1 of No. 4. It is difficult to decide whether the line should be scanned as five-foot or a four-foot verse, with slurred last foot; the latter is in Wiat's usual style.

Thou hast | no faith | of him | that hath nóne.

Perhaps the reasonable view is to regard these verses, that halt between four- and five-foot measure, as experiments of odd-syllable verse after the manner of the Italian verse, according to the precepts of Dante and Trissino.[1] Wiat abandoned the attempt later, finding, doubtless, that Italian metre is peculiarly adapted, by its richness in vocables, to odd numbers in verse; and for this very reason English metre, being a complete contrast to Italian, is seldom moulded in this manner with any degree of success for lyrical or serious verse.

[1] See Appendix E.

ll. 3–4. For the quotation of, or allusion to, proverbs, cf. Satire 3, opening lines; and Epigrams, Nos. 6, 13.

l. 12. Cf. Sonnet 23, l. 14. "That often chaunge doeth plese a woman's minde." A stock reflection on the sex from time immemorial. Wiat, however, puts the case in a nutshell in l. 4: "Like seeks like." The man who finds woman frail is frail himself. There is a dual note discernible in Wiat's poems. His attitude towards women is one of respect and honour, but occasionally he gives utterance to a very scornful indictment of a woman's faithlessness. Here, as in all else, Wiat is eminently just, being equally sincere in praise or blame. His attitude is direct and uncompromisingly candid when he tracks down want of faith or falseness in man or woman.[1] He is equally quick in recognizing and valuing noble traits in human nature. But he is quite free from the cynicism and innuendo, which disfigure every age, especially that of sixteenth-century literature. "Like to like the proverb saieth." John Donne, for example, ceases from his disfiguringly light judgments upon women when he has ceased from lightness himself, and sought graciousness in woman instead of allurement. Love of his wife brought out nobler qualities. Cf. with this Rondeau Clement Marot's rondering of "Amor et Foy."

Amor et Foy sont bien appariez
  Voyre trop mieulx ensemble mariez,
  Que les humains qu'en ce monde on marie;
  Car jamais Foy de l'Amour ne varie,
  Et vous humains, bien souvent variez.

Dames de cueurs icy estudiez,
  Ces deux beaulx dons Dieu vous a dediez,
  Et sont séans en haulte seigneurie.
      Amour et Foy

[1] Compare his scathing comments on fair-weather friends in his last Epigram, for example.

Tant sont uniz, tant sont bien alliez :
Qu'oubliant l'un, l'autre vous oubliez :
Si l'amour fault, la Foy n'est plus cherie :
Si Foy périt, l'Amour s'en va perie ;
Pour ce les ay, en devise liez
Amour et Foy.

No. 7. **Goo burnyng sighes.** A translation from Petrarch, see Appendix A. This is the first Rondeau in regular decasyllabic verse—the extra eleventh syllable, which characterizes No. 1 is avoided here. Notice the Romance stress in l. 3, *prayèr;* l. 12, *plaïnt*, scans as *two*, l. 13, *straynably*, as *four* syllables.

l. 6. *Take with the.* "the" is pronominal; it is the usual spelling of this text.

No. 8. **Ye olde mule.** This Rondeau is later than Nos. 1–7, and comes among the poems that mark the second Court period, 1533–6. This is the only poem of a realistic nature in the collection. It has been considered to be aimed at Anne Boleyn; there is no indication in Wiat's writings that such is the case. It is to Wiat's honour that he is free from the licentious blemish which marks sixteenth-century writers. But he is not alone in this respect: the greatest writers of the day keep their pens clean, among whom are Henry Surrey, A. Heroët, M. Sève, L. Alamanni, Boscàn, and Garcelasso de la Vega.

l. 8. *kappur*[1] is not found elsewhere. G. Nott changes the word and the sense to "keeper's" : of this Rondeau Nott says "it is coarse, but it is not offensive of the disgusting kind;" he remarks that it is probably intended for Anne Boleyn, and quotes Sanders. This latter writer is not worth

[1] *Kappur* is probably allied with *kipper*, a young colt, and used (dial. northern counties) for a gay or wanton person. It is evidently used here with the first meaning of *colt*, implying *wanton*. Cf. Danish *kippe*.

considering; since, being a partisan of a violent nature, his writing is coloured with virulence, and his aim was to place Anne Boleyn in the harshest and coarsest light possible.

No. 9. **What no perdy.** In octosyllabic metre, without experiments. It is one of the original compositions, and appears to be written under strong emotion. Wiat's best poetry is the expression of thought that surges in a strong brain forced into incisive speech by stress of feeling. Indignation and hurt pride thrill through the poem. Similar emotional power is to be seen in Sonnet No. 9. The sincerity and generosity of Wiat's nature was combined with extreme sensitiveness; the greatest troubles of his life came from hurt received through friends. Cf. one of his last utterances—

> Sure ame I Brian this wound will heal again
> But yet alas, the skarre shall still remaine.

THE SONNETS

THE Sonnets extend over the whole range of Wiat's poetry from the year 1528. This fact is suggestive of the proportionate influence that the French and Italian literary spirit exercised over him. The Rondeaus represent a passing (French) influence, whereas the Sonnets mark the permanent Italian influence, further exemplified by his use of ottava-rima and of terza-rima at a later stage in his literary career. Wiat wrote thirty-one Sonnets. Nineteen were probably written during the Calais period (1528–32).

The Sonnet "Like to these unmesurable montaynes" closes this period, and immediately precedes the group of miscellaneous poems which belong to Wiat's second Court period, 1533–6. This Sonnet further corroborates the theory of the chronological order of the poems in the E. MS. It is a translation of the sonnet, "Simile a questi, smisurati monti," by Sannazaro, whose poems were not published until after his death (1530). The first edition appeared in 1531, and contained Part III.; this part, including the above-mentioned Sonnet, is absent from many editions, and for this reason long escaped discovery as the source of Wiat's Sonnet; it appears again in the Florence edition of 1533.[1] It is probable that a copy came into Wiat's hands before he left Calais. The earliest date for translating the poem is *during 1531*. In 1532 he returned to England, was appointed Sheriff of Kent, and was busily occupied until

[1] See *Modern Language Quarterly*, Vol. V., 1902, for the paper on this subject by Mr. Arthur Tilley.

called to Court to assist at the Coronation of Anne Boleyn the following year (1533).

These events fit in with the place of the Sonnet in the MS. The Court poems immediately follow, and continue until the first Satire, *which was certainly composed in 1536.* Two Sonnets only are found amongst the Court poems: "The lyvely sparkes," probably written in honour of a Court lady, and "Such vayne thought." Four Sonnets in lighter vein, and found only in the D. MS. (the Court Album), most probably belong to this period. The Sonnet "Unstable dreme" was written in Spain in 1537. Another, celebrating May Day, "You that in love," was composed during Wiat's brief visit to England in May 1538. The last Sonnet in the E. MS., "If waker care," was composed in Spain, and must be assigned by its position to 1538–9. The last three Sonnets of the group are late compositions: "The pillar pearishd is," written on Cromwell's death in 1540, is found in the A. MS. as well as in Tottel. The two Sonnets "Such is the course" and "The flaming sighes" (a double sonnet) were probably written in prison, 1541, and survive only in Tottel.

No. 1. **Cesar, when that.** From Petrarch, see Appendix A.

l. 1. Classical allusions are rare in Wiat. When they occur they are generally translations.

l. 3. *Covering* scans as three syllables. Tottel inserts "hearts" before "gladnes."

The scansion marks in the text follow the MS. *cruel*, l. 8, and *chaunceth*, l. 9, have Wiat's sign for slurring.

Passion, l. 9, scans as three syllables—the usual sixteenth-century pronunciation.

l. 13 betrays the apprentice hand, and suggests a mere numbering of syllables. The Romance accent must be observed in the earlier Sonnets, *i. e.* until after 1532.

The first Sonnet was, perhaps, chosen for its reference to the classic figure of Julius Cæsar, whom Wiat held in admiration, according to Leland. See Appendix B. "Næniæ in Mortem Viati." [1] Leland relates that Wiat wore a ring engraved with the figure of Cæsar.

Cæsaris effigies in qua verissime Juli
Sculpta, occludendis signum spectabile chartes
Cæsaris at summam virtutem calcar imago
In genitas auxit vires animosque Viati.

Although this Sonnet is a translation, its temper reflects Wiat's attitude of mind in the disguising of sad thoughts under a similitude of gaiety (ll. 11–14).

l. 14. *To cloke my care but under sport and play.* These words recall the "Vita Nuova," Ch. VII., where Dante [2] calls the "faithful of Love" in the words of Jeremias the Prophet, Lamentations i. 12. The Sonnet begins with the lines—

Ovoi, che per la vico d'Amor passate
Attendete e guardate
S'egli è dolore alcun, quanto il mio grave.[3]

The last stanza runs—

Si che volendo far come alloro
Che per vergogna celan lor mancanza,
Di fuor mostro allegranza
E deutro dallo core struggo e ploro.

admirably translated by M. Henry Cochin—

[1] "Annulus Viati," Leland's *Næniæ*, 1542.

[2] Dante's interpretation —Intendo chiamare li fedeli d'Amore per quelle parole di Geremia profeta che dicono : O vos omnes qui transitis per viam attendite et videte si est dolor sicut dolor meus.

[3] Dante's interpretation, p. 22. King's Classics ed. 1908.

> Aussi voulant faire comme ceux-là
> Qui par vergogne ont caché leur faiblesse
> Au dehors je montre allégresse
> *Et au dedans du cœur je me consume et pleure.*

and by Dante Gabriel Rossetti—

> And thus it is that I, being like as one
> Who is ashamed and hides his poverty,
> Without seem full of glee,
> *And let my heart within travail and moan.*

This Sonnet was inserted in the *Nugæ Antiquæ*, I. p. 197. Ed. 1769.

No. 2. **The longe love.** From Petrarch, see Appendix A. This Sonnet is a good example of Wiat's selection of the conceited Sonnet, in preference to the more graceful examples portraying Petrarch's love of nature. Wiat, like Donne, enjoyed conceits, though there is a great difference in their method of handling. Wiat was the first to transplant the style, following the continental fashion. His work, therefore, had all the freshness of invention for his contemporaries and for those of the next generation, and the conceit had full play in the Elizabethan age. Donne, writing at the end of the conceited period, was obliged to invent new "ramifications of thought"; and, his genius being greater than his wit, he turned the original style of poetical fancy into rare figures of imaginative power.

lustes, l. 6, and *hideth*, l. 11, scan as two syllables.

hardines, l. 8, has the Romance accent on the second syllable.

where with all, l. 9, is a slurred foot scanning as two syllables.

l. 14 is an example of the very harsh method occasionally employed by Wiat, at this period, of cutting the ten-syllable line into two equal parts by the cæsura after the *fifth syllable.*

Since many of Wiat's characteristic rules of verse are exemplified here, it is not a success, as a sonnet. Without going into the controversy as to what *definite rules*[1] must be observed for a sonnet, it is universally acknowledged that Dante, and Dante's circle as well as Petrarch, set the example of *perfect harmony and modulation* of rhythm in the Sonnet form. This characteristic is discoverable in all great English sonnets. Wiat's rugged style of verse is very effective in Satire, but does not show to advantage in the sonnet. He was evidently conscious of the harsh note in the earlier Sonnets, for he not only employs the form rarely after 1536, but conforms to a more regular style in his later Sonnets.

Note that the various criticisms on Wiat's versification exemplified by this Sonnet *have not been drawn from Wiat's version, but from that of Tottel,* and therefore miss much of their application in Wiat's text.

No. 3. **Who so list to hount.** Adapted from Petrarch, see Appendix A. Romanello's version of the same theme is interesting. The only direct borrowing from Romanello appears in l. 13, "Cæsaris enim sum," *For Cæsar's I ame* (Wiat's version).

Even this is doubtful, for all three writers have adapted a well-known Latin motto, "Noli me tangere Cæsaris enim sum." Wiat quotes the first half of the motto (l. 13), and translates the second half. Romanello, on the contrary, translates and adds to the first half, and keeps the second half in the original. Petrarch gives the substance of the Latin in Italian.

l. 1. *Who so list to hount.* Note slurred second foot, "list to͡ hount."

[1] The so-called absolute division into octave and sestet has been broken by two of the greatest English sonneteers—Milton and Wordsworth. Petrarch himself does not keep to this division in at least *one* sonnet.

Wiat set the example, followed by Milton, in regarding initial "h" as no letter in the slurring of vocal syllables. (See R. Bridges on *Milton's Prosody*, Oxford, 1901.)

l. 14. *wylde* scans as two syllables by "poetical licence." (See note on Rondeau 3, l. 11.)

The free treatment of Petrarch's theme has suggested a personal application to Wiat's own experience in regard to Anne Boleyn. Cf. G. F. Nott,[1] H. H. Child,[2] and Prof. Courthope.[3] Nott regarded Wiat's feeling for Anne as a passion. I agree with Prof. Courthope that his intercourse with her was limited to a game of gallantry. See Appendix F on this subject.

No. 4. **Was I never yet.** From Petrarch, see Appendix A. There is a touch of humour discernible in Wiat's treatment of this Sonnet. He rebels against the utter subjugation of the lover as laid down in the old Code of the Court of Love, and followed by the Petrarchan school. He negatives Petrarch's line—

> Et voglio anzi in sepolcro bello et bianchi
> I will *nót* | yet ín | my gráve | be búr|ièd.

Macgregor translates the passage—

> I wish a tomb whose marble fine and fair,
> When this tired spirit and frail flesh are two
> May show your name to which my death is due.

Mr. Child finds this sentiment characteristically English and manly; but it is also found in the French sonnet by Louise Labé, Lyonnaise, "Tant que mes yeux," l. 9, "*Te ne sonharte encore point mourir.*" Wiat's own code in friendship is mutual respect and love and faithfulness. See next sonnet, ll. 9–14.

1 *Works*, Vol. II. 571.
2 *Cambridge History of English Literature*, Chap. VIII. p. 167.
3 *History of English Poetry*, Vol. II. p. 46.

No. 5. **Eche man me telleth.** No source has been discovered for this sonnet. From its temper it is probably original. The poet having been accused of changeableness, he retorts that it is the fashion; only those who would be considered wise are constant, and he is not "of such maner condition." The octave is in a bantering tone. The sestet is un-Petrarchan in its terse candour. Constancy in friendship must be mutual. Those who blame him for his "diversnes" are to blame for their instability. If they remain faithful to him, he will be loyal to them in word and deed.

l. 6 scans

And I͡ame | not of suche | manèr | condi|tion

l. 9. *Moost* has time equivalence of one foot.

l. 14. *Oon your owne.* "Oon" is substantival. The phrase is dialectal, meaning 'your own love,' or 'friend.'

No. 6. **If amours faith.** A close translation of the Italian, see Appendix A, except l. 6, where Wiat has "lower or higher" for the Italian "a pena intese."

The rhyme-ending "-aynèd" scans as three syllables. (sdrucciola rhyme) in ll. 1, 4, 5 and 8.

l. 11. *sorrowfull* scans as two syllables.

l. 13. The cæsura comes after the fifth syllable, cutting the verse into two equal parts, with very harsh effect. The best way of scanning is

Ar cáuse | that by | lóve || mysélf | I destróye.

Cf. Rondeau 1. 1, and Sonnet 2. 1, where "love" is a monosyllabic foot.

No. 7. **Farewell love.** The source of this Sonnet has not been found; it reads like an imitation, but contains personal touches, altered from the original version: cf. l. 3, "*Senec* *and Plato* call me from thy lore." The D. (probably earlier) version reads, "To sore a hope hath called." *Seneca* was a favourite author with Wiat. He writes from Spain to his son: "I would Seneca [be] your study"; and one of his late poems is a translation of a passage in Seneca's "Thyestes."

Plato. Expressions in the late poems indicate Platonic ideas. Wiat had probably begun the study of Greek in 1518 at Cambridge, when R. Croke was appointed the first Professor to the Greek chair.[1] He had also visited Florence, the centre of Neoplatonism, in 1527.

l. 9. *goo trouble younger hertes.* Wiat was about twenty-seven when he left England in 1528. The chapter of his youth was closed, from henceforth life had a sterner purpose. In the days when manhood was assumed at the age of fifteen, it is no wonder that men aged rapidly and were considered old at forty!

The Romance accent is to be observed in the rhyme-ending "-èr," ll. 1, 4, 5 and 8, with slurred feet, "for evèr," l. 1, "for to endevèr," l. 4.

No. 8. **My hert I gave.** From two Strambotti, Serafino, see Appendix A. The octave is a close translation of the first strambotto. The sestet is a free rendering of the second.

l. 10. *be craft.* "be" is dialectal for instrumental "by" (northern counties, including Yorkshire). Many phrases and peculiar words are to be traced to Wiat's Yorkshire origin.

l. 13. *bering in hand.* A common sixteenth-century phrase, with various meanings: to keep in expectation, to persuade, to accuse, to amuse with false pretences.

[1] Erasmus had lectured, unofficially, in Greek at an earlier date, see J. Bas. Mullinger, *The University of Cambridge to 1535.*

> *Bore* many gentleman, myself being one,
> *In hand*, with hope of action.—*Measure for Measure*, i. 5.
>
> His sickness, age, and impotence
> Was falsely *borne in hand.*—*Hamlet*, ii. 1.

The meaning here is that of expectation.

l. 14 exactly translates Serafino's line, "Zappa nel acqua et nella harena semina." The expression occurs in Chrestien de Troyes, "Cligès," [1] l. 1035–7. It is a commonplace that conceits are to be traced to Provençal writers and from thence, by two streams, to France and Italy. Hence England comes under the double influence of France and Italy in this respect.

No. 9. **There was never ffile.** No source has been discovered. The accentuation of termination "-èd" in the octave and "-èr" in the final couplet suggest early composition. It is also found in one of the earlier groups of the D MS.

l. 1 scans—

There was nêv|er ffí|le || half | so well | filèd |

The word *ffile* has various meanings besides the commonly accepted one—a polishing instrument. It is found in Northern England, substantively and predicatively, for a deceiver, coward, an immoral person and defiler.[2] There

[1] "Cligès," l. 1036 *et seq.*, "If he does not love and has not loved, then have I been sowing in the sea, where no seed can take root."

> Et s'il n'aimme ne n'a amé
> Donc si je an la mer semé,
> Ou semance ne puet reprandre.

[2] Cf. (1) Cupid with his filèd tongue.—Fairfax' *Tasso.*
(2) He most pricke and well affyle his tonge.—*Prol.* 714.
(3) Sory he was that fals fyle
And thogt more to begyle.—*Cursor Mundi.*

is a play upon the various meanings of the word in the first quatrain. The whole tenor of the poem expresses the deceiving of one who has formerly deceived in his youth, and has since repented. Nemesis falls at a later day from an unlooked quarter. The recompense is just : he cannot complain ; but the result of the deception is loss of confidence in the person who has deceived him. This Sonnet is obviously connected with the dark passage of his life to which Rondeau 9 refers. The Sonnet is entitled "To my ——," with no name inserted. Both poems are evidently original. Wiat is curiously modern here in his treatment of moral problems, because of his reasonable and fair attitude. He hated falseness and cowardice and want of faith, and regarded evil as such, apart from sex, not to be blamed in one and condoned in another.

l. 9. *I have* is slurred as one syllable.

No. 10. **Som fowles there be.** From Petrarch, see Appendix A. Puttenham praises this Sonnet,[1] saying, "Very well Englished by Sir Thomas Wiat," and adds his own version, which is much inferior. Wiat's style is increasing in flexibility. The first quatrain is very graceful. The latter part suffers through excessive use of slurred feet, ll. 6, 9, 10 and 12; with double slurring in l. 7, "The cón | trary of it |."

l. 12. *Tery yen*, translation of "gli occhi lagrimosi." Cf. Chaucer—

> Hir tery face atwixe hir armes hyde.—*T. & C.* IV. 821.

l. 14. *I run into the glede* is a happy rendering of the somewhat prosaic Italian, "I vo dietro a quel che vi arde," "I go again to that which burns me" : "glede" is commonly

[1] Arber English reprints, *Arte of English Poesy*, III. 249.

used in Chaucer.[1] Wiat's language is consciously archaic: he prefers the good old English words—a course approved by Gascoigne and Puttenham later. "I have always bene of opinion," says Gascoigne, "that it is not impossible eyther in Poemes or in Prose too write both compendiously, and perfectly in our Englishe tongue. And therefore although I chalenge not unto my selfe the name of an English Poet, yet may the Reader finde oute in my wrytings, that I have more faulted in keeping the olde English wordes (*quamvis iam obsoleta*) than in borowing of other languages, such Epithets and Adjectives as smell of the Inkhorne."—*The Epistle to the Reverend Divines Works*, I. 5. And Puttenham exhorts the "good maker" not to use words of great length "which have been fetched from the Latine inkhorne or borrowed of strangers; the use of them in rhyme is nothing pleasant."—*Arte of Englishe Poesie*, II. viii. 95.

Prof. Saintsbury and Mr. H. Child instance this Sonnet as showing a possible influence of the Troilus measure in Wiat's handling of the Sonnet form, because of the break after the seventh line. The reason, however, is found in the Italian. In this sonnet Petrarch breaks the rule of absolute division between octave and sestet, see ll. 7–9.

> Proran l'altra vertu, quella ch'encende.
> Lasso, el mio loco e'n questa ultima *schera !*
> *Ch'i'non* son forte ad aspectar la luce,

where the Italian has a definite break after the seventh, and an exclamatory line in the eighth, which runs on into the ninth. Here is an instance of the fallacy of the universal negative. Wiat translates the original closely here, and follows the Italian in the irregularity. Except for the deliberate imitation of Skelton's seven-lined stanza, in

[1] Cf. A thousand sykes (sighs) hottere than the glede.—*T.* IV. 337.
The cruel ire reede as any glede.—*K. T.* 1997.

"Myne olde dere enmy," Wiat seldom employs Troilus measure in his earlier studies.

No. 11. **Bicause I have.** From Petrarch, see Appendix A. The lover apostrophizes his tongue, his tears and his sighs, because they are not sufficiently under his command. This style of conceit had a long history, and specially commended itself to the troubled lover in the sixteenth century. The tongue which the lover has kept from falsehood for his lady's sake plays him tricks when he wishes to avow his love to her, and is either silent or else stammers. An old conceit, cf. Chrestien de Troyes, for example, in "Cligès"—

> They (lovers) speak by glances from their eyes; *but they are so craven with their tongues that in no wise dare they speak of the love which masters them.* God[1]! whence comes this fear to him that he fears a single maiden weak and timid, simple and shy? . . .

l. 7. *If thou speke towerd,* signifies if you come to the point in the sense of an avowal of love. "To be toord" is dialectal in northern counties; to speak of the matter in hand (W.D.D.); "towerd" was evidently unknown to Wiat's editors: it was changed to "koward" in E, and G. Nott altered to "if thou speak o' word." Such corrections are striking instances of the manner in which Wiat's text has suffered through alteration. Wiat's origin, as a native of Yorkshire, is a clue in such cases. The words altered are dialectal, and evidently unknown by his early editors. Grimould came from Huntingdon, Tottel was a Londoner; even Harrington, whose family originally came from Yorkshire, was ignorant of the meaning of "heins" (see Ps. 143, l. 16), and altered it in the 1549 edition of the Psalms.

l. 12. *And you so reddy sighes.* For a very beautiful

[1] .3845. Deus ! ceste crieme don li vient
Qu'une pucele sole crient,
Foible et coarde, simple et coie ?

rendering of the conceit of tears and sighs, see Dante, *N. V.*, XXXII. 21, where tears, the solace of grief, failing, the lover has resort to sighs.

> Venite a intender li sospiri miei,
> Oi cor gentili, che pietà'l disia
> Li quai disconsolati vanno via
> E s'e'non fosser, di dolor morrei ;
> Pero che gli occhi mi sarebber rei.

shright, found in Chaucer as past participle or preterite.

> The owle eek which that hight Ascaphilo
> Hath after me shright all thise nightes two.
> *T. & C.* V. 319–320.
>
> Shrighte Emelye and howleth Palamon.
> *Kt. T.* A. 2817.

No. 12. **I fynde no peace.** From Petrarch, see Appendix A. "Puttenham quotes the first two lines as a specimen of good Iambic verse, consisting wholly of monosyllables" (G. Nott, *Works*, II. 540). The conceit of the "contraries" is found in every language in the sixteenth century. Cf. the Rondeau of S. Gelay, "Jai trop de peine," and that of C. Marot, "Pas contradictions." It still flourished in Donne's time.

> Oh to vex me, contraryes meet in one
> Inconstancy unnaturally hath begott
> A constant habit.
> *Works of Donne*, Sonnet 18. Oxford Press, 1912.

Wiat recognizes the logical absurdity of the conceit in his song—

> To cause accord and to aggre

Like Sir Philip Sidney, and Shakespeare after him, he criticizes the fashion, but continues to employ it, as effective and really true in matters of love.

Notice the run of one-syllable words in this Sonnet. Gascoigne, in *Certaine Notes of Instruction*, § 5, says—

Here by the way I think it not amisse to forewarne you that you thrust as few wordes of many sillables into your verse as may be. And hereunto I might alledge many reasons : first the most auncient English wordes are of one sillable, so that the more monasyllables that you use, the truer Englishman you shall seeme, and the lesse you shall smell of the Inkehorne.—p. 463, Cambridge edition, 1907.

Puttenham, about ten years later, writes : "And ye shall find verses made all of monosillables to do very well : but lightly they be Iambickes bycause for the more part the accent falles sharpe upon every second word rather than contrariwise, as this of Sir Thomas Wiat's—which he quotes in somewhat free fashion as follows—

I finde no peace and yet mine warre is donne
I fearr and hope, and burn and freese like ise."

No. 13. **Though I my self.** This Sonnet is a lover's soliloquy, in which he views his situation on the one hand, and his responsibilities on the other, as "being instructed *in love*" that he may "faithfully uphold the customs and rites of his court."[1] The old chivalrous ideal of love mingles with the new platonic idealization of love. The old idea of the knight winning his lady by valour (as we read in "Cligès," for example) is interwoven with the intellectual ideal (ll. 1–4). The will restrains the senses. No man can hinder virtue while the will retains its mastery (ll. 5–8); the lover must be ever on the alert, trusting to time, truth and love to win his lady in the end (ll. 9–11); but the body wars against the spirit, causing the lover sorrow. For the platonic aspect, cf. M. Sève, "Délie," No. LVI.

[1] Quoting again from the "Cligès," which is a good example of a prevailing custom—

Vos qui d'Amor vos feites sage
Qui les costumes et l'usage
De sa cort maintenez a foi . . .

Le corps travaille a forces enervies,
Se resolvant l'Esprit en autre vie
Le sens troublé voit choses controuvées
Par la memoire en phantasmes ravie.
Et la Raison estant d'eux asservie
(Non aultrement de son propre delivre)
Me detenant sans mourir et sans vivre
En toy des quatres a mis leur guerison
Doncques a tort, ne t'ont voulu poursuyvre
Le corps, l'Esprit, le sens, and la Raison.

Notice the systematic use of Alexandrines for the concluding line of every part of the Sonnet, ll. 4, 8 and 11.

l. 6. scans—

Thy vér|tué | to lét || though that fró|werdnés,

with time equivalence on the second foot.

No. 14. **My galy**. From Petrarch. The likening a distressed lover to a ship in a storm is one of the most popular among the Petrarchists. It reappears in our time in H. Heine's *Verschiedene*, "Mit schwarzen Segeln," and in G. Carducci's Sonnet, "Passa la nave mia sola, tra il pianto." The earliest rendering of the conceit in English is traced back to the Old English poem, "Christ," where life is likened to a voyage.[1]

Prof. Courthope's just criticism of this Sonnet is as follows : "This is the production of an energetic mind ; nevertheless, the means employed are inadequate to the end, as

[1] Nu is þon ȝelicost, swa we on laȝuflode
Ofer cald wæter ceolum liðan,
ȝeon ' sidne sæ sundhenȝestum
Flodwudu ferȝen ; is þat frecne stream.
Yða ofermæta, þe we her on lacað
ȝeond þas wacan woruld, windȝe holmas
Ofer deop ȝelad wæs se drohtað stronȝ
Ær þon we on londe ȝeliden hæfden
Ofer hreone hrycg.—"Christ," 851-9 ; Grein. iii. 30.

may be specially noted in the unsuccessful attempt to render

> A ciaseun remo un pensier pronto e rio
> Che la tempesta e'l fin par ch'abbi a scherno.[1]—ll. 5-6.

and by the omission of any equivalent for "arte" in the thirteenth line caused by the necessity of rhyming. On the other hand, Wiat's strong individuality asserts itself in his alteration of Petrarch's "i duo miei dolci *usati* segni" ("my two sweet familiar stars") into the vehement

> The stars be hid that led me to this pain (l. 11).—
> *History of English Poetry*, II. 53.

Cf. the thought, finely rendered, in l. 11 to ll. 13-14 of the previous Sonnet.

Wiat's contemporary, M. Sève, expresses the metaphor in his characteristic symbolic style—

> Par maint orage ay secouru fortune
> Pour afferrer ce Port tant desiré
> Et tant me fut l'heur, et l'heure, importune
> Qu'a peine j'ay jusques ci respiré,
> Parquoy voyant, que mon bien aspiré
> Me menassait et mine et naufrage,
> Je fais carene attendant à l'umbrage
> Que voile fait mon aveugle Nocher.
> Qui depuis vint surgir en telle plage,
> Qu'il me perdit, lui sauve, en ton rocher.—"Délie," 39.

Margaret d'Angoulême derives the conceit from Petrarch, and employs the metaphor in the introduction to "Le Navire."

> *Navire loing du vrai port assablée*
> Feuille agitée de l'impetueux vent
> Ame qui es de douleur accablée
> Tire toy hors de ce corps non scavant
> Monte en espoir laisse ta vieille masse
> Sans regarder derriere viens avant.—"Le Navire," 1-6.

---

[1] At each oar a thought bold and guilty, which seems to think scorn alike of the tempest and the goal.—Courthope, *History of English Poetry* II. p. 53.

This conceit, though imitated by the school of Petrarch, belongs to all time; it is the most widely known poetic simile, whether we employ it for the heart, for the mind, or for the soul. The above illustrations of the same conceit give us three distinct aspects of thought amongst the eminent writers of Wiat's day. Wiat himself, as we have seen above, employed Petrarch with certain reservations of his own sincere, manly thought. Sève is symbolical and psychological, and Margaret d'Angoulême's verses flash with scintillations of poetic beauty, illuminated by her delicate imagination and mystical thought.

No. 15. **Avysing the bright bemes.** From Petrarch. The lover finds Love in the eyes of the lady, and is incited to "tread the old dance." The fruits of this experience being bitter, he rails at Love. Love, as ever among the Petrarchists, is a distinct personage, always working harm to lover or lady—never at one with both at the same time.

l. 1. *Avysing.* A translation of Italian "mirando." "Avysing," with the meanings of look at, consider, deliberate, observe, take heed, is common in Chaucer.

> This Juge his eyen caste
> Upon this mayde, avysinge him ful faste.—*C. T. C.*, 123–4.
> Lord ! so fast ye me avyse.—*T. & C.* ii. 276.

Wiat used the word in his dispatches, with the sense of observing closely. Cf. Spenser, *F. Q.*, II. ii. 7—

> He looked backe and her avizing well.

l. 10. In frossen though *nowe*, and *nowe ;* translation of the Italian "*or* com voglie gelate *or*"; rendered in French by "ore . . . ore": "qu'*ore* a joye, *ore* a deuil tu m'incites." [1]—
l. 12. *glad.* Monosyllable for second foot.

[1] M. Sève, "Délie," 344, 7.

l. 13. *hardines* has modern accent here. Cf. with "hardínes" in Sonnet 2.

l. 14. *ffruyte* scans as two syllables; *cometh* is slurred as one. Cf. with this line—

> A bliss in proof—and proved, a very woe.
> Shakespearean Sonnets, 129, l. 1.

No. 16. **Ever myn happ.** From Petrarch.

> l. 3. That leve | it or wait | it doth | me like | pain,

is entirely reconstructed in Tottel. The whole sonnet is faulty, the conceit overloaded and ungraceful. The Italian escapes failure through its harmony of rhythm. The sestet makes up for the want of taste in the octave by its lyrical beauty, brought out by reading aloud. Wiat, unfortunately, is harsh and irregular, and the faults of the Italian are increased tenfold, with the additional fault of the cæsura after the fifth syllable.

l. 6. *The See waterles, fisshe in the montain:* translated from

> e'l mar senz onda, et per l'alpa ogni pesce.

All Wiat's syllables are harsh, whereas those of the Italian are liquid. Moreover, his double rhymes overload the Sonnet and increase the harshness. Petrarch, no doubt, took the phrase from Boethius, one of the stock models of his day—

> Ne ye hiden not your gynnes on heye montaynes to kacchen fysshe.—Ch. translation of *De Consolatione* iii. Met. 8, 795.

l. 7. Wiat adds local colour by substituting "Tamys" (Thames) for Italian "Eufrate et Tigre."

l. 10. *rightwisely*, righteously, *i. e.* according to right; Wiat reverts to an archaic form < O.E. Riht wis-lice.

Right wis, rightwissnesse, are usual forms, but the adverb is not found, see Gavin Douglas, l. 8,

> **A blyst Byschop sone present in that place**
> **Off Canterbury he than was rychtwyss Lond.**
> *Blind Harry's Will*, **Wallace, l. 12–13.**

No. 17. **Love and fortune.** From Petrarch, see Appendix A. This is the most faulty Sonnet in the group.

l. 2. The presence of "that" four times is an unpardonable fault. Wiat has neither translated Petrarch nor managed his own version successfully in ll. 3–4.

l. 12. *not of steill but of brickell glasse.* The Italian reads "non di *diamente* ma d'un vetro"; Wiat's alteration is perhaps due to the fact that "steel or silver" was more commonly used for mirrors up to the sixteenth century; although glass mirrors are occasionally mentioned from the thirteenth century onwards, they were a novelty and an expensive luxury in Wiat's day. The beginning of the sixteenth century, however, saw glass mirrors introduced as a commodity. In 1507 two natives of Murano,[1] representing that they could make perfect mirrors of glass, obtained a monopoly for twenty years for the manufacture of glass mirrors. From this time onward for a century and a half Venetian glass mirrors were famous, and their manufacture was an important and lucrative trade.

ll. 13–14. The confusion of metaphors is inartistic. It is a matter of wonder that Wiat should have included so faulty a specimen in his manuscript. Its presence certainly strengthens the argument that this MS. was intended for his imitations of foreign verse and for his translations, which he

[1] Murano, an island and town of Italy one mile north of Venice, and celebrated from the eleventh century for its glassworks. It still manufactures mirror and other glass wares. In the fifteenth century it had a population of 30,000, and some efforts have been made to restore the glassworks to their old importance.—*Encyclopædia Britannica.*

regarded as more important than the occasional lyrics of his own composition.

No. 18. **How oft have I.** From Petrarch, see Appendix A. The conceit is intricate, and results in confusion of ideas. "Love" stands in the lady's eye; the lover's heart is conquered thereby and leaves his body, for it is now no longer his, but the lady will not give hers in exchange nor accept the lover's heart—hence the dilemma. The heart cannot live alone, neither can the lover without a heart. The sonnet concludes with this uncomfortable dilemma, and "points a moral" at the absurdity which was occasionally perpetrated in the name of conceit. After reading this with its involutions of thought leading to a "blind naye," compare the beautiful passage in "Cligès," from which extracts are quoted on pp. 20 *et seq.*

It is startling to find how inartistic Petrarch's ultra-conceited style is at times, when resolved into another language and robbed of the perfect grace of his setting. The beauty of the Italian language is answerable for the want of literary savour in the sixteenth century. Poets were carried away by the sweetness of the accents, relying more and more upon grace of style instead of quality of thought. This defect is glaring enough when seen through the medium of another language.

For a better and more manly rendering of the idea, compare Wiat's poem, "And if an Ie may save or sleye," with the refrain, "For the Ie is traitor of the Hert." In place of the extreme artificiality of the sonnet, we find sincere and deep sentiment in the later poem.

l. 2. *With those your Iyes.* Cf. Prol. I. of the Penitential Psalms, ll. 1–2—

> Love to give law unto his subjectes hertes.
> Stod in the Iye of Bersabe the bright.

l. 14. And *yowres . . . pain.* Wiat departs from the original, possibly on account of the need of a rhyming word. The Italian reads—

Et tanto piu de voi, quanto piu v'ama.
And yours the greater (harm) in as much as I love you more.

No. 19. **Like to these.** From Sannozaro, Part iii. *le rime*, printed in an edition of 1531 and in another of 1533. This Sonnet long eluded discovery because it only appears in Part iii. of *le Rime*, very seldom included in the editions of his poems, see Commentary, p. 26. Hence St. Gelais' French translation until recently was tâken for the source of Wiat's Sonnet. Mr. A. Tilley notified the correct source in the *Modern Language Quarterly.* The sonnet proves how misleading theories often are in the absence of fact, for the difference in Wiat's version, when compared with the French, has been regarded as originality in him.[2] When the Italian source came to light it was seen that Wiat's seeming departure from the French was in reality a close adherence to the Italian original. M. Sèves' dizaine, "De ces haultz monte jettant sur toy ma vue," is similar, but original. Puttenham, *Arte of English Poesy*, p. 142, quotes the first lines to show Wiat's use of acatalectic verse; he gives Tottel's rendering. This Sonnet marks the close of Wiat's poetical studies at Calais. The earliest date for the translation is 1531, being the year of the first appearance of the Italian sonnet. This fits in exactly with its position in the MS. The balance of the octave is disturbed by the double rhyme of "montayns," "fontayns," which breaks down in ll. 5, 8.

Wiat returned to England in 1532. Appointed Sheriff of Kent, he was busily employed "preparing his bills into Par-

[1] See article by A. Tilley, *Modern Language Quarterly*, Vol. V., 1902.
[2] Courthope, *History of English Poetry*, II. 53.

liament" (see Autograph Letter, p. 135), and had no leisure for poetry. In the October of 1532 he appears to have followed Henry VIII to France on a visit to Francis, and the following year he was again at Court. His presence there (1533–6) corresponds, I think, with the poems that follow this Sonnet.

In the later Sonnets, written at intervals between 1532 and the year of his death (1542), Wiat vindicates his position as a sonnet-writer. All undue harshness is gone; he seems to have recognized that the beauty of the sonnet lies in flowing rhythm and graceful language, and he manages to preserve his individuality without the harsh excrescences of his earlier attempts.

No. 20. **The lyvely sperkes.** Adapted from Petrarch. The conceit consists of the metaphor employed in lightning and thunder. The lightning is a glance from the lady's eye. The thunder is her "nay." "Nay" has been altered to "noise," in the D. MS. and in Tottel, thus obscuring the metaphor.

ll. 1–3. *The lyvely sperkes, that issue from those Iyes . . . Have prest myn heart.* See *Vita Nuova*, XIX., ll. 51–54.

> Degli occhi suoi, come ch'ella gli mova
> Escono spirti d'amore infiammati,
> Che feron gli occhi a qual che allor gli guati,
> E passan si che'l cor ciascun retrova.

l. 11. *I not.*, i. e. "I know not" (O.E. "ne wat"). Cf. No. 2, ll. 1–14.

The Sonnet is purposely uneven here in the sestet, and is not harsh from want of skill. The octave expresses the lover happy under the light of his lady's eye, then, dazed by her lightning glance, he stumbles as a blind man, ll. 10–11. The cæsura after the fifth syllable gives a halting movement to the verse, in keeping with the idea of the stumbling lover. This device is not infrequently used by Wiat.

l. 14. *nay*. G. Nott restored this reading, placing it between quotation marks.

No. 21. **Such vayn thought.** From Petrarch. The error of overmuch metaphor is due to the Italian. Wiat's rendering is remarkably fine.

l. 9. *disdaynfull browe* is a happy correction in Wiat's hand from the first reading, "the scornful brow." Mr. Padelford notes (*Sixteenth-Century Lyrics*, p. xxiv) the beauty of the Italian.

l. 11. *Which comforteth the mynde that erst for fere shoke*. The Italian reads: "Che'n parte rasserena il cor doglioso"; Wiat, as usual, ignoring nature touches, renders "which comforteth the mynde that erst for fere shoke," giving the idea of peace after mental storm; Petrarch has in mind the picture of the placid blue of the heaven when it has been gently brought back to serenity after the tempest clouds have lifted.

These differences bring out the essential qualities of the Italian and English poet. It is in such renderings that Wiat's individuality is clearly seen. Petrarch lavishes all his skill in painting nature with a loving hand, Wiat is equally observant in detecting and understanding attitudes of mind; but while the one is a past master of his art, the other is still at school.

It is by such lines as this, quoted above, that Petrarch has gained his place among the world's poets for the beauty and vividness of his poetic images derived from nature impressions.

No. 22. **I abide and abide.** Adapted from Serafino's "Lasso oimé." This and the following Sonnet are found only in the D. MS. Missing pages in the E. MS. may account for their absence, but this is original, following the ideas and language of Chaucer in the many references to Fortune, and copying the more regular type of Skeltonic verse. Wiat appears to have kept his MS. chiefly for his translations and for his experiments in metre in light verse, as well as his new metres from the Italian. The poems written for the pastime of the Court were evidently not considered worthy of being preserved, except the best examples, such as "A Robyn," and "My lute awake."

l. 1–2. The "olde proverbe" is found in the Envoy to the "Plaint," Thynne's edition of *Chaucer*, published in 1532—

> **Better is it to suffer and fortune abide**
> **Than hastily to clime and sodenly to slyde.**

Judging from the use Wiat and Surrey made of it, Chaucer was doubtless the favourite book of the Court circle.

Wiat, imitating Chaucer, constantly refers to Fortune, the fickle one, especially in the lighter, original poems. "my lady," l. 3, of course, refers to Fortune.

Cf. this metre with that of Rondeau 4, "Help me to seke."

The coupling of sound to sense is observable in the line—

> **Aye | me | this long abidyng**

The run of long-drawn-out vocal syllables has the effect of a long sigh.

No. 23. **Dyvers dothe use.** Wiat's sense of humour prompts him at times to oppose the slavish attitude of the wailing lover. The sonnet above alludes to the fickleness of Fortune, this alludes to fickleness in love.

l. 3. *to lynne*, to cease.

l. 14. Cf. Sonnet 25, l. 14, for this sentiment, *To long* delaies and chaunging at the laste. This is one view of the case; for another cf. the idea of "like to like."

The lover who finds fickleness is in most cases fickle himself. "Eche thing seketh his semblable."

No. 24. **My love toke skorne.** *toke*. T. and G. Nott both replace *toke* by "to." Wiat's language is superior. "My love became scornful and refused my service. She is to blame, since I lost my liberty to her in all good faith. But as things are so, I shall not fret." It is similar in tone to the last.

l. 4 is wanting in Tottel and the later printed editions, including the 1812 edition of John Nott. George Nott first replaced the line from the Devonshire MS. in his edition (1816).

No. 25. **To rayle or jest.** There is deep earnestness and even bitterness of feeling underlying this sonnet. It carries on the idea in the preceding sonnets, 22–24, of a woman's want of faith. Wiat had a contempt for want of sincerity; see Letter to his Son: "Be no mocker, mockes follow them that delyght therein; have your friends in reverence and think unkindnes to be the greatest offence.

The concluding couplet is bitter in tone: "Sincerity and faithfulness rewarded by ficklenes." These sonnets appear to reflect Wiat's passing attitude of mind resulting from some disappointment.

No. 26. **Unstable dreme.** From Filosseno's strambotta, "pareami in questa nocte," see Appendix A. Probably composed in Spain, as it follows the poem "Though this port," and precedes the Epigram "Of Catage he," containing direct reference to his place of residence in Spain. For carefulness of execution it is comparable to No. 21, but the last couplet is harsh. Cf. Scève's rendering of the same idea, striking in its restraint of language, beauty of simile, and purity of thought. It contains a graceful simile in the last line.

A l'embrunir des heures tenebreuses
Que somnus lent pacifie la Terre
Ensevely sous Cortines umbreuses,
Songe a moi vient qui mon esprit desserre.
Et tout aupres de celle là la serre
Qu'il reverait pour son royal maintien
Mais par son doulx et privé entretien,
L'attrait tant sien, que puis sans crainte aucune
Il m'est advis, certes que je la tien
Mais ainsi, comme Endimion la Lune.

No. 27. **You that in love.** An original poem and the best of the sonnets. It is Chaucerian in tone and rhythm, and is reminiscent of his phrasing. It is a May Song, and was probably composed in May 1538, when Wiat paid a brief visit to England with proposals from the Emperor concerning the treaty between Francis I, Charles V and the Pope. Henry VIII desired to act as mediator on this occasion.

The sonnet is in Wiat's happiest manner, and is of importance because of the personal touches.

ll. 3–4. Cf. Chaucer.

Til it fil ones in a morwe of May . . .
She was arisen and al redy dight
For May wol have no slogardye or nyght.

K. T., 1034, 1041–2.

And—

Do wey your bok rys up and lat us daunce
And lat us don to may som observaunce.

T. & C. II. iii. 2.

ll. 6–7. May was a fateful month in Wiat's life. He was imprisoned in the Fleet, May 1534, for an affray in the London streets, and in May 1536 on account of a hasty quarrel with the Duke of Suffolk. He had been imprisoned in Italy in 1527 (probably May), at the time of Sir John Russell's mission to the Papal Court.

In May, at the time of this Sonnet, he was in the midst of very difficult and anxious diplomatic work for Henry VIII, being conscious that his master's interests were not gaining ground with the Emperor. See Biographical Table, Vol. I. p. xv.

l. 9. *Sephanes* refers to a person (unknown) who had drawn up Wiat's horoscope.

Turberville has expanded this Sonnet into a long poem beginning—

> You that in May have bathde in blis
>   And founde a salve to ease you sore
> Do May observaunce : reason is
>   That May should honord be therfore.

No. 28. **If waker care.** The opening lines only are based on Petrarch. The Sonnet contains personal touches. *Brunet*, ll. 8, 10, clearly refers to Anne Boleyn. The original version in E. MS. is

> Brunet that set our country in a rore. l. 8.

During the seven years' duration of the Divorce Suit, public opinion had steadily gained ground against Anne, culminating at the death of Queen Catherine, who was beloved by the nation and respected at Court. But a graver aspect of the case had been experienced by Wiat during his embassy in Spain, in the odium that attached to Henry's name in that country. The Emperor himself could not politically, and would not socially, overlook the indignity offered to his aunt, Catherine of Aragon.

l. 9. *Phillis*. The name introduces a pleasanter aspect. The friend of his later years, whom he had in mind when writing the Epigram, "A face that shuld content me." This friend was probably Mary, Duchess of Richmond, and sister to Henry Howard, the Earl of Surrey. The brother and sister were alike in their intellectual and artistic tastes.

Mary had some part in the D. MS., and her initials are on the cover. Henry was an enthusiastic admirer of Wiat, and the few facts known about Wiat's circle of friends encourage the belief that Mary was the friend of Wiat's later years. She appears to have been a woman of character. Intellectual, musical, sympathetic and cheerful, with a combination of grace and dignity, she was likely to appeal to a man of Wiat's temperament.

This is the last Sonnet in Wiat's manuscript.

No. 29. **The piller pearishd is.** From Petrarch. This Sonnet is in the A. MS., fol. 37b, and in Tottel. The difference of spelling is to be noted. It records Wiat's grief at the fall of Cromwell. The situation described is Wiat's own position, ll. 5–14. The last tercet is original, replacing the Italian.

> O nostra vita, ch' è si bella in vista
> Com'perde agevolmente in un mattiono
> Quel che'n molt annia gran pena s'acquista,

which is translated as follows in the version of this Sonnet by an "uncertayne" author (P. MS.)—

> O brittel lief w[t] face so faire ystained
> How easly lost th'art in a moment's space
> That many yeares w[t] muche a doo a tained.

Wiat states his own feelings and his position at the moment, knowing that his downfall is imminent, as the friend and servant of Cromwell.

We gather much concerning Wiat's attitude of mind from his selection or rejection of Petrarch's passages.

No. 30. **Such is the course.** Found only in Tottel. The Sonnet scheme is noteworthy, consisting of *three quatrains* in alternate rhymes, a b, with final couplet on a third rhyme, c.[1] It forms the link between the Petrarchean Sonnet in octave and sestet and the (so-called) Shakespearean Sonnet in three distinct quatrains and final couplet. This is the only example of the kind in Wiat, and it originated from the ottava-rima stanza, *the normal type for Wiat's short poems* in the middle and latter part of his life. In this Sonnet he merely doubled the first six lines of his Epigram form, and concluded with the couplet. For suggestion in Trissino concerning the three-quatrain form, see Appendix E.

ll. 1–2. These lines no doubt suggested the following in Surrey's "The sote season"—

The hart hath hung his old head on the pale,
  The buck in brake his winter coat he flings
The fishes flete with new repaired scale;
  The adder all her slough away she flings.

Cf. l. 5—

Why shoulde such spight be nursed in thy thought,

and l. 9—

Consider eke that spight availeth naught,

with "Blame not my lute," stanza four, and "Spite hath no power." From the sentiment it is not to be placed among the last sonnets, yet the facility of expression suggests maturity. It probably belongs to the second Court period, when Wiat composed a number of Epigrams.

Nos. 31–2. **The flaming sighes.** This Sonnet was written in prison, 1541. It is closely connected in thought with the Epigram, "Sighes ar my fode, drink are my teres."

Cf. l. 1, "The flaming sighes . . ." and l. 5, "the watred eyen . . ." with the above line of the Epigram, and ll. 13–14,

[1] Surrey's sonnet, "The sote season" is in the same scheme with the final couplet on the *a* rhyme.

The wound alas! happe in some othr place
From whence no toole away the skar can race,

with ll. 7–8 of the Epigram.

Sure I am Bryan this wounde shall heale agayn
But yet alas! the scarre shall styll remayne.

The same idea is repeated in the oration.[1]

ll. 19–20.

And wher as you, in weightie matters great
Of fortune, saw the shadow, that you know.

Like the Epigram, it was composed for a friend who had served his country.

ll. 22–23. Wiat remarks on the foulness of his dungeon in the Epigram "Sighes ar my fode"; he contracted fever there, and his health was shattered. The difference between the two Holbein portraits is remarkable. The one at Windsor, taken before his ambassadorship, is that of a young man; the other, taken less than six years later, portrays a face emaciated and considerably aged, with hollow temples and thinning hair.

The *individual* quality of Wiat's verse comes out in the last Sonnet and Epigram. When he had surmounted the difficulties of rhythm, his natural proclivity for strong, rapid, condensed utterance had fair play. This virile quality, combined with simplicity and directness of speech, are the vitalizing forces of his genius. The note of sincerity is as delightful as it is rare.

[1] As often, Wiat uses a proverbial expression: he quoted it in his oration: "These men thinketh it enough to accuse, and as all these slanderers use for a general rule: "Whom thou lovest not accuse: *for though he hele the wound yet the scarre shall remayne.*

THE EPIGRAMS

Sir Thomas Wiat's reputation as a poet in his own day rests largely on the Epigrams. The earlier Epigrams mark his return to Court and were written for ladies. In this respect he undoubtedly conceded to the French fashion set by C. Marot and M. de St. Gelais. But the style of Epigram is not French but Italian. It is modelled on the strambotti of Cimino Serafino d'Aquilano, an Italian Petrarchist of the Quincento, whose love of conceits and bombastic language led him into grave errors of taste. Wiat had already translated two of the strambotti into sonnet form.

Since Serafino's day, ottava-rima had developed into a perfect instrument of Italian metre. Bembo had polished and refined, Ariosto had perfected the form in the "Orlando Furioso," showing what a perfect instrument ottava-rima could become in the hands of a genius. Later, Tasso,[1] was to discover fresh founts of beauty in this wonderful measure. The sonnet, among sixteenth-century Italians, was the conventional form for conventional sentiment; ottava-rima was the form to conjure with. Wiat, with his customary penetration, had discovered its essential qualities in contemporary Italian poetry, and, what was more to the point, he found in it a measure peculiarly adapted to his own needs.

His wit, his condensed form of utterance, and his glowing style, were set out to the best advantage in ottava-rima; and the Epigrams represent his most finished work in slight forms of verse.

The earliest Epigram was written about 1532. The first thirteen are among the Court poems (1533–6), all light, but

[1] The author of the "Gerusalemme Liberata."

sufficiently varied: compliments, riddles, mock quarrels, with occasional graceful renderings of commonplaces, comprise this early group.

Nos. 14–15 are biographical, and present experiences of May 1536, when Wiat suffered a short imprisonment for striking the Duke of Suffolk. These two Epigrams are placed between the first and second Satires, poems certainly not written before May 1536.

Nos. 16–19 deal with life in Spain, and were written in Spain.

No. 20 is the farewell to Spain. It is written in Wiat's handwriting and is the last Epigram to be entered in his MS. during his lifetime. One other, "Vulcan begat me," is entered by a later hand.

The last poems deal with events, 1540–1.

Although direct influence is due to the Italian, there is a dual influence to account for Wiat's employment of the Epigram for Court poems. It was the medium in vogue at the French Court. Marot and St. Gelais derived a great part of their popularity from their witty *tours-de-force* in the shape of epigrams in the octave stanza, and its popularity at the English Court was largely due to its vogue at the French Court. Contemporary events had brought about a close union between the French and English Courts. Anne Boleyn was at length crowned in 1533, and Wiat acted as Chief Ewer, in the place of his father, at the wedding festivities. The Queen had been brought up in France, following Mary, the sister of Henry VIII, to Court, on her marriage with Louis of France in 1514, and remaining as lady-in-waiting to Queen Claude of France,[1] when Mary

[1] Apres que Marie fust revenu
En ce pays elle fust retenu
Par Claude que Royne apres succeda
Ch. Hist. de la roine Anne de Bouillant.

returned to England on her husband's death. Again, in 1532–3, Henry Duke of Richmond, son of Henry VIII, spent a year at the Court of Francis I, in company with Henry Howard, Earl of Surrey; they were treated with the same honour as the sons of France. These two young noblemen, returning from France early in 1533, took the places at Court due to their rank. The Duke of Richmond was an accomplished musician. Henry Surrey had early inherited the poetic instincts for which his older relatives were reputed, amongst whom Bourchier, Lord Berners and George Boleyn may be cited, as well as Henry Parker, Lord Morley. The King had honoured George Boleyn with important diplomatic service in France. Hence those in the immediate circle of the King had not only experienced French influence but were lovers of poetry and music. Politically, the King was strengthening his friendship with France, on account of the estranged relationship between England and Spain consequent upon the divorce and death [1] of Queen Catherine. In consideration of these facts, and the appearance of Wiat's Epigrams at this particular period, French influence must be conceded for the vogue of the Epigram, while the actual composition is derived from Italian sources.

No. 1. **Who hath herd.** The idea is derived from a passage in Skelton's "Philip Sparow." The curious inequality which is so remarkable in Wiat's verse is seen in still greater contrast in Skelton. A perfectly charming lyrical gift is portrayed in the "Philip Sparow," drawn with a grace and delicacy of touch that astounds, coming as it does in the midst of much that is either dull, or else lively in a way far from edifying.

[1] It was universally believed that the Queen had succumbed to poisoning, and that an attempt had been made on the life of Princess Mary.

Skelton had been the Court poet of Henry VII's reign, as well as tutor to Prince Henry. Cf. his lines—

> The Honour of England I learnt to speke
> And acquainted him with the Muses IX.

These lines give a clue to the rhythm of Wiat's "Help me to seke," Rondeau 4. It is at first sight surprising that Wiat does not show more imitation of Skelton, but the older poet died in 1529, when Wiat was abroad, and deep in the study of Italian verse.[1] Moreover, his early compositions are lyrical songs to be sung to the lute, Skelton's verse was meant for recitation. When Wiat began to study prosody in real earnest, he had great aspirations for English poetry, and in order to realize them he concentrated his efforts upon the introduction of Italian forms of verse—a work which left him neither time nor inclination to follow any English poet other than Chaucer. But the lyrical grace and humour of "Philip Sparow" made an impression upon him, and the idea of the following lines is to be seen in the first Epigram.

> I toke my *sampler ones*
> Of purpose for the nones
> *To sow* in stiches of silke
> My sparow white as milke,
> . . . .
> But when I was sowing his beke,
> Me thought my sparow did speke
> And open his pretty bill,
> Saying : maid ye are in will
> Again me for to kill,
> Ye prick me in the hed.
> With that my *nedle were red*,
> Methought of Philip's blode,
> Mine here right upstode.
>
> "Philip Sparow," 26–29 ; 35–43.

---

[1] See note on the Rondeau, p. 17. Wiat seems to have paid a passing compliment to Skelton, about the year 1529, when he composed "Myne olde dere enmy."

l. 2. *that when my plaint remembred her my woo*, etc., that is to say, "When my complaint reminded her of my woe which actuated it, she in cruel wise wished that each stitch as she sewed had pricked my heart." "remember" has the meaning "remind . . . of."

No. 2. **She sat and sowde.** A more graceful rendering of the same idea as the preceding Epigram; it is placed here for the sake of comparison. Its place in the MS. is fol. 37a. It is possible that Wiat was acquainted with the following dizaine of M. Sève; if so, the reason is more obvious for the inclusion of two Epigrams on the same theme in the Egerton MS.

Ouvrant ma Dame au labeur trop ardente
Son Dé luy cheut, mais Amour le luy dresse :
Et le voyant sans raison évidente
Ainsi trouve, vers Delie s'addresse.
C'est luy dit elle, afin que ne m'oppresse
L'aiguille aigue, et que point ne m'offence,
Donc, respond il, je croy que la deffence
Fais que par moy ton cœur n'est point vaincu.
Mais bien du mien, dy ie, a ferme essence
Encontre toi lui sert toujours d'ecu.

Note the opening of both poems, and the inclusion of "Amour" in the French version corresponding with the "blind maister" in Wiat, which suggests an imitation of the French poet in this Epigram. The notable difference between the preceding poem and "She sat and sowde," is the inclusion of this third person "Love"—always a distinct identity in Petrarch and his followers.

No. 3. **Alas madame.** A translation from Serafino. See Appendix A. From a textual point of view the poem is interesting; the MS. page contains two sets of corrections in Wiat's hand, easily detected by the difference in the ink.

There are besides two later hands. *See facsimile page of MS. reproduced on* p. 45, Vol. I.

l. 4. A characteristic phrase, *it may be amended*, which was common in Wiat's day, *and occurs in his dispatches*, is corrected to the more modern and more prosaic "mattr may be mended." The hand may be that of J. Harrington, but more probably that of G. Nott. The same hand appears in a correction of the Psalms. The conceit in ll. 5–8 found much favour among the sixteenth-century poets. The theme was employed for Sonnet as well as Epigram; we find it in C. Marot's Rondeau "En la baisant," ll. 9–13.

Bref mon esprit sans cognoissance d'ame
Vivoit alors sur la bouche à ma dame
Dont se mouvoit le corps enamouré
Et si le lievre eust gueres demouré
Contre la mienne, elle m'a sucie l'ame
En la baisant.

The Sonnet of Louise Labé, No. xviii, is derived from the same source. An ardent Petrarchist and passionate in tone, she has added still more colour to a theme which was already lacking in artistic restraint.

Baise m'encor, rebaise moy et baise
Donne m'en un de tes plus savoureus :
Donne m'en un de tes plus amoureus :
Je t'en rendray quatre plus chaus que braise.

No. 4. **The wandering gadlyng.** Prof. Koeppel has found the source in Ariosto's *Orlando Furioso*.

l. 1. *gadlyng*. Old English "gædeling," companion, degenerates in meaning in Middle English to a man of base degree, vagabond—the sole instance of the word in Wiat.

The expression that likens a lover's annoyed surprise to one that stumbles upon an adder is common in sixteenth-century writers. Cf. Shakespeare, *V. & A.*, 877.

Whereat she starts like one that spies an adder.

l. 5. Note absence of weak syllable after cæsura.

No. 5. **What nedeth these threning wordes.** From Serafino. See Appendix A.

l. 7 is an Alexandrine.

l. 8. *thothr*, usually a monosyllable, has the force of two syllables in this line.

No. 6. **Ryght true it is.** An instance of Wiat's many references to proverbial sayings. This and the next are in a seven-line stanza. The rhyming scheme is ababb, bb. No. 7 is in octosyllabic verse, with Troilus rhyme ababbcc.

l. 2. *that by thy back the claweth.* The expression "claw the back" is common both substantivally and predicatively for a flatterer. Cf. "Mirror for Magistrates"—

> And I had *claw-backs* even at court full rife
> Which sowght by outrage golden gains to win.

And Latimer's Sermons :—

> "These flattering *clawbacks* are original roots of all mischief." (Second Sermon before Edward VI, 1549.)

No. 7. **What wourde is that.** An example of a favourite Court device of setting riddles in verse. See also No. 8 and No. 22.

l. 3. *It is myn aunswer.* Corrected to "It is myn Anna" in Tottel; Nott follows Tottel. This is a flagrant example of the alteration of the MS. by Nott without duly recording it. The word "Anna" is written above the Epigram in the MS. In respect of Epigrams 6–7, the A. MS. shows evidence of blind copying; they are run together to form a poem of fourteen lines and are placed amongst the group of Sonnets.

No. 8. **A layde gave me.** Another riddle in rhyme; it is

found in A. and Tottel and is placed here as a companion poem to the preceding. The answer to the riddle is a kiss. Nott says (*Works*, 1816), "Selden ventures with some diffidence on the interpretation: 'I think it is a kiss.'" The kiss was the usual high-bred form of salutation between the sexes of the upper classes in England in Wiat's day. Erasmus remarks upon the custom with much relish. See his Letter to Faustus Andrelinus: "Wherever you go you are received on all hands with kisses; . . . when a visit is paid the first act of hospitality is a kiss, and when guests depart the same entertainment is repeated. . . . Oh! Faustus, if you had once tasted how sweet and fragrant those kisses are, you would wish to be a traveller not for ten years, like Solon, but for *your whole life, in England*."[1] It is only fair to add, however, that besides the "nymphs with divine features so gentle and kind"[2] enthusiastically worshipped by Erasmus, he experienced another type in the form of landladies—veritable sharks, concerning whom he makes opprobrious remarks!

Gascoigne imitated Wiat's poem as follows:—

A RIDDLE

A lady once did aske of me
  This preatie thing in privitie:
Good sir, quod she, faine would I crave,
One thing which you your selfe not have:
Nor never had yet in times past,
Nor never shall while life doth last.
And if you seeke to find it out,
You loose your labour out of doubt:
Yet if you love me as you say,
Then give it me for sure you may.
    Meritum petere, grave.
        Hearbes, I. p. 340. Camb. ed. 1907.
            Edited John W. Cunliffe.

---

[1] *Letters of Erasmus*, No. 98, p. 203, Ed. Nichols, 1901–4. [2] *Ibid.*

No. 9. **Some tyme I fled.** This is probably a translation, with local colour inserted to suit Wiat's case (l. 4).

It appears to be a reference to the King's visit to Calais, October 1532, to meet Francis I. Anne Boleyn was included in the party. Wiat's name is not amongst those in personal attendance on the King, but it is probable that he was chosen to superintend the arrangements for Henry's visit, being peculiarly fitted for the duty after his recent four years' experience at Calais. The whole trend of the poem corresponds to the contrast between his former and his present attitude towards Anne. Seven years before he had at least been interested in her, though there was probably no serious attachment. See Appendix F. Now his tone is one of thankfulness that the connection was broken (ll. 6–7). The period of the divorce suit corresponds with Wiat's absence from Court. The year that Henry VIII seriously considered making Anne his wife, Wiat left the Court. He went to France 1526, to Italy 1527, to Calais 1528–32. Returning to England 1532, he was made Justice of the Peace for Essex, and did not reappear at Court until the event of Anne Boleyn's coronation, May 1533. His presence at Calais in 1532 was probably merely official. The Epigram records Wiat's reflections on the irony of the situation. For seven years his absence from Court had been required, for fear his attractive personality should harm the King's suit. Now that the divorce arrangements are complete he is called to follow her whom he was forced to avoid in times past. But Wiat's present feelings are of surprise that he ever felt any attraction, l. 5: "Lo how desire is both sprung and spent." As a matter of fact, Wiat saw a very different woman in 1532; utterly changed from the vivacious and accomplished maid-of-honour, seven years of anxious scheming for Catherine's divorce, and the knowledge that she was doing her former mistress, the Queen, a grievous wrong, had hardened and embittered her character, and she had developed an insolence of bearing with an ungoverned temper. Wiat looked for noble qualities in a woman, and he found them in Mary Howard, sister of Henry, Earl of Surrey, shortly to be betrothed to the King's son Henry Fitzroy. Mary and her brother became the devoted friends of Wiat in later years.

l. 8. *Mashed . . . to-torne.* Wiat is now merely caught by the "briars that formerly had torn him severely," "to-torn" (with old intensitive prefix "to") meaning "torn to shreds." Tottel completely reverses Wiat's idea.

No. 10. **He is not ded.** From Serafino, see Appendix A. The alteration from the particular sense "I" to the general "he" is to be noticed. This change exemplifies one of the differences between Wiat's MS. and the D. MS. The particular (and earlier) sense is to be found in D.; the corrected form (in a general sense) is the reading of E.

The Epigram contains a personal reference to Wiat's imprisonment in the Fleet in May 1534. A fray occurred between his men and the citizens of London, and a sergeant was killed. Wiat was required to pay the penalty. A similar punishment was meted out to Henry, Earl of Surrey, recorded in the poem—

> London hast thou accused me
> Of breche of lawes the roote of stryfe.

ll. 7–8. *And eke the willowe.* Cf. Third Penitential Psalm, ll. 19–20—

> Under the wich I stowp and bowe to ground
> As willowe plant.

The simile of the willow is very dear to the conceited poets. Cf. willow, willow waly refrains in English songs.

No. 11. **The furyous gonne**, from Serafino. See Appendix. Cf. M. Sève, who, like Wiat, was drawing upon Petrarch and Serafino about the same time.

> Et le Canon qui peur et horreur mène
> Ne territ point par son bruit furieux
> Si durement les circonvoisins lieux
> Qui se ruine et sa fureur soutiennent.
> Que mes sanglots penetrants jusqu'aux c ieulx
> Esmeuvent cieux qui en cruaute règne.

Wiat follows the Italian; Sève takes the simile and applies it in his own fashion. He is hardly to be commended in this instance for the extravagant conceit of likening his sobs to the bursting of a cannon.

Turberville has imitated Wiat in an extended Sonnet of four quatrains and couplet in his *Songs and Sonets*, 1567: "Lyke as the gunne that hath to great a charge"; he introduces a new element, and weakens the poem by calling upon the lady, in conclusion, "to assist the gunner and seeke to quite his wo, Least in short time his gunne to peeces go."

No. 12. **Thenmy of liff.** Prof. Koeppel derives this Epigram from St. Gelais: it is probable that both English and French poems have a common Italian source.

No. 13. **Nature that gave the bee.** One of the "common sayings" woven into an Epigram in Wiat's most graceful manner. For other examples cf. No. 15 for a collection of proverbs (though it is a translation), No. 6, "Ryght true it is," for another popular saying, and Satire 3, ll. 1–4. A reference to the bee who gathers honey, and the spider, poison, from the same place, is to be found in Latimer's Sermons. Gascoigne says: "I had alledged of late by a right reverende father, that although in deede out of everie floure the industrious Bee may gather honie, yet by proofe the Spider thereout sucks mischeevous poyson." *Works:* "The Epistle to the Reverend Divines," p. 6, Cambridge Edition, 1907. The conceit is worked out with a moral significance by Latimer. Intended as a courtly compliment by Wiat, the setting is singularly harmonious.

No. 14. **Desire alas.** This Epigram suggests imitation of M. Sève, who was becoming renowned as the prize-winner of the best "blason," awarded by Renée, Duchess of Ferrara, and her Court. His work was distinguished by purity of sentiment and a platonic attitude of thought, attributes which won high praise from the woman whose intellect, manners and morals were the means of gathering round her the most brilliant and the most moral Court in Europe. Sève's dizaine is as follows—

Tant est Nature en volonté puissante
Et volonteuse en son foible povoir,
Que bien souvent a son veuil blandissan
Se voit par soy grandement decevoir.
A mon instinct je laisse concevoir
Un doulx souhait qui, non encor bien né,
Est de plaisirs nourry, et gouverné,
Se paissant puis de chose plus haultaine;
Lors estant creu en desir effrené,
Plus je l'attire plus a soy m'entraine.

The D. version varies considerably. It is given entire in the text.

No. 15. **Venemus thornes.** One of the most well-known Epigrams in Wiat's day. It is found in the E, D, P, and Harln. MSS. and in Tottel, with considerable variations; but *there is no doubt whatever* as to the correct version, since this Epigram is written in Wiat's own hand.

ll. 5-7. Cf. "Troilus and Cressida," iii. 1213-1216—

> O soth is said *that heled for to be*
> Men most drinke as men may alday see
> Full bittre drink.

No. 16. **In dowtfull brest.** One of the most forcible examples of the bad taste which lovers of conceits display at times. This incident is taken from Josephus' *History of the Jews*, Book VII. chap. viii., as follows: "There was a certain woman named Mary, rich and well born, who took sanctuary in Jerusalem." "Stript" of all her possessions and reduced to starvation by her cruel oppressors, "she delivered herself up to fury and necessity, and pitched upon the most unnatural resolution that was ever heard of.

"She had a child sucking at her breast, which she snatched up, and looking tenderly upon it, 'What,' says she, 'shall I say now to thee, thou most unfortunate infant, to be brought into the world under a complication of three such dreadful judgments as war, famine, and rebellion. . . . What canst thou do better now than to supply the want of a meal's meat to thy starving mother, and hag out the faction with the horror of the fact. And thus fully crown the history of the Jews with the only execrable abomination that is yet wanting to the perfection of their misery. . . ." So she partook of this ghastly meal, and left the remainder for the enemy. The news getting abroad, and the faction coming to her house and seeing this horror: "They stood like statues upon the very sight of it, and so fell trembling and ran, stark mad. The news of this deed was presently over the city, and such an abhorrence of it in general as if every man had had a part in the crime" (L'Estrange's Translation). *Josephus* was widely read in the sixteenth century. Latin editions were issued from the Paris press in 1513 and 15 9, and from the Lyons press in 1528. French translations followed. The Lyons edition appeared 1538. The first translation done in English was *The famous workes of*

Josephus' history out of the Latin and French by T. Lodge, 1602. Another edition from the French appeared in 1676 and L'Estrange's translation in 1702. *Josephus* came to be one of the books without which no library was complete, and within which few cared to venture.

A small item of interest attaches to this Epigram. Written in Spain, it is the only poem that suggests connection with Spanish men of letters. Diego Hurtado de Mendoza (1503–75) was one of the greatest figures in Spanish letters and politics; ambassador to the Venetian Republic, and the patron of the Aldine Press, he was also a great collector of MSS. The *first complete edition of Josephus* was printed from Mendoza's copies. He appears to have been at the Spanish Court in 1537. Intercourse between de Mendoza and Wiat probably led to a discussion on *Josephus*, and its perusal by Wiat. He, carried away by his excessive zeal for striking situations, immortalized this singularly gruesome incident in an epigram.

No. 17. **Off Cartage he.** Imitated from Petrarch. See Appendix A. This Epigram contains one of the few direct personal facts recorded by Wiat of his residence at Mountzon (l. 8), thus fixing the date of the composition. Such clues are the sign-posts, pointing unerringly to the fact that the E. MS. is in chronological order. Wiat lived at Barbastra, near Mountzon, while the Emperor Charles held his Court there in 1537. The tenor of the Epigram is Wiat's difficult position as ambassador. He was sent over to bring about what was impossible of achievement—the drawing together of England and Spain in a closer union, and the prevention of a treaty between France, Spain and the Pope. Henry VIII, now that Anne Boleyn was executed and Jane Seymour was Queen, thought the present a good opportunity to bury the past, particularly in connection with his treatment of Queen

Catherine, the Emperor's aunt, and his breaking away from Rome.

Wiat personally pleased the Emperor; he "could overcome" the Emperor's dislike of England by personal attachment, but "could not use his chance" by forcing Charles into a plan to benefit England while it frustrated the Emperor's own schemes of stamping out Protestantism by a triple alliance between France, Spain and the Pope. Wiat saw that Henry was to be left out in the cold (ll. 5-7), and expressed his opinion in such terms as were afterwards made one of the points of accusation by Bonner that "Wyat said his Master (*i. e.* Henry VIII) would be let out at the tayle of the cart" (see Wiat's Oration, § 4).

l. 1. *Off Cartage he*, i. e. Hannibal.

l. 8. *Mountzon.* Near Barbastra, Huesca Province, N. Spain, bordering on the Pyrenees. Wiat wrote to Lord Lisle, deputy of Calais, about this time (R. O. letter [1] dated October 16, 1537, from Barbastra, beside Mountzon).

Pardon me y^r lordshipp that I wryt not unto you off o^r news here / for sins this berer can Informe you off thm / at full. I besech yow let y^t suffice for my excusis in this litill leysir. And that this may recommaund me humbly to my good lady. Always redy to do y^r lordshipp the s^er^vice that in me lyth as knowth o^r lord who send the same good lyff and long.

Yo^rs alway at com̃aundemēt,
Tho. Wiat.

To the right honorable and very singular
good lord, my Lord Lysle.

No. 18. **I lede a liff.** This and the next Epigram is a record of Wiat's residence in Spain as ambassador. Disappointment met him at every turn in his inability to obtain what Henry VIII desired; shortness of money, and even personal danger, were constant sources of annoyance. In May 1538 the Emperor suddenly made overtures to Henry, which, however, Wiat must carry to England himself and

[1] Record Office. Lisle Papers 1537.

be back by the middle of June. Wiat, thinking success at last seemed in view for his master, joyfully obtained leave; but while he was away, Charles broke the promise made to him to *do nothing in his absence*, and completed the treaty between Spain, France and the Pope. It was, of course, a mere political device to get rid of Wiat at an awkward moment. This Epigram is a good example of the state of his mind when he discovered the deceit practised upon him.[1]

No. 19. **From thes hye hilles.** The Pyrenees, with their well-watered slopes, faced Mountzon, and probably suggested the Epigram, which is imitated from Ariosto, see Appendix A.

l. 3. Note correction of "still" to "ay" to avoid the harshness of the presence of "still" and "shall" in the same line. Wiat's corrections always aim at a neater turn of thought, a more apt expression, a more fitting word. This is the never-failing test between Wiat's text and his correctors; unauthorized corrections aim at regular iambics; the text is often weakened and sometimes rendered faulty, especially in A.

No. 20. **Tagus, fare well.** Wiat's joy at returning to England after all his troubles in Spain finds vent in this Epigram, written in 1539. The patriotic sentiment and loyal service which had distinguished Sir Henry Wiat's career was handed on to his son Sir Thomas Wiat as his most precious heritage. This finds expression in l. 7.

ll. 1–2. Derived from Chaucer's "Boethius," Thynne's Edition, 1532: "All the thinges that the ryver Tagus gyveth yow with his goldene gravelis."

l. 5. *the town which Brutus sowght by dremis.* London. An allusion to the legendary account of the building of

[1] See Appendix G. for the facts stated in Wiat's letter to the Privy Council.

London by Brutus, descendant of Æneas. He, in a vision, was told by Diana to sail to the "shining Clives of Albion and there to found a Kingdom" (see Holinshed, Bk. II. Chap. II., and *Mirror of Magistrates*). Geoffrey of Monmouth is the ultimate source of sixteenth-century allusions to this legend.

l. 6. *like bendyd mone*, i. e. crescent moon. Cf. *T. & C.* III. 549 : "The bente mone with hir hornes pale."

l. 7. *Country* comprehends friends and loved ones, as well as patriotic feeling.

Turberville imitates Wiat in the song—

> Thou stately streame y[t] with the swelling tide
> Gainst London walles incessantly dost beate.

l. 8. Tottel's emendation to *O mighty Jove the windes for this me geve* is logical, since Wiat needed favourable winds for the crossing, but he misses all the poetry as well as the noble feeling which is gathered up into the last line of Wiat's text : "Of myghty love the winges for this me gyve."

No. 21. **Off purpos love.** Cf. this Epigram with Sonnet 28, "If waker care," written the same year, 1539; it is autobiographical, and records a deep attachment for some unknown friend, possibly Mary, Duchess of Richmond. The Epigram is adapted from some original; Wiat's customary method of recording some personal experience is by means of a translation or imitation of an Italian or French poet, which he finds suitable as expressing his own feelings. Paradoxical as it may seem, Wiat is sincere when he is imitating.

The idea that Love was blind was very popular, particularly amongst Wiat's French contemporaries. L. Labé's prose story, called "Le Debut de Folie et D'Amour," had a great reputation, and was translated into English a few years later by R. Greene, the dramatist. M. Sève wrote a fine dizaine on the same subject—

Bien paindre sceut, qui feit Amour aveugle
Enfant, Archier, pasle, maigre, volage:
Car en tirant ses Amans il aveugle
Amolissant comme enfantz, leur courage :
Pâles par cure et maigres par grand rage.—" Délie."

No. 22. **Vulcane bygat me.** Translated from the Latin of Pandulpho and inserted in the *E. MS. by a later hand*, probably that of Mary Harrington. It is written in the space intended for another poem, *begun in Wiat's own hand*, but after the first two lines left unfinished. The fragment is a translation of Petrarch's Canzone, "Di pensier in pensier," and begins—

From thought to thought, from hill to hill love doth me lede
Clene contrary from restfull lyff, these common paths I trede.

The poem is begun in the long couplet, produced by writing short measure in two lines instead of four, lately introduced by Wiat in "So feble is the threde." He employed it again in his last (unfinished) poem, "When Dido festid." The authority for this Epigram is the Harleian MS., there inserted with the title "A Riddle"—Thos. W. At the foot of the poem is the legend "idem latine ex Pandulpho." [1] The latter runs—

Vulcanus genuit, peperit Natura, Minerva
  Edocuit : Nutrix Ars fuit, atque genitrix
Vis mea de Nihilo est ; tria dant mihi corpora pastum ;
  Sunt nati, Strages, Ira, Ruina, Fragor,
Dic hospes, qui sim : num terræ an bellua ponti
  An neutrum : an prosint facta, vel orta modo.

Wiat has translated the six lines of this Epigram and has added his own couplet in ll. 7–8.

Epigrams 23–30 are collected from various MSS. to complete the group. The first four, Nos. 23–26, judging by

[1] Flourished *circ.* 1500.

their style, belong to the middle period, and were probably written between 1533 and 1536. No. 23 is found only in D., No. 24 in D. and in Tottel, Nos. 25–26 in Tottel only. Nos. 27–30 are later poems.

No. 23. **All yn thi sight.** This Epigram deals with the old conceit, never too much worn for the sixteenth-century poet. Cf. Sonnet 15, "Avysing the bright bemes of these fayer Iyes," Sonnet 18, "How oft have I," and Sonnet 20, "The lyvely sperkes," for a similar conceit.

No. 24. **The fructe of all the servise.** The theme of the contraries is in Wiat's earlier manner; the reference to "Tantalus" suggests a translation. Allusions to classical fable is very rare in Wiat.

No. 25. **Within my brest.** This is written in Wiat's most sincere manner. It is one of the poems forged from his own heart; falsehood, insincerity, breach of faith, always moved him to great indignation. His ideal of manhood, inculcated by Sir Henry Wiat, a Christian knight of the old school, was embodied in Chaucer's *Knight*—

> That from the tyme that he first began
> To riden out he loved chivalrie
> Trouth and honour, fredom and courtesie.

No. 26. **For shamefast harm.** A translation of an Epigram ascribed to Plato—

> *χρυσὸν ἀνὴρ εὑρὼν ἔλιπεν βρόχον · αὐτὰρ ὁ χρυσὸν*
> *ὃν λίπεν οὐχ εὑρὼν ἧψεν ὃν εὗρε βρόχον.*

Ausonius translated into a Latin Epigram—

> Thesauro invento qui limina mortis inibat
> Liquit ovans laqueum quo periturus erat.
> At qui quod terræ abdiderat non repperit aurum
> Quem laqueum invenit nexuit et periit.
>
> *Epigrammata*, xxii.

Prof. Courthope, *History of English Literature*, Vol. II. p. 58, renders as follows—

> A man about to hang himself one day
> By chance found gold, and flung his noose away.
> The owner came and—each thing has its use—
> Finding his gold was gone, employed the noose.

Courthope observes that Wiat requires eight lines, and Ausonius four, to translate the original Greek couplet, and Turberville later produced it in a twelve-lined poem, "A man in deepe dispaire with hemp in hand."

Mr. Arundell Esdaile, Brit. Mus., has kindly furnished more details: Plato's Epigram is imitated by Statilius Flaccus, *Anth. Pal.* IX. 44. Ausonius made *two* versions, the above and Epigram 23; L'Estrange included it amongst his *Fables*, and finally Coleridge returned it to its original force—

> Tom, finding some gold, left a rope on the ground
> Jack, missing his gold, used the rope which he found.

Now the question to consider is whether Wiat derived his source from the Greek or from the Latin. He certainly knew his Plato, and on Leland's evidence he was an accomplished Latin scholar. Certain facts throw light on the matter. Richard Croke was appointed first official Greek Professor [1] at Cambridge 1518–1519, when Wiat was resident. Some years previously he had edited the Ausonius. Richard Croke's installation at Cambridge gives a clue to the study of the Ausonius, since he was the editor of that work, and it was probably made the Latin medium of the scholars' Greek studies. It is significant that the last two lines of Wiat's Epigram exactly translate the Ausonius version. Wiat probably knew the Greek as well as the Latin version, but being a good Latin scholar he chose the Latin version to translate.

[1] Erasmus lectured *unofficially* as early as 1511.

No. 27. **My love ys lyke.** This Epigram is in the form of a madrigal. It is interesting as the second example[1] in Wiat's poetry of a very popular Italian lyrical poem, later imitated by the Elizabethan poets.

It will be remembered that Wiat's first Rondeau was a translation of Petrarch's Madrigal "Or vedi Amor," with the rhyming scheme aba, bcc, cdd, *in three tercets*. Wiat adopted the rhyming scheme, but the division of his Madrigal is in quatrain, tercet and final couplet, thus: abab, ccc, dd, instead of the Italian tercet group. The style and treatment of the poem mark it as a late composition.

l. 7. Compare the sentiment expressed with the Sonnet "If waker care." The last couplet is finely modulated. The merits of such poems as these easily procure for Wiat a front place amongst sixteenth-century lyrists.

No. 28. **In court to serve.** Found only in Tottel. It is a late Epigram from its style.

l. 3. *bankets*. This word becomes blankets in later editions of Tottel.

No. 29. **A face that shuld content me.** Found only in the P. MS. (Add. 36529) and in Tottel. This description of a woman is the only one in Wiat. Constant to his rule, he gives us no portrait, but rather a character sketch. Honest and sincere himself, with a deep scorn of anything false or inconstant, his ideal of a woman is displayed here in strength of character and gravity of thought, a cheerful, sympathetic and graceful woman. Mary, Duchess of Richmond, "Maiden-wife, and widow," possessed the qualities he admired, and was a staunch friend as well as admirer

[1] The other example is the stanza "To his bed," and entitled "Sonet." No. 2, *Miscellaneous Poems*, 1528–1536.

of Wiat's poems. She was the friend of his later years, and, with her brother Henry, Earl of Surrey, was probably instrumental in gaining pardon for Wiat in 1541, through Catherine Howard, her aunt, the new consort of Henry VIII.

The date of this poem is probably late in 1539, before his visit to Flanders 1539–40. There is no suggestion of coming evil here, as all the poems written in 1540 and before his imprisonment show.

Again, the last year of his life, 1541–2, is not probable, for the latest poems express moral or philosophical reflections on life, as from a man who had finished with worldly interests, after many sufferings and trials, surveying life from an eminence, with the calm of one who has battled through it, and can await his end with unruffled demeanour.

No. 30. **Luckes my faire falcon.** Found only in the P. MS. and in Tottel. To this latest MS. we are indebted for two of the finest Epigrams, this and No. 29 above. From the context we gather that it was written after Cromwell's execution (July 1540) and before Wiat's arrest early in 1541. The situation described exactly answers to Wiat's position. Those who were instrumental in procuring Cromwell's downfall were seeking to bring about Wiat's ruin. He was hated by the prominent party for his adherence to Cromwell, and for his favour with the king. His former friends feared to show him any sympathy, lest they should be involved in his ruin (ll. 3–5); Wiat's scathing comment on the situation is: "Loe what a profe in light adversytie" (l. 6).

This Epigram reveals, by the way, Wiat's interest in sport. The reference to his favourite falcon is graceful.

l. 7. *but . . . belles.* Holbein's drawing of the master falconer of Henry VIII is executed with a falcon on his wrist; the ring attached to the claw is ornamented with bells. The drawing of the falcon is one of the finest pieces of detailed work by Holbein.

No. 31. **Sighes ar my foode.** Written during Wiat's imprisonment, January 17–March 21, 1541, and addressed to Sir Francis Brian. It is absent from the E. MS.

Brian was a friend, and had managed with consummate diplomacy to keep clear of the shoals and quicksands which had shipwrecked most of the statesmen in Henry's reign. He had achieved his easy position at Court by changing his policy whenever the exigencies of the moment required it, both in domestic and private affairs, and if there was a man who could save him from the intense rigours of the law (ll. 1–4), Wiat considered that man to be Brian.

Yet although Wiat was in the greatest danger he had a firm belief in his ultimate release, knowing his innocence (ll. 13–14). He knew, too, that Henry VIII had received lifelong service from his father, and that he himself had been trained from his earliest years for the King's service and for his country. Henry VIII, in spite of all his failings, possessed extraordinary perspicacity, and realized the disinterestedness of the Wiats in their loyal service to him, and he was probably glad of the opportunity that allowed him to grant Wiat a full and free pardon on the occasion of the coronation of Catherine Howard.

MISCELLANEOUS POEMS

FIRST GROUP, 1528–36

THE first few poems of this group belong to the Calais period, and are clearly imitations of Italian stanzas; they come amongst the early Rondeaus and Sonnets. The douzaine "Madame withouten any wordes" (No. 9) is probably the first poem in the E. MS. composed as a Court song. The lyrical poems, in lighter vein, continue until No. 33, "Comfort thyself." Then follows the first Satire, written in 1536, with an Italian stanza and Italian imitation. At this point we not only see a return to foreign influence, but a change in the life, environment and thought of Wiat. The last poem in the group, "To cause accorde," is a reflection on a literary habit, and follows the second Satire in the MS.

Throughout the group, from No. 9 to No. 34 of the Court poems, there is no trace of direct Italian influence. A chance expression of Wiat occasionally makes one feel that he had read Dante's *Vita Nuova*, but there is no imitation. In certain stanza forms and modes of expression French influence is undeniable, and in No. 9 there is direct imitation, but on the whole the influence is merely the reaction of the French upon the English lyric which takes us back to the eleventh century, and is closely interwoven into the history of English verse through the Middle English period.

A striking difference is noticeable in the earlier and later poems of this group. Nos. 9–21 are essentially light court poems, some trifling or complimentary, others merely set to a musical air with refrains. The latter poems, especially Nos. 25–26, 29–30, 32–33, consist of a series of extremely fine odes distinguished by a richness of quality hitherto lacking in Wiat's work. His musical talent had developed from his earliest years a capacity for lyrical sweetness; but in these poems, for the first time, a depth and intensity of thought is combined with great beauty of expression. At this stage the musician and the poet part company, for the poet has at last discovered that he is a musician of language and has learnt the secret of its harmony.

No. 1. **Alas the greiff.** This is the fifth entry in the MS., and follows three Sonnets and a Rondeau, all translated from Petrarch. The form is a six-line stanza, running in two tercets, aab, abb, after the Italian style. It is evidently an attempt to copy the Italian sestina without the recurring rhyme in every stanza; either Wiat had not analyzed the exact system of rhyme-grouping in the Italian sestina, or he realized that it would be difficult or impossible in English. He merely adopted the stanza length and the Italian grouping of two tercets.

Petrarch's "rime" consists largely of Sonnets, varied by an occasional madrigal, sestina or canzone. It is interesting to find that in the first few pages of the MS. Wiat has imitated all these varieties.

ll. 1–2. Imitation of Chaucer—

> Love hath his fyry dart so brenningly
> Y stiked thurgh my trewe careful herte
> That *shapen was my death erst than my sherte.*
>
> *K.T.*, ll. 1564–6.

And Skelton writes—

> Of Philip Sparowe the lamentable fate
> The dolefull destiny and the *carefull chaunce.*

carefull in the original sense of "full of care," troubled.

l. 24. *And price hath privilege.* Cf. "Myne olde dere enmy," l. 140. "Price" is a dialectical word (Yorkshire and northern counties) meaning a bargain; to make a bargain, particularly in the sense of marriage. The meaning is that the disdainful lady is privileged to set the lover's faithful intent at defiance. Note Wiat's slurring marks under "cruell," l. 4, "dowblenes," l. 6, "Causer of," l. 13, "I have," l. 19. Instances of the usual complement of syllables in "cruel," "dowblenes," occur in stanza 3.

No. 2. **O restfull place.** From Petrarch. The handwriting of this poem betrays a later hand; it is that of one of the correctors of the early pages of the MS. It is entitled "Sonet to his bedde." This title rouses suspicion for two reasons. Wiat was versed in the Italian Sonnet; his first efforts were directed to translating Petrarch, and there is no *other instance in his MS.* of using the title "Sonet" for a short stanza. But "Sonet" was commonly employed for short poems in Gascoigne's day. He says, "Then have you Sonnets, *some thinke that all Poemes* (being short) *may be called Sonets*, as in deede it is a diminutive worde derived of *Sonare*, but yet I can beste allowe to call those Sonets whiche are of fouretene lynes, every line conteyning tenne syllables." [1] In Turberville's works short poems are entitled "Sonets," as, for example, the "Sonet" to Googe, as follows—

Mayster Googe his sonet.

Accuse not God if fansie fonde
Doe moove thy foolish braine
To wayle for love : for thou thy selfe
Art cause of all the paine

[1] *Certayne Notes of Instruction*, § 14, p. 417. *Works*, Cambridge edition 1907.

Turbervile's aunswere.

Not God (friend Googe) ye lover blames
As worker of his woes ;
But Cupid that his fierie flames
So frantically bestowes.

Epitaphs, Songs and Sonnets, p. 19, 1567.

The second title, "To his bedde," is still more suspicious, for Wiat never names his poems. One riddle, whose solution is Anna, has "Anna" above it, and poems written in Spain are marked "Out of Spayne." The editor of Tottel's *Miscellany* inserted titles, and this one has crept into Wiat's MS. through the later hand that copied the poem.

"O restfull place" is, I think, an adaptation of a longer poem, "The restfull place" (No. 3). A similar instance may be seen in Sidney's "My true love hath my hert," written as a Sonnet, and turned into a song with a refrain, and quoted by Puttenham, *Art of English Poesy*, p. 233, as an instance of the Greek *Epimone* or Latin *versus intercalaris*. In respect to this poem, however, the order is reversed and the later version assumes a shorter, epigrammatic form, with a madrigal setting. This very form and the crystallization of the thought are the reasons which suggest later composition than its place here denotes, and this view is further corroborated by the fact that it is entered in the hand of the main unauthorized corrector of the MS.

The arrangement of this stanza, which I believe to have been set to music as an adaptation of No. 3, is in *madrigal form*, and should be compared with the second madrigal, "My love is like unto the eternall fyre." These are the only two poems of this kind in Wiat's poetry. Both are derived from Petrarch, and are well-known madrigal forms; whereas the second poem is taken from the triple-tercet arrangement of madrigal (seen in the "Or vedi Amor" poem), this is composed of a double tercet, aba, bba, with a concluding couplet, cc. The finished form of the poem marks it as later than the Sonnet and Rondeau group in which it is found.

No. 3. **The restfull place.** This poem, found only in the D. MS., is inserted here as the probable first draft of the preceding form. It is written in the well-known Troilus Measure, and the last line forms a refrain to every stanza. Turberville, *Works*, p. 62, has elaborated this song in five six-lined stanzas of fourteeners with refrain, "(O bed) I thee forsake."

No. 4. **Myne olde dere enmy.** From Petrarch's canzone, see Appendix A. Stanzas 1–3 are supplied from A., owing to a missing page in E. It will be noted, however, from stanza 4 and onwards, that A. presents many variations from the authoritative MS.

l. 13. *oppressed patience.* Both words scan as three syllables.

Stanza 3. There are several harsh lines in this stanza. Wiat is purposely writing in the Skeltonic Troilus measure, for the reason already named, that Wiat probably paid a tribute to Skelton in his choice of the measure at the time of his death, 1529, when this poem was written.

l. 25, *traced*, and l. 26, *ataced*, are instances of adapting Italian words. He appears to have confused the two forms. We should expect "atraced" (l. 25) and "taced" (l. 26) from the Italian—

> La quel *m'atrasse* a l'amorosa schiera,

translated by Wiat—

> With the amourous daunce have made me *traced*,

l. 26. Nott alters "ataced" to "araised," altering the sense without justification. "ataced," in the sense of silenced, subdued, quieted, fits in perfectly with the context.

l. 54. *hevynly goodenes.* A difficult point. Nott and Tottel read "heavenly gods." The Italian is—

> . . . *pieta celeste* a cura
> Di mia salute non questo tyranno.

"Heavenly pity" would naturally be personified as feminine.

The first reading, translated correctly as "hevynly goodenes," is altered to *Goddes*, evidently meant for *Goddess*, personifying goodness as a woman, thereby bringing out the force of the idea in the canzone. A later correction has altered to "Goddz," and is adopted by Tottel and Nott. The correction to "Goddes" is, I think, Wiat's, and harmonizes with the general run of the poem. The original reading, however, is kept, on the usual plan of accepting no alteration unless undeniably that of Wiat.

The corrections of the MS., which are clearly later, and at variance with Wiat's method, are nearly always to be found as the Tottel version. This coincidence is a strong proof of such corrections being regarded as unauthorized. Mr. Padelford has shown in his introduction to "The MS. Poems of Henry Howard, Earl of Surrey," that Tottel is as unreliable for Surrey's poems as Wiat's.—*Anglia*, Vol. XXIX.

There is a link still missing in the chain, for the editor of Tottel's *Miscellany* did not work from Wiat's MS., because some of the poems *found only in the E. MS.* are absent from the *Miscellany*. It may be that Tottel's edition corrected Wiat's poems for his *Miscellany* in 1557, and *later*, Wiat's MS. was corrected to conform with that printed edition.

l. 65. An alexandrine.

l. 70. An octosyllabic line.

ll. 75–6. Cf. with the "Testament of Love," I. 2, ll. 52–3, "Wost thou not that I am Love that brought thee to this service?" This prose work was included in Thynne's 1532 edition of *Chaucer* too late for imitation by Wiat. It merely shows that Petrarch was well versed in the Romance as well as the Classical literature of his day.

l. 84. *Daskard*, i. e. "dastard." Wiat's rendering is original. The Italian is "or alzato per se non fora mai."

l. 101. *sterred*, i. e. "steered."

l. 105. *The ignoraunt ffole.* Wiat adds piquancy to the translation by these touches. The expletive is not in the Italian, cf. ll. 111–2.

l. 109. Cf. Sonnet 15, l. 14: "Of suche a rote cometh ffruyte fruytles."

ll. 111–2. *I . . . serpent.* Not in the Italian. ll. 118–9 of following stanza are original. *dowting*, i. e. "fearing."

Stanza 19. A very beautiful stanza, following the Italian.

ll. 128–131. *I gave him winges.* Petrarch probably had in mind the Boethius' "De Consolatione." "I have forsothe *swifte fetheres that surmounten the heighte of hevene.* When the swifte thought hath clothed itself in the fetheres, it despyseth the hateful erthes, and surmounteth the roundnesse of the grete ayr; . . . till *that he areyseth him into the houses that beren the sterres* and he y maked an knight of the clere sterre. . . . And yif they wey ledern thee ayein so that thou be brought thider, thanne wolt thou seye now that that is the contree that thou requerest, of which thou ne haddest no minde."

l. 140. *Not I quoth he but price that is well worth.* Cf. "Alas the greffe," l. 24, for this use of "price," meaning bargain, particularly in marriage. The meaning is "*I* did not take her from you, but a (better) bargain removed her from your sight," *i. e.* from earth. The Italian is—

Io non : *ma chi per se la volse.*

Not I, but he who wanted her for himself.

The poem is picturesque. Petrarch adopted the old

mediæval setting of the Court of Love, with the accused and accuser brought face to face with the arbitrator. The dramatic element appealed to Wiat, specially the raucous passages, to which he added more colour by such epithets as "ignoraunt ffole"; and the introduction of such proverbs as "Nourishing a serpent in one's bosom."

With No. 5 a lighter strain of verse follows.

No. 5. **Farewell the rayn** is a slight poem in monorhymed quatrains, a type common in Middle English lyrics.

l. 4. *nedë* is *two syllables.*

Nos. 6–8 are varieties of the seven-line stanza with Troilus *rhyme.*

No. 6. **It may be good.** Octosyllabic verse with Troilus rhyme.

l. 5. *Ies*, i. e. "eyes," the spelling of this word varies.

l. 9. *to accorde two contraries*, see No. 34 for this idea.

l. 19. *Nay sir in faith.* Introduction of dialogue suggests two speakers; either this represents the woman's point of view, or the speaker is a man, as in "A Robyn Joly Robyn," where two men converse. The argument "It may be good for some people, but I dislike 'fayned' ways" is a sentiment often pronounced by Wiat, and exhibits a very marked side of his character.

No. 7. **Resound my voyse.** A fine ode. The Chaucerian Troilus measure, in seven-line decasyllables rhyming ababbcc, is followed here so successfully that one feels that the rhythm of "Mine olde dere enmy" (No. 4) is consciously employed for a particular (Skeltonic) type. The poem is remarkable as one of the very few poems with references to nature, and suggests translation. Nott finds a source in Serafino.

l. 13. *The howgy okes*, a fine touch, is reminiscent of the wind among the oaks on his father's estate of Allington. Nature lovers will know that there is a peculiar music in the wind among oaks.

ll. 18–19. Suggests "La Belle Dame sans Mercy" included in Pynson's 1526 edition of Chaucer. *Beaultie* scans as three syllables.

No. 8. **In faith I wot not.** Another variation of seven-lined stanza. Wiat appears to be experimenting with the old fifteener (the *Poeme Morale*, twelfth century), broken into eights and sevens as in the *Ormulum*. The first stanza is arranged 8787788, cf. ll. 1–2.

> **In faith | I wot not | well what | to say**
> **Thy chaun|ces ben | so won|derous.**

"Wonderous" scans as two syllables following the rhythm of "dolours," l. 4, and "joyus," l. 5.

Stanzas 2–3 revert to octosyllables.

l. 3. *Fortune.* Wiat is a close disciple of Chaucer in his many references to fortune.

l. 7. The refrain is a typical instance of Wiat's fondness for word-play.

No. 9. **Madame withouten.** Imitated from Mellin de S. Gelais' douzaine. This entry marks a special division of the MS. The Court poems, 1533–6, begin here. The general idea of the French poem is expressed in ll. 1–10. The last two lines are a close translation. The method of imitation suggests memory work and not translation. Had Wiat studied the original, he would doubtless have followed the scheme of the douzaine, which is a four-tercet movement, since he had a very careful eye for form; but he set his rendering simply in three octosyllabic quatrains. It is worth while comparing with the original. Both poems were written for a lady of the Court.

L'amour vous a donne un cueur en gage?
De quoi vous sert user tant de langage?
Or vous voulez or vous ne voulez point;
Quand vous voudrez deus mille ans deviser,
Si foudroit il a la fin s'aviser
Quon s'en ennuye et venir a un point;
Si vous voulez me faites que branler
Car j'entendray le moindre signe en l'air
Et vous serez ami non decevant.
S'il ne vous plaist? amis comme devant
Un autre aurez et moy ne pouvant estre
Servant de vous, de moi je seray maistre.

No. 10. **Suche happe as I.** These Court poems run in eights, sixes and fours, or combinations of these, following the English lyrical types. Variation is attained by refrains. In this instance the tag of every stanza forms the opening words of the following stanza. The rhyme-scheme is interesting, ababcb^{c}.

ll. 6–7. The poem is (intentionally) obscure. Wiat was criticized for obscurity in his own day. Cf.—

My songes were to diffuse,
They made *men to muse.*

ll. 13–14. Cf. Epigram 27, l. 7, for a more direct allusion to Tantalus.

l. 30. *So hawkes be taught.* Hawks were tamed by deprivation of light and food.

No. 11. **They fle from me.** For form and style cf. with No. 7.

l. 2. *stalking.* Walking gently.

l. 5. *daunger.* "Governaunce" as in Shakespeare.

l. 9. *in speciall.* Cf. Chaucer, *T. & C.*, I. 260—

But for to tellen forth in speciall.

l. 13. *did me kysse.* The kiss was the ordinary form of salutation amongst the upper classes of Wiat's day.

l. 19. *new fangilnes,* i. e. Inconstancy. Cf. Chaucer, *Analida and Arcite,* l. 140—

This fals Arcite of his new fangilnesse.

The word is general, sixteenth century.

No. 12. **There was never nothing.** In the old ballad metre with refrain.

Alas the whyle; cf. Chaucer, *Amorous Complayte,* "Alas, alas, the while," with the same meaning as the exclamatory: "Alack the day!"

No. 13. **Patience tho I have not.** This and the companion poem (No. 14), "Paciens for my devise," represent two points of view. The first states the philosophy of the disappointed lover, the second his attitude towards, and condemnation of, the lady. But the poem is meant in playful vein. Above the second poem in the D. MS. is written the reason for its composition, namely, that a lady having remarked, on hearing the poem "Patiens tho I have not," that such patience as the poet recommended *was not for her, but that the contrary was most meet for her purpose,* the poet replied in the poem, "Paciens for my devise." The idea is derived from Serafino. Notice the different spelling, "paciens," in the second poem. Wiat displays the tendency, so strong in Browning, of presenting various points of view on given questions. The best example in dialogue form of the poem that presents two points of view is "It burneth yet alas."

No. 15. **Ye know my herte.** One of the most graceful lyrics with a simple sincerity that strikes home to the reader. The stanza (a treizaine) is elaborate; stanzas 1–2 are supplied from D. owing to a missing leaf. Judging from the third stanza, this version varies from the original lost version. Stanza 3 is supplied from E., and differs considerably from D. The stanza form shows French imitation.

No. 16. **If fansy would favor.** The whole poem is a play on the word "fancy"; evidently a trifle for the Court circle, like the riddles. Such verses are examples of Wiat's wit, and explain his popularity at Court as a "ballate-maker." [1]

No. 17. **At moost myschief.** A lute song in the short measure, greatly favoured at the Court of Henry VIII. There are many examples in the sixteenth century song-books. Skelton's lines to Margaret Tudor run in this two-foot verse—

Of Margarite
Perle orient
Lode sterre of lyght
Moche relucent
Madame regent
I maye you call
Of vertues all;

but Skelton's has the rhyming scheme of Troilus measure. Wiat's runs aaab, cccb.

The opening and concluding stanzas form a refrain.

l. 25. *No Tigres hert.* Example of Petrarchan conceit.

No. 18. **Marvaill no more.** Written as an *eight-lined stanza* in the D. MS.

l. 29. *Souch* was inserted by a later hand.

l. 31. *Such.* Altered in Tottel and Nott to "Souch" on the ground that it was meant as an allusion to a certain Mistress Souch [2] at Court. There is no authority for the change of spelling in the original version.

[1] *State Papers*, May 1536.

[2] Madame Souch, or Zouche, was one of the Court ladies; she is mentioned in the Domestic State Papers about this time. She was one of the mourners at Jane Seymour's funeral in 1537.

No. 19. **Where shall I have.** There is a noticeable use of enjambement or overflow here; for example: ll. 2–3, ll. 17–18, ll. 39–40.

l. 24. *Like to like.* The expression occurs more than once. Cf. Rondeau 6, l. 4, "Eche thing seketh his sembable."

No. 20. **A Robyn Joly Robyn.** One of the best known of Wiat's songs, and a great favourite in his day. It is possibly his version of a well-known theme. Other similar poems are in Henry VIII's song-book. It is a French type known as the *Chansor-à-personnages.*[1] See *Study of Sir Thomas Wyatt*, Chap. X. A fascimile of the poem is given in Vol. I. p. 62 set to music by Cornysshe, the Court musician. The song is sung by the Clown in *Twelfth Night*, IV. ii. 70, *et seq.* It is included in Percy's *Reliques.*

The name *Robyn* was, no doubt, popularized in the Robin Hood ballads, and the attribute *Joly* is derived from the same source.

The Pastoral eclogue on the classical model was generally adopted by Italian poets. Marot composed his famous "Pan et Robin eclogue" about this time, 1536, but some years elapsed before the Pastoral "Eclogue" was established in England.

The poem is not complete in the E. MS. The scribe evidently omitted a stanza. Prof. Padelford remarks (*Sixteenth Century Lyrics*, p. 117): "Certain lines would *seem to belong to the Plaintif*, the concluding stanza to the Response. These lines are reversed in the E. MS. for *Response and Plantif.*" The scribe appears to have omitted stanza 4, which is in the D. version. *This is inserted from the D. MS.* for Response. Then the following stanza falls

[1] Jeauroy, *Lais du treizième siècle*, and *ibid.*, *Les Origines de la poésie lyrique en France.*

to the Plaintif as the sense requires, and the poem concludes (stanza 6) with Response. I have taken the liberty of inserting the stanza in order to keep the logical sequence of thought, which is disjointed as it stands in the E. MS.

No. 21. **Tho I cannot.** The increasing facility of arrangement and structure is observable. The combination of tens, eights and sixes, have produced, in artistic hands, some of the finest lyrics in our language. The poet joins sound with sense in the long-drawn-out syllables to express sorrow, cf. l. 8. A happy variety is given to the last refrain by the substitution of "Rejoyce" for "rew" (l. 20).

No. 22. **To wisshe or want.** Stanzas in monorhymed triplets, with refrain as here, are found in the Percy Collection. Note the proverbial phrases in ll. 25–26.

No. 23. **My hope alas.** In the same metre as "It may be good."

l 3. *lust and joye;* Chaucerian use of "lust" for "pleasure."

l. 4. *Carefull*, i. e. "full of care." Cf. "Carefull chaunce," No. 1, l. 2.

ll. 10–11. *In fortunes forge.* Wiat experienced sudden revulsions of fortune all through his public career. Not once or twice is he stripped of the favours that the king heaped upon him so lavishly. But he had a facility for extricating himself from every dilemma.

ll. 18–21. A personal reflection. Truth is the keynote of manly character. Cf. Letters to his Son, Appendix G. Sincerity often brought him into trouble, but as surely released him. The perusal of his letters, dispatches and oration throws a strong light on this side of his character.

No. 24. **What deth is worse then this.** Cf. this lyric with

"And wylt thow leve me thus?" (Vol. I. p. 272), for its energetic movement and sincere feeling.

ll. 7–8. *My hert is hens;* the old Provençal conceit so beautifully expressed in Middle English in the "Cligès," for example. See note on Rondeau 5. Wiat has produced a very graceful little poem here; it is well worth comparing these little pieces tinged with the fire of Wiat's genius, with the stiff and artificial results of the Petrarchian translations.

No. 25. **Ons as methought.** This song is conspicuous for the gladness it expresses. Fortune is personified as a gracious personage, giving the lover all he desires. The long vogue of the "Roman de la Rose" is responsible for the allegorical impersonation. The vogue still lingered at the French and English Courts.

No. 26. **My lute awake** is one of the most beautiful farewell songs in our language. It is, perhaps, the best known of Wiat's poems.

l. 26. *Perchaunce the lye.* The favourite method of turning the tables, and is as old as literature itself. Cf. M. Sève, "Délie," 310.

Tu te *verras ton ivoire cresper*
Par l'oultrageuse et *tardive vieiellesse*
Lors sans pouvoir en rien participer
D'aucune joye et humaine liesse

And a well-known sonnet of Ronsard begins—

Quand vous serez bien vieille au soir à la chandelle
Assise auprès du feu, dividant et filant,
Par les ombres myrteux je prendrai mon repos
Vous serez au foyer *une vieille accroupie.*

No. 27. **If chaunce assynd.** The same style of short-metre lute song as "In moost mischief." This was probably composed during Wiat's short imprisonment occasioned by his quarrel with the Duke of Suffolk in May 1536. The gossip of the time ascribed his arrest to his former intimacy with Anne Boleyn. Facts and Wiat's own statements disprove such an idea.

No. 28. **I have sought long.**

ll. 3–4. Cf. the Old English proverb, "A folys bolt is sone yshott." The homely reference in the last stanza is difficult to trace. For a more poetic homely allusion see "My Mother's Maydes," ll. 1–2.

ll. 5–8. References to proverbs.

No. 29. **Lyk as the Swanne.** A torn leaf in the E. MS. has almost obliterated this poem and the next. They are inserted from the D. MS. "The complaynte of Dido" (Pynson's edition of *Chaucer*) begins in a similar manner.

The doubling of word and phrase at the end of a line is used by Serafino and carried to excess. Wiat employs this device with great success in No. 32, "Hevyn and Erth."

No. 30. **In Eternum.** Another refrain song.

l. 7. *To trace this daunse.* Cf. "Myne olde dere enmy," l. 25.

l. 14. *Feble . . . grounde.* Cf. Sonnet 8, ll. 13–14.

l. 16. *kest*, for "cast" is dialectal (Yorkshire and northern counties).

No. 31. **Syns ye delite to knowe.** This stanza is based on the short measure 6686, by breaking up the third verse into fours; and concludes with an additional broken fourteener for the last two lines, thus, 66,446,68. The first two lines of the stanza combined become the Alexandrine, the next three lines become the fourteener, and these five lines together make up the long-lined couplet that Wiat used later in "So feble is the threde" and "When Dido festid."

It affords, too, a striking proof of the architectural quality of verse, and gives a clue as to the reason of the Provençal ambition for stanza structure rather than the expression of new emotions, for they knew that in matters of the heart the old way must be trodden either in storm or sunshine, tragedy or happiness, whereas the mind of man continually soars out and beyond to new vistas of thought, new complexities of structure. This stanza is graceful, flexible, varied, and capable of much beauty; but put together into a couplet of twelve and fourteen syllables, it at once becomes inflexible, hard and monotonous if used by mediocre poets. It is hard to forgive Wiat for running a light lyrical form of verse into the weighty, even dull, measure of the long-lined couplet. One wonders whether it were rather grim humour on his part. After being criticized for harshness, and for obscurity, he produced a measure that required regularity, and was dangerously open to dulness of delivery. Certainly Wiat cannot be blamed for the absence of poetic fire from Surrey's death five years after his own until the dawn of Elizabethan literature; and, *in spite of the metre*, Wiat has proved himself a poet in the poem, "So feble is the threde."

But in the hands of mediocre rhymesters, who stuck to this measure with remarkable pertinacity, it became a fatal clog upon poetry. All the miscellanies and anthologies that followed Tottel's edition were overweighted with this kind of verse; the exceptions to mediocrity were Chapman's translation of the *Iliad* in the fourteener and Lord Brooke's poem of *Romeo and Juliet* in the long-lined couplet, 12, 14.

No. 32. **Hevyn and erth.** One of the finest odes. There is a certain quiet dignity of sorrow very beautifully expressed, and a higher artistic excellence is reached than in the favourite, "My Lute Awake." The doubling of the last word or phrase is very effective. Wiat, one feels, has at length learnt the secret of the music of language, apart from actual musical accompaniment. He has succeeded in putting new beauty into an old conceit by sheer beauty of expression, and sincerity of feeling.

Notice the increasing tendency to overflow, 3.3; 4.1.

l. 22. *that fleith as fast*. Cf. Sonnet, "Such vague hope," l. 5.

No. 33. **Comfort thyself.** A song on an old conceit. The Provençal singer, when he had exhausted the fount of tears, turned to sighs. Henri Cochin [1] says, concerning the significance of *sighs* in the *Vita Nuova*, "Je me convaincs que les soupirs représentent toujours dans la *Vita Nova* des *vers douloureux*. Ce sont les esprits d'amour qui sortent en parlant." For example—

. . . Amore . . .
Fa li miei sospiri gir parlando ;
Et escon for chiamando
La donna mia.

And compare *Vita Nuova*, XXXII.—

Venite a intender li sospiri miei
Oi cor gentili, che pieta'l disia
Li quai disconsolati vanno via
E s'e non fosser, di dolor morrei

"Come listen to my sighs, ye gentle hearts, for pity requires it, inconsolable, they break forth, and if it were not so, I should die of grief."

Wiat's verses often suggest a knowledge of the *Vita Nuova*.

No. 34. **To cause accord.** Wiat utters his reflection upon

[1] *Vita Nova*, ed. Henri Cochin, 1905.

the absurdity of conceits; like Shakespeare and Sidney, he commented on the fashion, but followed it. The last verse strikes a deeper note; the light-hearted reflection is followed by the great truth that life is made up of contraries—rain and sunshine, pleasure and pain, comedy and tragedy, are closely allied. And in Love, as in any other phase of the human soul, the ultimate beauty is only brought out by light and shade, by the height and depth of feeling in the heart of man.

SATIRES

The Satires not only mark an advance in form and style, but are characterized by a grip of thought and intensity of expression rarely found outside the works of the humanists in sixteenth-century contemporary literature. The Italians had allowed their garden of poetry to run wild in a rank profusion of mediocre thought. Beguiled by the sweetness of their language and the richness of their vocal syllables, form and melody were becoming more and more the ultimate end of poetry.

Every ambitious poet, following the example of Bembo, the dictator of verse, refined and polished the form, while the matter was regarded as of secondary importance. The lack of virility in the nation was felt in the literature; luxury and sensuality in life perforce left its mark on the intellectual productiveness of the time, and with the exception of a "giant like Michael Angelo," literature is largely that of soulless imitations from the death of Ariosto to the publication of Torquato Tasso's masterpiece. It is significant of the times that the two authors who contributed most to the literature of their day and attained to European fame, were regarded—the one as a devil,[1] the other as a madman,[2] by their contemporaries.

The few Italians who had some definite purpose beyond form, employed the Satire, and the most vigorous poems are in this kind of verse. The Satire was no new growth in Italian literature, being an inheritance from the days of

[1] Machiavelli (d. 1527).

[2] Torquato Tasso would be regarded to-day as a genius with a tendency to overstrung nerves.

Horace. Dante and his contemporaries had wielded a graver form of satire. In the first half of the sixteenth century L. Alamanni, Ariosto, and Aretino, amongst others, wrote in satiric vein. Alamanni appealed more to the foreigner than to his own countrymen; Ariosto was the most renowned, Aretino the most notorious of satirists. Machiavelli's "Capitoli" came under the category of the good-humoured Horatian Satire, the type essayed by the Italian because "easy garrulity," to quote Dr. Garnett, "was preferred to the invective of the Juvenalian Satire."

Wiat was a fine classical scholar, and was thoroughly conversant with the Horatian Satire—a fact easily proved by his borrowing from Horace for his Second Satire. Alamanni was also a Latin scholar, and directly imitated Horace; while affecting the Horatian type in the dialogue form and the good-humoured style of unveiling human weaknesses, he drew his illustrations from his own times. Wiat, who was always observant of contemporary fashion in literature as well as in special verse forms, borrowed from Alamanni the terza-rima, as well as the substance of his Tenth Satire, for his first essay in the satiric vein.

But in this instance he has borrowed merely to reconstruct, and his fine utterances in the vivid expression of his subject, as well as the special point of view set forward, are original and personal.

As a matter of fact, Wiat was far superior in poetic genius to his Italian contemporary, and had become a facile writer when he imitated him. Comparing Wiat's Satires with those of Horace, it will be seen how closely he has imitated the Latin poet in the easy, familiar style of language, the elasticity of his subject, and the dramatic element in the vivid touches of character, and the indications of dialogue. This dramatic force and freedom of style is absent from Alamanni.

But there is another reason for the development in Wiat's poetry at this particular time of these masterly traits. The study of the "Knight's Tale" and the "Troilus and Cressida" gave Wiat the impetus. The traits which he had learnt in Horace were vividly presented in his own language by Chaucer in these two great masterpieces,[1] and the three Satires were written not only in the spirit but in the very language of Chaucer.

THE FIRST SATIRE

The Italian model for the First Satire is the Tenth Satire of Luigi Alamanni, an exiled Florentine who had thrown in his lot with the French nation. His writings appealed far more to the foreigner than to his own people. He was a dignified, courteous, scholarly person, and his poetry reflects his character. Luigi wrote his Satire in Provence when an exile from Florence. Brought up amongst the wealthiest of the Florentines, he was in his youth intimate with the son of Bernando Rucellai, whose estates and magnificent gardens were the rendezvous of scholars and artists in the grounds known as the "Orti Oricellari." Added to his artistic upbringing was a love of study, and he early acquired Greek and Latin. Exiled for opposing the Medici party in 1522, he was a wanderer for five years, living in Provence, and paying prolonged visits to Venice and Lyons. Returning to Florence, he was again exiled in 1530, and made France his home for the rest of his life. He received a place at Court, and brought out his poems under the patronage of Francis I in 1532.

Wiat, exiled from the English Court for a short while to learn restraint under his father's roof at Allington Castle,

[1] Included in Thynne's edition, 1532, as well as in Pynson's edition.

found much in Alamanni's Tenth Satire which suited his own views of Court life.

Wiat was marching with the times in the choice of his subject. The Satire on Court Life was the fashion, having its origin, by way of contrast, in Baldassare Castiglione's "Il Cortegiano." Castiglione was a dreamer and an idealist, uniting scholarship with an artistic and sensitive mind, viewing life with platonic ideals, and suffering, as all such kindred spirits have done, through contact with the harsh realities of life. The standard of living set up in "Il Cortegiano" being too ideal for the average gentleman, the cynic and the humorist saw their opportunity in contrasting the actual with the perfect courtier. Hence so many Satires on the life of the courtier.

Alamanni's Tenth Satire, published 1532; Ariosto's First Satire,[1] published 1534; Wiat's First and Third Satires, written 1536–7 and printed in Tottel 1557; Guevara's "Menos precio de Corti," and his "Aviso de privados," both published in 1539; L'Alaigre's "Mepris du Cour," 1542, and "Le Favovi du Court," 1556, both translations of Guevara's Satires; and Sir Francis Brian's "Dispraise of the Life of a Courtier" (see Satire 3, l. 7), all give an indication of the prevalence, not only of the mode of verse, but of the subject. All writers agree in the essentials, the hollowness and vanity of Court life; but the Satire varies in the attitude towards the ruler, and the requirements of the courtier according to the nationality of the writer. For example, the Spanish courtier has before him the pride and dignity of his profession,[2] the reverence towards the sovereign and the magnificence surrounding the Court. The Italian Alamanni,

[1] The Second Satire in the final edition.

[2] The courtier of the sixteenth century entered the *profession* of the Court as surely as a surgeon the medical profession to-day, and had an arduous apprenticeship.

writing in the spirit of the Florentine Republic, is naturally more free, and Wiat, with the honesty and sincerity which characterized his temperament, and which naturally became mirrored in his writings, admired these special traits in the Italian, and translated them in more pronounced fashion.

Myn owne John Poynz. The first two Satires are written to this friend, of whom little is known. His name appears among the challengers at the famous feat of arms at the Feast of Christmas, 1525, in which Wiat took part (Hall's *Chr.*, p. 683, edition 1809). His uncle, Sir Anthony Poynz, was a brilliant statesman, whose untimely death by plague in 1528 probably accounts for the nephew's return to private life. From Holbein's portrait of John Poynz he appears as a scholar, and wears a scholar's garb.

l. 27. *Sely*, "foolish," by deterioration of meaning, ∠ "selig," O.E. "happy."

l. 38. *Cato*. Wiat's illustration. Alamanni refers to Brutus.

l. 40. *Cesares hands*. Alamanni mentions other Roman celebrities which Wiat omits. It is the Italian fashion in the Satire. Machiavelli and Ariosto illustrate copiously from classical figures.

ll. 40–50. Wiat's original illustrations.

ll. 50–1. Wiat's satirical observation here shows his proper appreciation of the "Knight's Tale," which comes out in his later poems indirectly in many phrases imitated from this work; his opinion of Sir Thopas evidently agrees with that of Chaucer's Host.

ll. 53–4. Wiat's ironical observations on a courtier's training.

l. 67. *Favell*. Deception by flattery. The fashion for personification which had its origin in the "Roman de la

Rose" still lingered, and but a short time was to elapse before it was renewed to vigorous life in Spenser's "Faery Queene."

ll. 76–8. Wiat's position was analogous with that of Alamanni. The Italian exiled from Florence, Wiat from Court. There are many points of likeness in character of the two poets—both possessed a graceful manner, and a generous nature, combined with noble qualities of mind.

l. 79. *A chipp of chaunce . . . witt.* Wiat's several imprisonments were due to a sudden change in the temper or the policy of the king.

ll. 80–1. *This maketh me at home. . . .* Wiat's imprisonment was put down to his former intimacy with Anne Boleyn—a supposition proved to be false by definite statements concerning his quarrel with the Duke of Suffolk. He was released conditionally: he was obliged to retire to Allington under his father's control.

l. 86. *A clogg.* Wiat was free to go about on his father's property, but he was on parole, in his father's custody. His detention came to an end in October 15, 1536, when he was sent north to assist in putting down the Northern insurrection.

ll. 89–90. *saffry*, i. e. "savory." Wiat asked and received permission to export wine during his residence at Calais in 1529. The references to France, l. 89, Spain, l. 91, and Flanders, l. 94, are in the original.

l. 97. *Where Christe is geven in pray.* A notable instance of change of text is seen in Tottel's version, evidently for religious and political reasons. Wiat's version expresses the view of the nobler spirits in the Roman Catholic Church as well as the Reform attitude towards Rome; these words were carefully altered in Mary's reign.

l. 100. *In Kent.* Provence in the original. Wiat introduces local colour, and makes his version living and personal by the concluding lines. The Italian reads—

Con le rare muse in solitario loco.

ll. 101–2. original. For the Italian ending see the Italian source, Appendix A.

THE SECOND SATIRE

My mothers maydes. This reference to home life at Allington Castle is one of the pleasant touches in Wiat's poems. His mother was a reputed character, not only governing domestic affairs, but keeping law and order on her husband's estate during his frequent absences on the King's business. A complaint being made to the Court of Lady Wiat's summary treatment of a neighbouring Abbot, and the matter being brought to her husband, Sir Henry Wiat deftly turned the tables by asking what licence the world would take if Lady Wiat should be reprimanded for upholding a moral standard.

The Satire is based upon Horace's "Town and Country Mouse," which is inserted as a nursery tale ("aniles ex re fabellas") into the dialogue between Tiresias and Ulysses, Satire II, 6. As the opening lines show, the fable was popular and well known. Henryson's fable of the "Uponlondis Mous and the Burges Mous" may have been known to Wiat. S. F. Nott cites the expression, "Pepe quod the other," l. 42, with Henryson's "Cry peip anis" (iv. 5). This is the only likeness, and the course of the Scotch fable differs considerably from Wiat's. The imitation in this Satire is, in fact, Chaucerian throughout, the likeness to a part of the Troilus poem is striking, and is the neatest and most sparkling piece of work that Wiat ever accomplished.

l. 26. *Cater.* Provisions. Cater is the general term for purveyor, < O.F. *Acateur* > "acheteur."

l. 31. *Jape.* "Jest." Constantly found in Chaucer.

> And al his ernest turneth til a jape.

ll. 36–46. This interview between the Town and Country Mouse brings out the dramatic element in Wiat. The dialogue is inimitable. Wiat had caught the art, as he appreciated the genius, of the "Troilus and Cressida" poems. It was this new impetus, added to his previous knowledge of the Horatian satire that brought out the fine quality in this masterpiece of style.

l. 49. *She chered her with . . . what chiere.* "Chere" (chiere) common in Chaucer.

> And ther-with al he lough and made chere.—A, 4363.

l. 50. *befell a sorry chaunce.* Cf. Chaucer A—

> Lord what me is tid a sory chaunce

l. 51. *Well awaye.* Cf. *T. & C.*, III. 1695.

> But cruel day, *so wel-away the staunde,*

(i. e. Alas the while !).

l. 52. *A scaunce.* "Askance," the general meaning is "slantwise," "sideways." Cf. *T. & C.*, I. 204.

> And with that word he gan cast up the brow
> Askances.

Rarely used in Shakespeare. It is found in *R. of L.*, 637, and also in the early Hamlet quarto, but is replaced in the 1623 folio by "aslant."

l. 53. *Stemyng Ise*, i. e. gleaming eyes, borrowed from Chaucer.

> His eyen stepe and rollyng in his hed
> That *stemed* as a forneys of a led.—*Prologue.*

The word *stemyng* has been strangely misunderstood.

G. F. Nott proposed "streaming"! It is found in Middle English romances to express light that "gleams forth." In modern language the expression "*lightning* glance" is a fairly good parallel.

l. 55. The rhyming word to match "Ise," "gyse," is omitted; such a word as "ywys" is required.

l. 63. *Hevyn it would lo.* Cf. Chaucer,

> fortune wolde that he most twinne.—F. 557.

l. 64. *her sely fote.* "Sely" common in Chaucer for "foolish," "unfortunate." One of the words that has depreciated in meaning. O.E. *selig*, "happy," "blessed." Cf.

> To helpen sely Troilus of his wo.—*T. & C.*, II. 683.

l. 68. *her poure suretie. poure*, i. e. "poor," the usual spelling in this text. A. and T. take the meaning as "power." Wiat is drawing the contrast between secure poverty and perilous wealth.

l. 70. *Alas my Poynz.* The morality to the fable begins here. Henryson divides his Satire into the Fable and Moralitas, the latter beginning—

> Friendis ye may find an ye will take heide
> Into this fable ane gud moralitie.

The person addressed is John Poynz. See Satire 1, l. 1.

ll. 75–80. *O wretched myndes there is no gold that may* . . . This fine passage surely suggested Shakespeare's speech on Ceremony. *Henry V.*, IV. i., and the speech beginning—

> Within the hollow crown
> That rounds the mortal temples of a king.
> *Richard II.* 3, ii. 160.

Shakespeare learned from his mother Nature on the banks of the Avon, but amongst the literary sources from whence he derived inspiration we must include the *Songs and*

Sonnets. Note the speech put into Slender's mouth. *M.W.W.*, I. i. 179. "I had rather than forty shillings I had my Songs and Sonnets here"—one of the very few utterances in Shakespeare that we might consider to reflect the dramatist's own point of view!

l. 80. *disease.* Want of ease, trouble.

l. 88. *Conys.* Possibly meant as a satirical allusion to the cheats, who were termed "cony-catchers." Cf. the title of pamphlet published by R. Greene, "Frauds and Tricks of Coney-Catchers and Couzeners."

l. 100. The thought is much condensed here. The meaning is that when a remedy is known it is madness to allow the disease to continue. I consider that *mad* is meant in the modern sense. G. F. Nott interprets as *made*, following the A. MS.

l. 101–2. Work is the remedy suggested by philosophers and poets for the ills of life. Mrs. Browning adds love, in that splendid passage of the "Aurora Leigh," Bk. IX.

> The world waits
> For help. Beloved, let us love so well.
> Our work shall still be better for our love,
> And still our love be sweeter for our work,
> And both commended, for the sake of each,
> By all true workers and true lovers born.

This combination of work allied with a great human sympathy is the great force which is drawing men and women nearer together to-day. The idea of work undertaken in love, meeting the problems and difficulties of life on an equal footing, with mutual help and mutual joy in life, is one of the ideals of the age, and must be partially realized, because of the purity and integrity of the purpose that it involves.

l. 105. *But to the great God.* Imitated from Perseus, Satire iii.

> Magne Pater Divum, saevos punire tyrannos
> Haud alia ratione velim cum diva libido
> Moverit ingenium ferventi tincta veneno
> Virtutem videant intabescantque relicta.

l. 112. *To frete inward.* Cf. "the gruging of the worm within," *i. e.* the prick of conscience.

ll. 108–112. G. F. Nott justly remarks that Wiat's fine rendering may have influenced Milton's lines; *P. L.*, iv. 846—

> Abashed the devil stood
> And felt how awful goodness is, and saw
> Virtue in her shape how lovely ;
> Saw, and pined his loss.

THE THIRD SATIRE

A spending hand. The last Satire was written a little later than the two preceding—1537 is the probable date. It is an imitation of Horace, Satire 2, l. 5. The turn of speech and general style is Chaucerian, but it bears the stamp of Wiat's own personality.

Wiat's homely allusions are a dominant feature of his style (ll. 1–4). Contrast the domestic allusion in the opening of Satire 2.

The Satire is addressed to Sir Francis Brian (see ll. 7–9), than whom no one knew better the tricks of a courtier's life, and the constant tacking needed in order to keep within the fair wind of the Court.

Sir Francis Brian is the most constant, though by no means the greatest figure at Henry's Court. Diplomatist, courtier and favourite of Henry VIII all through the reign, he was also a scholar and a keen lover of literature; his culture and strong literary tastes formed the chief bond of intimacy between Wiat and Brian, while similar ambassadorial duties necessitated an official correspondence between them about this time (1537).

Brian's uncle, Lord Berners,[1] translated Guevara's "Libro Aureo" at his nephew's suggestion. Brian himself translated a French work, "The Dispraise of the Life of a Courtier,"[2] thus making a fresh link in the chain of Satires on the courtier. It was probably undertaken in acknowledgment of Wiat's third Satire, addressed to him. Imprisoned in 1541, Wiat wrote the Epigram "Sighes ar my food" to Brian as the person most intimately connected with the King, and therefore more able than any other to assist in Wiat's release. His help came, however, from another quarter.

Brian retained his position in the King's favour by a trimming policy. At one time Anne's chief supporter, he was the chief mover in her downfall; he was chosen to carry the news of her execution to Jane Seymour, and was a prominent figure at the christening of Prince Edward.

In April 1537, about the time of Wiat's departure for Spain, he was sent as special ambassador to France with Gardner, the then resident ambassador, but was back in England at the end of the year.

This Satire, from its tenor, appears to have been addressed by Wiat to Brian in France, either before he left England (between April and May) or from the Spanish Court a month or two later.

[1] Lord Berner's "Golden Boke" has the following colophon: "Thus endeth the volume of Marke Aurelie emperour otherwise called the golden boke translated out of Frenche into englyshe by John Bourchier knyghte lorde Berners deputie general of the kynges towne of Caleys and marches of the same at the instant desyre of his neuewe syr Francis Bryan knyghte, ended at Caleys the teneth day of Marche in the yere of the reygne of our soverayne lorde Kinge Henry viii the xxiii.

[2] This is an *English* version of the French translation of Guevara's satire, published some years after Wiat's death.

ll. 1–4 appear to be an implied analogy with Brian's life.

ll. 7–9. Brian needed all the courtier's art to carry out successfully the diplomacy required of him.

ll. 9–10. *Who knows how great a grace In writing is.* An implied compliment to Brian's scholarship and appreciation of literature.

ll. 11–12. Brian had a share in the leading events of the reign, whether domestic or foreign.

ll. 12–13. *Reaulme to Reaulme.* Many important missions were entrusted to Brian. In 1528 he was sent to Rome to obtain the papal sanction for the Divorce. In 1531 he was ambassador to the French Court : in 1533 he was travelling in France with the purpose of preventing an interview between Francis and the Pope ; again in France in 1535 ; and in 1537, to obtain the expulsion of Pole.[1]

l. 15. *bed of downe.* Cf. Satire 2, l. 21.

l. 16. *drynck goode ale so noppy,* i. e. "heady." (Cf. Skelton : "Ale . . . so nappy for the nonce." A general expression of the times was "nappy as ale is," *i. e.* "vigorous."

l. 18. The imagined dialogue forms a great contrast to the lively dialogue between the Town Mouse and the Country Mouse (Satire 2). Here the Satire cuts deep. *Swyne so groyns,* i. e. "ferrets with its snout."

l. 20 combines the pagan and Christian metaphor in the allusion to the Circean swine added to the metaphor from the Gospel text : "Cast not your pearls before swine."

l. 21. *Then of the harp the asse.* "As pearls to swine, so is good music to the ass." The expression is derived from Chaucer's Boethius Iprosa 4, "Artow like an asse to the harpe?" The original Greek, εἰνε ὄνος πρὸς λύραν and the Latin "Esne asinus ad liram?" became proverbial phrases for dulness of understanding. In the 1656 edition of Boethius, R. Vallinus quotes for this line, "Ii liberi si

[1] *Vide* N.D.B.

erunt ὀνοιλύρας exheredes sunto." Chaucer himself explained the allusion in *T. & C.*, 730–5—

> What, slombrestow as in a lytargye !
> Or arlow lyk an asse to the harpe,
> That hereth soun when men the strenges play,
> But in his minde of that no melodye
> May sinken, him to glade, for that he
> So dull is of his bestialitee.

Wiat is thinking of Chaucer's interpretation in this passage.

l. 22. A very biting reference to the evils in cloistral life; expunged in Tottel's edition.

l. 25. Sir Henry and Sir Thomas Wiat both gave their life-service to the King.

ll. 26–27. Wiat was tall and spare of figure, his later portraits present an emaciated appearance.

ll. 28–30. The Latin Satire begins in this manner (the previous lines in Wiat are original)—

> Hoc quoque Tiresia præter narrata petenti
> Responde, quibus amissas reparare queam res
> Artibus atque modis.

ll. 34–37. A very cutting Satire on the evils of Court life, its falseness (34–7), its hypocrisy (37–41), its cozening (41–51), its flattery (51–8), and its viciousness (59–75).

l. 44. *As to a dogge a chese;* the origin of this expression is not known. Tottel alters to "as to a calfe a chese." The sense, of course, is "Don't lend unless you can make a bargain out of it."

ll. 51–53. Cf. Horace II. v. 93–5.

l. 54. *and if he koggh to sore*, taken from Horace, cf. Serm. II. v. 106.

> Siquis
> Forte coheredum senior male tussiet . . .

Wiat, however, enlarges on the illustration.

ll. 82–4. Wiat's lofty moral purpose comes out here, cf. Letter to his Son : "I call not Honesty that men commonly call Honesty as reputation for riches for authority or such like thing; but that Honesty that I dare say your grandfather, whose soul God pardon, had rather left me than all the lands he did leave me; that was Wisdom, gentleness, soberness, desire to do good, Friendliness to get the love of many and *Truth above the rest.*" Cf. l. 34 above, Wiat first of all attacks the want of truth at Court.

ll. 87–8. Wiat's own case, his tongue was always free. He insisted upon honest dealings, hence many of his troubles —hence also his final victory. Truth had never a greater victory, nor falseness greater discomfiture, than in Wiat's exposure of the ignominious character of Bonner his accuser, in 1541. See the Oration.

ll. 90–1. Wiat suffered greatly through want of ready money. In Spain he was greatly harassed by the straitness of his exchequer, and the need of keeping up appearances at Court, notwithstanding the fact that, on his father's death, November 1537, he was said to be the greatest landowner in England.

MISCELLANEOUS POEMS AFTER 1536

THE Miscellaneous Poems are divided into the earlier and later groups for the purpose of keeping the chronological order of the MS., and differentiating between the quality of the poems. While the first group consists mainly of light Court songs, which occasionally reach the highest lyrical excellence, this group contains many fine poems, and includes Wiat's most original work; here he has attained maturity of thought with elegance of expression. There are two new tendencies to notice: an interest in astrology in the first poem, "Though this port," and the last, "When Dido festid" does not merely mark personal taste, but is an example of the interest taken in this subject by Western Europe. Secondly, Wiat contributes to the literary argument that was interesting France on the platonic aspect of love, by the poem, in three parts, "Lo what it is to love." Both tendencies are due to the influence of the Lyons School[1] upon Wiat, which coincides with his embassy to Spain.

The majority of the poems in this section are peculiar to the E. MS.

No. 1. **Though this port.** Elliptical for "though this *be* port." Nott inserts "the" before port. The poem was probably written when Wiat was crossing the Channel on his way to Spain in 1537.

The meaning of the first stanza is: though I am coming

[1] See Appendix G.

safely into port, and am thy (*i. e.* Venus') true servant; although you are propitious, being in your seventh heaven (*i. e.* chief house); yet I am sad because I am separated from the one I love. The whole is imitated from Chaucer. Cf. *T. & C.* II. 680—

> And also blisful Venus wel arayed,
> Sat in her seventhe hous of heaven tho,
> Disposed well.

And *T. & C.* III., stanzas 1–4, being the translation from the Filostrato [1] of the beautiful hymn to Venus.

And again, *T. & C.* III. 1254–7—

> O Love, O Charite
> Thy mother eke, Citherea the swete,
> After thyself next heried be she;
> Venus mene I, the well-willy planete.

Wiat's unbounded admiration of Chaucer, and his critical appreciation of "Troilus and Cresida," is evident in his later poems. That his interest in astronomy is originally derived from Chaucer, is clearly seen here. We find it developed in the last poem.

l. 3. *chieff howse.* "House" in astrology meant (i) the zodiacal sign; as Taurus is the house or mansion of Venus, and (ii) the division of the celestial sphere into twelve equal parts, or houses, by six great circles passing through the north and south points of the horizon. Reckoning from the eastern horizon was the first house; the seventh house was opposite to it, being reckoned downwards from the western horizon.[2] Both the first and seventh houses were propitious, therefore "chief." The popular phrase "in the seventh heaven of delight" no doubt originates from the astrological "chief house," or "seventhe house of heaven."

[1] See Boccaccio Filostrato, stanzas 74–79.
[2] Skeat's note, *Works of Chaucer.*

l. 7. *En vogant la galere.* A refrain of a French boat song. Possibly imitated by Wiat from the sailors, while composing this song. Cf. l. 17, "In stede of slepe, thus I occupy the nyght. "Galere" varies in spelling, in ll. 14, 21, 28, written "galerie."

ll. 10–14. *The ferme faith . . .* Supplication to Venus, to guard her faithful servant, now on the sea.

l. 16. *reducing*, i. e. "recalling."

l. 18. *A thowsand thoughtes and many dowbtes.* Wiat had come to a parting of the ways, his new life as ambassador to the Spanish Court lay before him with all the anxieties involved in the task of trying to effect conciliation between Henry VIII and the Emperor Charles. He refers to his *doubt* concerning the task laid upon him in the Oration. "I confess frankly," he says, "I never begged the office, and but for the obedience to my master I would have utterly refused it; and how I excused the taking of it, my Lords of the Council can bear me record; as well for that I knew my own inability . . . meddling with wise men, having no council but my own foolish head, a great zeal that the King might be well served by me, *a great fear lest anything should* quail through my fault. *This solicitude, this care* troubled me. But the still starlight night, the unruffled sea, and the chant of the sailors reduce Wiat's troubled spirit to quiescence, and the song continues—

But still I trust thou canst not be unkinde.

Stanza 4. There is a curious mingling of pagan and Christian metaphor in this poem; he begins with a supplication to Venus, but clothes her in the Christian figure of Charity—this image easily connects itself with faith (stanza 2) and hope (l. 19). The best example of the mingling of pagan and Christian metaphor is Milton's "Lycidas," with a deeper spiritual meaning in his case.

No. 2. **Processe of tyme.** Based on Petrarch and full of the usual conceits. Notice the trisyllabic beat throughout the poem.

No. 3. **After great stormes.** The whole poem suggests phrases from the Psalms. Cf. ll. 5–6, 10, 13–14, 18, which are adaptations of Bible verses. Wiat wrote his paraphrase of Psalm 37 when he was in Spain. His Protestant attitude became very pronounced from 1537 and onwards. At this time the letters to his son were written, wherein he lays down the principle of "the dread and reverence of God" as the "infallible ground of Honesty." And by honesty Wiat includes all the virtues that go to form the character of a noble-minded human being.

No. 4. **All hevy myndes.** This song seems to have been composed to beguile the poet amidst the cares of life at the Spanish Court. Music exerted a powerful influence upon Wiat, and he turned to it as his great consolation after physical and mental strain. His duties in Spain were not only fatiguing but hazardous, and music was possibly his only resource. See ll. 57–8—

> And with my lute
> Sum tyme to ease my pain.

ll. 33–34. *Who . . . fethered wings.* For a similar experience see "Myne olde dere enmy," stanza 19, and the note. Cf. the verse of the Psalmist, "Oh had I the wings of a dove, then would I flee and be at rest."

No. 5. **To seke eche where.** This poem is of special interest. Long after the early and fleeting French influence, Wiat arranged it from Marot's beautiful little "Etrenne," one of the most graceful little madrigals he ever wrote. It runs—

Ce nouvel an pour etrenne vous donne
Mon cueur blessé d'une nouvelle plaie,
Contraint j'y suis, amour ainsi l'ordonne
En qui un cas bien contraire j'essaie :
Car ce cueur là c'est ma richesse vraie :
Le demeurant n'est rien où je ne fonde :
Et faut donner le meilleur bien que j'aie,
Si j'ay vouloir d'estre riche en ce monde.

M. Emile Faguet quotes this in his "Seizième siècle" (1900), saying : "Ce joli talent de dire agréablement des choses obligeantes l'a conduit naturellement au madrigal, et les madrigaux de Marot *sont parmi les plus jolies petites choses de la littérature française.* Les Etrennes à Neère de Tibulle, bien gracieuses du reste, sont-elles aussi jolies que celles-ci, précieuses un peu, sans doute, mais d'un si libre ton et d'une chute si heureuse?"

This is high praise indeed, and Wiat has not come short of the original. His rendering is worth analyzing. He has taken Marot's octave, abab, baba, and expanded it into four stanzas of two tercets, aab, abb, with octosyllables in the first four, and decasyllables for the last two, lines.

The idea in Marot's first line is made the refrain of Wiat's song, "I give to yere," *i. e.* "I give as a New Year's gift." He alters the idea in Marot's second line, the weakest in the poem, to the very beautiful

It is both whole and pure withouten peer.—l. 17,

and by so doing removes the artificiality which spoils Marot's version. From ll. 6–7 in the original Wiat composes stanzas 1–3. But Wiat adds greatly to the charm of the poem by keeping the nature of the gift until the last lines—

Dare I well gyve I say *my hert* to yere.

l. 3. *Ffraunce, Spayne, and Inde.* The mention of Ffraunce here and in l. 21 is accounted for by the fact that

Wiat has adapted Marot's French poem; *Spayne*, Wiat composed this Etrenne in Spain; *Inde* represented the farthest corner of the world. This is the best instance among the lyrics of Wiat's masterly handling of material, in stamping his own individuality upon it.

No. 6. **O goodely hand.** This conceit is probably derived from Giusto di Conti's "La Bella Mane." It is a slight, but graceful, poem.

The form of stanza is a double fourteener split up into fours and sixes.

No. 7. **Lo what it is to love.** This poem is in three parts, in the same metre as "Sins ye delite to know." It is Wiat's contribution to a certain phase of thought, and is the result of the influence of the school of Lyons upon him. He was in touch with Lyons during the time of his embassy in Spain, for it was the great highway, and formed a junction for travellers to all parts of Europe; and since dispatches and communications came by way of Lyons, Wiat necessarily became conversant of the life there. The city was passing through a phase of extraordinary activity at this very period.

The poem expresses Wiat's attitude towards love, and is no chance production. "La Querelle des Dames" was occupying France at this moment, and the battle waged hottest at Lyons, where women had been regarded as individual and had possessed a great amount of freedom from its earliest history. The women of Lyons, their beauty and grace, their intellectual and moral force, and their equal share in the social and moral needs of the race, is one of the fine things in civilization.

The position was briefly this: at the very time that the later school of Petrarch tended to develop a sensual type of love, encouraged by the laxity of moral and general exuberant enthusiasm in life so prevalent in the early sixteenth century, the close study of Plato carried on in the schools at Florence and elsewhere had brought into prominence the ideal of spiritual and intellectual love, of which Dante had been the great exponent in the thirteenth century, and Michael Angelo [1] in the sixteenth century carried on the tradition. Different poets took sides upon the question as to the baseness or purity of love.

The nobler spirits took up their position for the ideal. Heroët, Sève, Pernette du Gueillet, Wiat and many others took the nobler view, while the lesser and generality of poets frankly regarded love as a mere passing pleasure. Heroët's "Parfaicte Amie," published in 1542, and preceded by a translation of Plato's "Androgyne," Marguerite d'Angoulême's "spiritual" poems, Sève's "Délie" (1544), Pernette du Gueillet's "Songs, including La Parfaicte Amie" (1545), are all tinged with the platonic ideal, and are expressions of this movement. "Lo, what it is to love," is Wiat's contribution, written about 1539. The *querelle* raged from about 1537 to 1545, and the poems mentioned above were probably written some years before their publication. Wiat puts the case as simply and tersely as we settle the question to-day. A low view of love merely shows ignorance concerning love, and a capacity in the person who holds this view for the low things of life. He who abuses love has acted unworthily, and therefore has not known love. He who really loves is of necessity true of heart, and will never slander love, because true love requires above all else sincerity and purity. "E se creato a Dio non fusse equalæ."

Each part consists of five stanzas, each stanza in the first part occupies the same position in the argument as the

[1] Among the poets. Prose-writing on the subject was enormous, including the critical as well as the mystic school of Plato students.

corresponding stanzas of the other parts. Reference to dicing appears in stanza 3 of every part.

Part III. l. 21. *zyns*, i. e. fives, was the lucky throw in dice. l. 22. *ambs-as*, i. e. the double ace, was the unlucky throw.

No. 8. **Yf in the world.** A good example of Wiat's skill in technique. An example of a treizaine, in lines of tens, eights and sixes; the rhyme scheme shows a certain amount of ingenuity in welding together the thirteen lines as one stanza by the following structure, ababb, cbdc, eded. Cf. "Ye know my hert," for another form of treizaine. l. 12 indicates a personal touch. Wiat alludes to this "unkyndeness" several times. See "Letter to his Son" concerning unkindness, quoted on p. 259.

Park, the antiquary, notes in the revised edition of Warton's *History of English Poetry*, IV. 40: "Ascham in his discourse of the state of 'Germanie,' has the following tributary remark, 'A knight of England of worthie memorie for wit, learnyng, and experience, old syr Thomas Wiatt, wrote to his sonne that the greatest mischief amongst men, and least punished, is unkyndness.'"

No. 9. **Thanswere that ye made.** A very noble sentiment pervades this poem. See ll. 6–7, in very different vein from the typical railing lover who finds his lady cold.

Stanza 3 was begun at the bottom of the page in the MS. Then the leaf was turned and the scribe started off with stanza 4, leaving three lines wanting to stanza 3.

l. 12. *Ffre hert* . . . Cf. Sonnet, *Though I myself*, ll. 3-4. The treizaine "Ye know my hert," expresses similar ideas of disinterested love, *i. e.* the platonic type.

No. 10. **Most wretched hart.** A debate, in which the argument and reply runs in alternate quatrains with the appropriate refrain. It is imitated from "The Playnte to Fortune" in the 1532 edition of Chaucer. In the Chaucerian poem Pleintif complains and Fortune replies—

> **No man is wretched but himself it wene**
> **He that hath himself hath sufficaunce**
> **And eke thou hast thy best friend on lyve.**

The first four stanzas are written in a new hand, probably that of Wiat's secretary in Spain; the fifth stanza is continued in a new hand, on a fresh page, and for this reason was regarded by the intending editor of Wiat's poems as another composition.

The group of poems written towards the close of Wiat's residence in Spain reflect Wiat's anxiety and unhappy state of mind. The political situation in England was gloomy. Wiat was harassed and persecuted at the Spanish Court, and Cromwell's power was waning.

The debate represents the pessimistic versus the optimistic view. Optimism wins, though the prospect is dark (stanza 6); yet it is not outer circumstances, but the soul of man that wins or loses, cf. ll. 23, 30.

ll. 31–2. *And he that knoweth what is what, Sayeth.* An indirect reference to Chaucer, to whom he is indebted for the refrain : "And he is wretched."

l. 33. *Seist thou not how they whet their teth.* A personal allusion; Wiat's enemies were extremely hostile, and Bonner was spreading false reports at home. The last stanza expresses the same optimism as the poems in prison (1541) : "Yet sure I know the wound will hele again." Wiat, aging before his time with the stress of official duties and private troubles, is developing that same quiet confidence that his father, Sir Henry Wiat, had possessed.

No. 11. **And if an Iye.** This poem is of a higher quality

than that of the old conceit of the glance wounding the lover's heart. It is in a dramatic vein, in the form of a monologue, but the lover speaks with such art that we can easily imagine the dialogue. The definite parts of the discussion are made out at l. 5, "How can ye say . . ."; l. 10, "But yet I say . . ."; l. 15, "But yet alas . . ."; l. 23, "For as ye saye . . ."; l. 29, "But I your frende . . ." And the very fine conclusion is typical of Wiat: "Well, never mind the past, but be stedfast *in Truth*, then "feres not the Iye to shewe the hert." In defining the virtues to his son, he places *Truth* above all the rest. Cf. the fine spirit of the Sonnet 13, ll. 9–11, and especially the lines—

> Still under the defence
> Of time, trouth and love to save thee from offence.

An interesting parallel to this poem may be seen in the romantic correspondence [1] in verse between Bonaventure des Periers and Claude, Abbess of St. Honorat, during the years 1536–1539. Bonaventure des Periers was a brilliant writer and a leading figure of the literary clique at Lyons when Wiat was at the Spanish Court. One verse runs (B. des Periers—

> Mais l'œil je n'accuse
> Qui mon cœur ravit,
> Ni le cœur excuse
> Qui pour l'œil servit.

And the Abbess replies—

> Vous faictes justice
> D'excuser mon œil,
> Qui fait son office
> Vous faisant accueil.

No. 12. **What rage is this.** The poem originally began with the second stanza. It is in Wiat's handwriting. The first stanza must have been inserted when the poem was

[1] *Studies of the Renaissance.* In hand.

corrected, for stanzas 2–5 are in black ink, whereas the corrected portions of stanza 1 are in faded ink. It is the last poem in the MS. before the Psalms, excepting "Vulcan begat me," which was certainly inserted later (see note on this poem, Epigram 2). The corrections are later than the poem, which was written about 1539, and definitely proves that Wiat revised the E. MS. after this date.

In this and the previous poem Wiat definitely writes of himself as the friend, and in the poems of this group—peculiar to the MS., and written in Spain—he addresses his friend as "my dear." Such familiar phrases are not often found, and are confined to the poems in this group.

No. 13. **So feble is the threde.** A very fine translation of Petrarch's Canzone "Si e debile." The short lines of "Sins ye delite to know," and "Lo what it is to love," are welded together to form a couplet consisting of an Alexandrine [1] followed by a fourteener, and called Poulter's Measure by Puttenham. It is hard to understand why such an unwieldy and monotonous measure should have been adopted by Wiat at this stage. He had become singularly fluent in the ten-syllable line; he had shown his skill in the use of every variety of lyrical form, and after all his achievements he deliberately seems to have left this measure as his last legacy.[2] (See also the last fragment.) Surrey wrote seven poems in this long couplet, and succeeded tolerably well. The versifiers, they are not poets, who followed him, adopted it most faithfully, and employed it

[1] Puttenham, *Arte of Poesie*, II. p. 86, Arber's Reprints. "This metre of twellve silables the French man calleth a verse Alexandrine and is with our modern rimers most usuall; with the auncient makers it was not so. For before Sir Thomas Wiat's time they were not used in our vulgar."

[2] Cf. Ronsard's choice of metre for *La Franciade*, which was never finished, for which "Dieu Merci," says M. Faguet, an ejaculation which every one re-echoes.

ad nauseam. It is a measure that insists on regularity, and with regularity of measure, simplicity of speech. Wiat recognized these essentials, and with all its drawbacks he has achieved success. The poem is living, and in parts compares very favourably with the model where Wiat has not only caught the beauty of the Italian, but expressed it with great vividness in English. Had Wiat attempted this verse in the early days, it would have been a failure. This fine poem is perhaps the most conclusive example of the height which Wiat had gained in the structure of verse. He tended to irregularity and was at times obscure, being criticized for these features in his day. The Canzone is an evidence of his power to be regular in metre and clear in speech when he so desired, without the loss of those inherent qualities which fascinate by their charm and convince by their manliness and sincerity of tone.

Still, it must be owned that we feel grateful to Wiat for not finishing the second example of the long couplet.

The poem carefully follows the build of the "Canzone," which is in seven stanzas of sixteen lines, and a concluding envoy of eight lines. The divisions corresponding to the Italian stanzas are in fourteen-line lengths, with one division of twelve lines for the fifth stanza. The concluding envoy is in six lines. Thus the stanza in fourteen, with an occasional twelve, lines, harmonizes with the structure of the verse of fourteen, or twelve, syllables.

The following first lines show the correspondence in the Italian and English—

I. So feble is the threde.	I. Si e debile il filo.
II. The tyme doth flete.	II. Il tempo passa.
III. Eche place doth bryng me grieff.	III. Ogni loco m'atrista.
IV. If suche record alas.	IV. Lasso, se ragionando.
V. These new kyndes of plesurs.	V. Novo piacer.
VI. The cryspid gold.	VI. Le treccie d'or.

VII. And yet with more delyght to mone my woful cace.	VII. Et per pranger anchor con piu diletto.
VIII. My song thou shalt attune to fynd that plesant place.	VIII. Canzone, s'al dolce loco la Donna nostro vedi.

Reading through this poem single lines stand out for forcible language and tender feeling—Wiat's thoughts revert to that *friend*, to whom so many of these later poems are addressed. The sixth stanza of ll. 5–10 is doubtless personal, in the reference to happy meetings and pleasant converse.

The envoy is original. A similar ending is found in Tasso, but Tasso is later than Wiat.

The division into stanzas, though not marked in the MS., is authorized by the above correspondence with Petrarch's canzone, and the poem is rendered less cumbersome by making the divisions obvious. Stanza 6 has rendered the Petrarchan references to Nature with a delicacy of touch rarely seen in Wiat's poetry.

The various allusions to the heavens in this poem is a preparation for the last fragment, "When Dido festid first."

No. 14. **When Dido festid first.** This fragment seems to-day intolerably dull. Yet without it we should miss a link in the chain of evidence gained from the study of Wiat's poems. Apart from the opening lines, 1–4, suggested by *Æneid*, I—

> Cithara crinitus Iopas
> Personat aurata docuit quæ maxima Atlas
> Hic canit errantem lunam, solisque labores,

the precise source is unknown. Wiat's taste for astronomy had first been aroused by his study of Chaucer (see Note on "Though this port"); and was deepened by his study of Plato, for the general interest in astronomy was largely due to the cult of Plato at the end of the fifteenth century and early sixteenth century. Take, for example, the passage from the *Republic*, Book VII, "Concerning harmony and astronomy": "Every one as I think must see that astronomy compels the soul to look upwards and leads us from this world to another"; and in Book X Plato illustrates his theory concerning the immortality of the soul by the mythical treatment of the Ptolemaic theory of the heavens in the "Vision of Er." M. Sève, steeped in neoplatonism, represents his Adam in the "Microcosme" as a good geometrician, and better astronomer—

> Adam si tost soit fait bon geomètre
> Et meilleur Astronome.

And Eve, equally intelligent, both "hears and asks questions" concerning

> L'Astronome joyeux que son docte propos
> Ait rencontré cerveau et gentil et propos
> Et capable assès plus d'autre difficulté,
> En l'entendemente.

Scholars wrote treatises, and poets composed verses on the subject. Editions of Ptolemy were issued: at Venice in 1518; at Basle in 1533, including a later poem on the subject; *in 1536 Thomas Linacre* issued his Commentary on the subject in Greek and Latin. In France, a few years later, Pontus des Tyard published his discourses, and M. Sève his "Microcosme."

Meanwhile Copernicus had propounded his theory in 1530, and the news of his discovery soon became known to the astronomers. His work was not published until 1542, but the idea of a rival to Ptolemy was intolerable to all those who regarded him as "Prince of Astronomers." Many writers hastened to vindicate his theory, and set forth treatise after treatise to establish, and hold people firm to, the old (Ptolemaic) belief.

In 1536 the subject was considered so important that a tiny popular edition was issued with the title of "*The Compost of Ptolemy Prynce of Astronomye translated out of the*

Frenche with Englysshe for them that wolde have knowledge of the Compost." *By Robert Wyre* "*in Saint Martin's Parysshe in the feldes besyde Charing X.*"

The translation was made, so it said, "for them that be littell or no clerkes," and the Preface set forth that "*a man is a lytel world by himselfe for the likeness and similitude he hath to the great worlde.*" Here we find how widespread was the idea of man's relation to the universe as the Microcosme to the Macrocosme, an idea which J. Donne takes some pains to disprove later. See "*Letters to Severall Personages.*" Works, 1912.

The *Compost* was meant for the people, Wiat's poem for the upper classes; the one gave in popular language an account of the spheres and their relation to and influence upon the human body, the other aimed at setting before a cultivated society a *résumé* in English verse of the scientific theories of Ptolemy. Wiat's poem is possibly based on Plato's "Vision of Er," for he was a student of Plato; there were besides many treatises on the subject in Greek and Latin, both in prose and verse; Linacre's edition of 1536 may have yielded the scientific facts. The calculations in the poems are fairly correct, those in the Compost are approximations. Cf. l. 44 with Compost: "Saturn is so high that astronomers cannot well measure it . . . but it is more than xxx year or he may runne his course."

ll. 5–6. The treatises on this subject begin with the earth, and its roundness, and its central position. Then follows an account of the poles and axis. See ll. 17–28.

l. 46. "Saturn is an enmy to all thing" (Compost).

l. 47. "Jove in twelve yeare or thereabout passeth all the seven synes" (Compost).

l. 50. "This planet doth of good and none evill" (Compost).

l. 51. "Mars . . . causeth all wars and bataylles" (Compost).

ll. 53–4. The Compost adds a poetical touch : "all things ben glad of th sonne. . . . After that the sunne gothe out *th fayre flowers close themselves*."

l. 55. "Venus the gentylle planet . . . is a lady over all lovers" (Compost).

l. 63. "The lowest planet of the seven is named Luna . . . called the Lady of the nyght" (Compost).

Whether death or the knowledge of the Copernican theory hindered the completion is unknown. We can only guess that Wiat had in mind the connection of man with the heavens, as the Microcosme to the Macrocosme, beginning with the heavens, and continuing with the Creation of Man. M. Sève's *Microcosme* begins with the Creation and continues with the Ptolemaic [1] theory, which is unfolded to Adam and Eve in the Garden of Eden.

Wiat was familiar with the words of Plato at the end of the "Vision of Er" : "Mortal souls, behold a new cycle of life and mortality : virtue is free, and as a man honours or dishonours her he will have more or less of her. The responsibility is with the chosen. God is justified." (*The Word of Lachesis*. Rep. X. Jowett's translation.)

This is the underlying meaning of Wiat's late work.

Much has been said in favour of the Satires; equally important, I think, is this group of miscellaneous poems that extends from his setting out to Spain in 1537 to (possibly) the last month of his life. They prove, I think, that Wiat possessed many more qualities necessary to a strong, finely intellectual poet such as he was, than critics have hitherto credited him. Above all, they bring out in a marked degree that Wiat not only had a firm grasp of contemporary thought, but definitely contributed to subjects that interested continental writers.

[1] M. Sève's poem in 3003 lines was finished in 1538, but not published until 1562.

PARAPHRASE OF PSALMS

Ps. 37. Altho thou se. There are two reasons for assigning the date 1538 to this paraphrase: first, the place it occupies in the MS.; and secondly, the political situation in which Wiat was involved, as ambassador at the Court of the Emperor Charles V. The paraphrase follows the Sonnet "You that in love" and the song "And if an Iye"; and precedes the Epigram "From thes hye hilles," and the canzone "So feble is the threde." All these poems belong to the period of Wiat's embassy in Spain, and were written in 1538, or the early part of 1539. Again, in 1538, a treaty was pending between the Emperor and Francis I, with the Pope as mediator. Wiat's chief duty was to prevent a Roman Catholic coalition. He had won the Emperor's favour by his wit and courtly bearing, as well as by the sincerity of his personality; on the other hand his importunity in his master's affairs made his presence a serious obstacle to the plans of Charles V.

Suddenly, therefore, in May 1538, the Emperor laid favourable proposals before Wiat, stipulating that he himself should carry them to Henry VIII and return within twenty-five days. Wiat landed in England on June 3,[1] having consumed ten days on the journey. He re-embarked for Spain on June 21.[2] Meanwhile a ten years' truce had been concluded between Charles and Francis, with the Pope as

[1] State Papers. [2] *Ibid.*

mediator, at Nice[1] on June 18,[2] in spite of the Emperor's promise to do nothing until Wiat's return. The successful move of the Roman Catholic party, and their open triumph at the Spanish Court, Wiat's strong leanings towards the reformed faith, his intense disappointment at his ill-success, and anger at finding himself the Emperor's dupe, are all reasons that give special point to the paraphrase. All Wiat's more serious poems and translations reflect a certain attitude of mind at a given moment, and reading the paraphrase in the light of the events of 1538, it appears that the "owtragius" of the Psalm represented the Roman Catholic party, and the composition provided a vent for Wiat's feelings.

Slight indications in the later poems, the letters to his son from Spain, and this paraphrase, are all evidences of the strong faith that Wiat had at this period of his life in a higher power than earthly kingship.

An interesting point is brought to light in connection with the version of the Psalm[3] used for this paraphrase. In 1530 a beautiful little edition of the Psalter appeared in the English tongue. A short preface begins as follows—

"John Aleph greteth the Englishe nacion. Be glad in ye Lorde dere brothern, and geve him thankes *which nowe at the laste hath sente ye* his Psalter in Englisshe." The

[1] M. Sève records the event, "Délie," 318—

> Que diray donc de ceste abouchement,
> Que Ligurie & Provence & Venisce
> Ont veu (en vain) assembles richement
> *Espaigne, France, et Italie a Nice.*

[2] Egerton MS. 990. Brit. Mus.

[3] It is out of the question to consider one of the issues of the Great Bible as in Wiat's possession at the time. Even had the size not excluded it from the Ambassador's baggage, it would have been seized as heretical literature, for Wiat's baggage was rigorously searched at the Spanish frontier.

colophon states: "Emprinted at Argentine/in the yeare of our lorde/1530 the 6 daye of January/by me Francis Foye/

"Praise ye the Lord."

While the version of this edition is inferior to that of the Great Bible the minor details are beyond praise in the matter of printing, division into verses, rubrics, and above all the size, which must have commended itself particularly to Wiat, as "small to be carried in the bosom." [1]

Comparing the versions of the Great Bible and the 1530 Psalter with Wiat's paraphrase, it is clear that Wiat followed the 1530 Psalter. Take the first verse. The Bible versions, with little variety, read, "Fret not thyself at the ungodly, be not thou envious agaynst the evell doers."

The 1530 Psalter reads, "Frete not thy selve with theis kursed harmfull men, nether envye angrely theis workers of wikednes." This highly coloured version must have been extremely soothing to Wiat, when he was smarting under the uncomfortable situation at the end of June 1538, and gives a clue to the intense word "owtragius" which he employs in l. 1 of the paraphrase, and to the spirit of his own parenthetical l. 17. Again, l. 24, "Restrayne thy mind from wrath that ay offendes," is taken from the 1530 Psalter, "Restraine thyselfe from wrathe."

On the other hand, the likening of the wicked to a laurel is omitted from the 1530 Psalter. In the matter of orthography, too, there is a close likeness between the 1530 Psalter and the spelling of the paraphrases, including the Penitential Psalms, whereas the spelling of the English Bible versions is nearer to the A. MS. and to Tottel.

The Psalm is incomplete in the E. MS., wanting l. 37 to the end. It is continued from the A. MS., which is the

[1] See Letter to his Son, regarding Epictetus and Seneca.

only other version known of this paraphrase. It is absent from the 1549 edition.

l. 23. *To wicked folke.* The line is incomplete in E. and A. See also l. 43. In both cases the line is tentatively completed, to preserve the terza-rima chain.

l. 29. *heire to hayre*, i. e. "heir to heir." A great diversity of spelling is found in the Psalms.

l. 39. *the tyde . . . the full*, a spirited rendering of the original, for which see foot of p. 191.

l. 43. *To overthrowe the.* The completion of this line is supplied from the context of the Psalter, v. 14.

l. 69. *Catchinge his hand*, a fine touch. Cf. R. Browning—

> . . . The man
> Stood erect, caught at God's skirts and prayed!
> So I was afraid.—" Instans Tyrannus."

ll. 70–71 are missing; the context is: "I have been young and now am old, yet saw I never the righteous forsaken. . . ."

ll. 72–80. A very fine passage. l. 72 resumes the context, "nor his sede . . ."

l. 89. *Suffer.* The scansion requires the accent on the second syllable.

l. 97. *Shene lyke golde.* The metaphor is employed for the rhyme's sake. It is omitted from the Psalter and the Bible version.

l. 102. *freshe arraye.* Cf. the single-stanza poem, found only in Tottel, beginning—

> In court to serve, decked with *fresh aray.*

l. 108. *Helthe to the juste.* Here and in l. 111 Wiat renders *helpe* of the Bible version as *helthe.*

ll. 109–112 form the concluding quatrain, which is the recognized ending for poems in terza-rima.

THE PENITENTIAL PSALMS

RAYNALD and Harrington's edition of the Psalms in 1549 was the only portion of Wiat's writings published, apart from Miscellanies, before the nineteenth century.

The Title-page, which is reproduced in this edition (see p. 203), has come down to us through the medium of the projected 1807[1] edition of Bishop Percy and G. Steevens. As far as we know there is no extant copy of the 1549 edition. The one used by the compilers of the 1807 edition was destroyed. But the title-page reproduced for the 1807 edition is to be seen in the British Museum in one of the four copies which left the printers for final revision. The MSS. and Tottel were employed in compiling this text, with the additional authority, which the editors call PC., i. e. the *printed copy of 1549*. This reference is especially valuable, as a comparison of the PC. variants with the original text of Wiat in the E. MS. proves that it is carefully reproduced, except in small details and the important alterations of "heins," Ps. 143, v. 16 of the Paraphrase.

The source of Wiat's Psalms has recently been discovered by Mr. Arundell Esdaile (Brit. Mus.) in Pietro Aretino's prose paraphrase of the Penitential Psalms. Though the unworthiness of the model calls forth some surprise, it confirms the merits of Wiat's Paraphrase by force of contrast.

[1] The 1807 edition, destroyed by the printer's fire at Nichols' offices, in February 1808, was a two-volume edition of the "Miscellany and uncertayne Authors, with additional pieces including Wiat's Psalms."

The question arises why Wiat should have turned to this poor specimen of the literary profession for his last work after having drawn from Petrarch, the prince of lyrists, after showing a knowledge of at least Dante's "Vita Nuova," of Ariosto, Alamanni, of Serafino and Trissino, besides lesser Italian poets. It is another link in a long chain of evidence that Wiat was thoroughly in touch with literary fashions of his own day, whether in France, Italy or Spain. Paraphrase of the Psalms was the vogue, and Aretino was the most notorious man of the day.[1] He stands as the type of the later decadence of Italian Art, where sensuality ruled, and higher aspirations were forgotten; where, however, the genius of the south still kept the torch alight, in a

[1] Aretino settled at Venice in 1527, the year Wiat visited Italy, and remained there until his death in 1556. He lived in princely state on the profits of his blackmailing. His methods were simple. He sent to all the heads of Europe in turn for pension or present. If given, the patron was flattered, if refused, he came under Aretino's lashing tongue. Notorious in his day for "Maldicentia," Nash, in 1592, refers to him in his double character of ill-speaking and blackmailing. "We want an Aretino amongst us that might strip their golden asses" (*Piers Peniles*).

In 1533 Francis I sent him a wonderful chain of gold formed of interlaced tongues with the legend, "lingua ejus loquetur judicium."

In 1536 Charles V gave him a pension of 200 crowns, and Aretino's first volume of letters was dedicated to him.

In 1539 he wrote to Cromwell for Henry VIII's patronage. Henry sent him 300 crowns, and the second volume of letters was dedicated to "Magnanimo Henrico Ottavo," 1542.

One of the last entries in Cromwell's diary was to "remember Aretino for some gyft."—(State Papers, 1540.)

Aretino was a prolific writer: mostly rubbish. Some was suppressed as unfit for reading in his own day, and there is much extant that is not catalogued. His moral(!) writing is so trite and so palpably hypocritical that it irritates the reader. Nevertheless, he holds a place in literature for certain striking qualities. Aretino helps the literary historian to get a right view of the times. It would be impossible to understand the Renaissance and all it stood for without the work of Aretino and Cellini.

sensitiveness to colour, and clear perception of thought. The two prominent features in Titian's art were possessed by his friend Aretino in a vivid degree; and he is practically the first exponent of a true and natural criticism that was new in his day, and not found again until many years later in French writers.

Aretino knew how to translate intense observation into vivid speech, and his description of a Venetian sunset is justly famous.[1] But the process of finding these traits is like picking out jewels from a rubbish-heap. There is too much rubbish for a modern reader.

The same vivid handling of material is exemplified in the Paraphrase. The seven Psalms are linked together to form one dramatic episode by means of Prologues. Aretino's Paraphrase was published in 1536, and had reached its third edition by 1540.

Wiat's friend, C. Marot, had already followed the fashion and had composed his metrical paraphrase of the Psalms, which immediately became popular on account of their extreme lyrical beauty. They were set to popular airs, and for many years were held in high estimation. In fact, their vogue has never died out. To-day at the Oratoire in Paris you may hear Marot's words sung to a sixteenth-century air.

When Wiat was at the French Court in December 1539, on the occasion of the Emperor's passing through France to the Netherlands, C. Marot presented these Psalms to Charles V.

Probably the presentation of Marot's metrical version put Wiat in mind of a similar task, but he chose his favourite metre, terza-rima, for the medium, while adopting the dramatic arrangement of Aretino's prose version.

[1] See *Letters*, III. No. 48, "To Titian"; the description concludes with the remark "O Titiano dove sete mo."

Wiat's developed power is in evidence in the handling of his subject. He borrows the best in Aretino, imitating the picturesque outlines and striking metaphors. Aretino ceases to become a model in the substance of the Psalms. Then Wiat relies upon the English version, and keeps close to the Great Bible, or to the 1530 Psalter.

In the Italian the scene of the episode is a dark cave. David with his harp is the solitary figure. In Wiat's version, another figure, unseen but felt, is constantly before us, of the Jehovah, as Michael Angelo paints him, with godlike strength and dignity united with human paternal solicitude. All the best qualities in Wiat are found in the Psalms : a wealth of language, vigorous and clear thought, rising to fine moral expression. Our poet, carried away by his own intense conviction, is moved to powerful emotions crystallized in grandeur of language, and convincing in clarity of thought. He touches at times the mystical vision which to Blake was the only domain of poetry and the only reality of life. And for the first time, on account of the dramatic setting, Wiat has an eye to the background, and there is a presentment of natural scenery hitherto lacking [1] in his poetry. Not the least part of the merit due to him in the Psalms is the skilful handling of terza-rima (see Introduction). The disuse of this measure in English literature for nearly three centuries, until the Romantic revival, is accounted for by the fact that no poet followed Wiat skilful enough to wield it, and with the Elizabethan age came blank verse.

The Introductory Sonnet, "The Great Macedon," is Henry Earl of Surrey's contribution to the appreciation of Wiat's Psalms. It is written on a blank page of the MS.

[1] Slight indications show his power, when he chooses, *e.g.* "The howgy okes have rored in the wynde" is a phrase that gives an insight into his observations of nature.

immediately preceding the First Prologue, and appears to have been written as the complimentary verse preface for the edition of the Psalms. It was, therefore, evidently in hand before the death of Surrey. Surrey's initials, H. S., are placed at the head of the Sonnet; and those of I. H., John Harington, the joint editor of the Psalms, are in the margin.

The MS. came into John Harington's possession on Wiat's death.

Prologue I. This episode is very popular among sixteenth-century writers. The 1537 edition of the Bible illustrates the first page of the Psalms with the incident of David giving to his captain Uriah the place of honour which means certain death. In the foreground stands the King giving command to the kneeling warrior; in the background is the battlefield. See ll. 21–4.

The numerous paraphrases of the Psalms were the outcome of the enthusiasm and admiration for the beautiful vernacular versions of the Bible.

l. 48. *himsellff*. Wiat's spelling is not so simple as that of the scribe. A definite principle is observable, that of employing double consonants after a short vowel, and a single consonant after a long vowel; occasionally the spelling is obscure; when this happens, Wiat's spelling is given in the footnote, and the normal spelling is used in the text.

l. 50. *rabates*. Commonly used for abate, diminish.

First Psalm (Ps. 6). l. 9. *Chastyse* scans as three syllables.

ll. 12–31. A very fine passage.

ll. 28–81. Continued from A., absent in the MS. through a missing page.

l. 48. *the flesshe; the wretch*. This harshness in rhyme

would no doubt have been corrected had Wiat revised the Psalms.

ll. 55–6. Touches of Calvinistic doctrine.

ll. 58–64. No MS. is complete except the 1807 edition, which was copied from Harrington's 1549 edition. By the comparison of this edition it has been possible to insert l. 59 (absent from all the editions of the Psalms).

ll. 81–96. A very picturesque passage, for which the text is simply, "I have so many enemes." Wiat follows Aretino here, including under *enemy* the temptations of the world, the flesh, and the devil.

ll. 90–1. Cf. Shakespeare's speech on "Ceremony" in *Henry V*.

l. 93. *Marmaydes*. Translated from Aretino, "Chiudendo le orecchie a le *sirene*."

ll. 96 *et seq*. This passage is very characteristic. Cf. Wiat's epistolary style.

l. 97. *Avoyd*. Here Wiat appears to follow closely the 1530 Psalter version.

Prologue II. The dramatic setting is strong. The darkness of the cave, the connection of physical with moral fear, and the dissipating of both by a return to grace is powerfully brought out.

l. 25. *vapord Iyes*. One of the many phrases imitated by Surrey. Cf. "When Windsor walles," l. 12.

l. 29. Translated from the Italian. Aretino and Wiat were musicians.

Second Psalm (Ps. 32). l. 19. For allusion to *adder* see "The wandryng gadlyng." Cf. also Ariosto, Satire I, "On Courts," l. 2, "A giusa delli serpi mitan spoglia."

ll. 73–6. A very spirited conclusion.

l. 74. The spelling of *makth* and *holdyth* is to be noticed as exemplifying Wiat's counting "-eth" as a syllable or not as occasion required.

Third Prologue. ll. 25–6. From the Italian "infiammarto dello amor di Dio che non fu di quel di Bersabe."

ll. 27–30. Paraphrased from the Italian.

Third Psalm (Ps. 30). l. 27. *Gruging off the worme within*, i. e. "the pricking of conscience." See Letter to his Son, No. 2. "Never do that that within yourself you finde a certayn *gruging* againste." Cf. Satire 2, last line, "*to frete* inward for losing suche a losse."

l. 28. *that never dyth.* The Gospel text, "Where their worm dieth not," is evidently running in Wiat's head.

l. 39. Cf. "Hevyn and Erth"—"My face, my lowke, my teres. . . ."

l. 42. *Myn own vertus.* Wiat's reading was in the 1549 edition. Percy and Stevens have this reading. The insertion of "acquaintance" is probably Nott's, following the A. Version.

l. 44. *as kyn unkynd.* Cf. Shakespeare, *Hamlet*, "A little more than kin, and less than kind," I. ii.

l. 48. *yede.* Archaic in Wiat's time; imitated from Chaucer for the rhyme's sake.

ll. 43–56. Wiat's own situation at this time.

Fourth Prologue. ll. 9–10. Taken from the Italian. Aretino was a lute-player, like Wiat.

l. 13. *As he that bledes in baigne.* The sense is seen in the Italian: "Sangue tutto, chi con le *vene a perte* si giace in una ampia conca di acque a tepidate."

l. 25. Follows the Italian.

Fourth Psalm (Ps. 51). ll. 1–4. A very beautiful beginning; the whole rendering is very fine.

l. 43. *Juyz.* The spelling of this word misled Harrington, for PC. has "juyce." Percy and Stevens note this, and decide to alter the text to "Jewes," which is Wiat's meaning, of course.

A perusal of this Psalm at once shows how near it is to the English Bible version. Wiat confines himself to imitating the Italian in the Prologue alone.

Fifth Prologue. The bare idea is taken from Aretino; the form it takes is original. Cf. stanza 1 for Wiat's conversational style, when he is vigorous and picturesque.

Fifth Psalm (Ps. 103). Wiat keeps close to the English version, whereas Aretino makes long digressions, cf. ll. 13–15. Wiat keeps to the text, Aretino enters upon a long dissertation on the "brede of lyff."

Again, ll. 16–18 follow the text closely, Aretino proceeds to a long account of the ills of the flesh.

l. 20. Aretino goes into chatty details on the habits of the pelican.

l. 21. *Owle.* Here Wiat follows the Great Bible Version. The 1530 Psalter reads "ostrege" (*i. e.* ostrich).

Dante, in his version, and Aretino, both use (different) words signifying "bat."

ll. 37–48. A particularly fine passage.

l. 43. Not the Sion of the "chosen people," but of all faithful believers.

l. 72. A striking instance of the faulty A. MS. See Variant.

Sixth Prologue. l. 31. *His knee, his arme, his hand, sustenid his chyn.* "Chyn." The Italian has *barba* (beard). Surrey imitates this expression in the poem beginning "When Windsor walles susteyned my wearied arme, My hand, my chyn."

Sixth Psalm (Ps. 130). l. 27. *thrust*, for "thirst" (by metathesis of "r").

Seventh Prologue. The Italian version introduces the word of the Angel, and the subsequent incidents in the birth and life of Christ, concluding with the phrases of the Apostles' Creed—purely doctrinal—Wiat's vision is mystic and compares with John i. The first two stanzas are particularly fine; the last stanza contains a personal touch.

Seventh Psalm (Ps. 143). l. 16. *In heins to fle his rage so ryff*. *heins*,[1] or *hains*, is a dialectal word (North Yorkshire), with the meaning of (1) a hedge, (2) *refuge* in a figurative sense. The first reading (see Variants) makes the meaning of "heins" as "refuge" still more clear. The expression "hayning" for hedging is still in use in the north. Wiat's spelling "heins" is characteristic. His editors were southerners, the word was unknown, so the line was amended even in the 1549 edition. This is the only instance of important variation in the 1549 copy.

l. 49. A conclusion not devoid of humour. This is Wiat's epistolary style. See reproduction of letter from the Cotton MS. F. xiii. f. 160, p. 135.

[1] This word is also found among the forest laws of the New Forest.

THE POEMS OF THE D. MS.

THE D. MS. is a Court album consisting mainly of Wiat's poems. It presents a great contrast to the E. MS. There we find all Wiat's work in chronological order, in translation and imitation of foreign masters, with a small selection of lyrics composed during the three years at Court, 1533–6. In this MS. there is no attempt at chronological order; the poems are scattered singly or in small groups from fol. 1 to fol. 64, and consist mainly of Court songs with an occasional Sonnet or Epigram. Here and there a late poem has made its way into the MS.; for example, on fol. 49 is the poem, written in Spain about 1538, beginning "So feble is the threde." The first pieces include the earliest lyrics, probably composed during the years 1524–7.

At fol. 65' a long group of Wiat's poems begins, copied in one hand, and signed with Wiat's interlaced initals T.V. (Thomas Viatus). They are not in chronological order. The first entry, "To cause accord," marks the conclusion of the first group of lyrics in the E. MS., and the last entry is a fragment of the Second Satire (1536–7).

A different purpose is discernible in the long group of poems entered continuously from fol. 69a onwards. The collection of Wiat's poems in their entirety appears to have been the aim, and although the majority of these are songs found nowhere else, there are many poems included, such as Sonnets, Epigrams and parts of the two Satires, that are inserted in the E. MS. The collected group of poems possibly marks the change in the ownership of the album about 1533 (see Appendix D on this question). But the scattered entries still continued, judging by the presence of late poems amongst them. Where poems are common to D. and E. there is often to be noted a difference in the version; in this case the D. version is the earlier. Occasionally this version appears in E. as the first reading, afterwards corrected by Wiat. The D. MS. was not under Wiat's control; the scattered poems were evidently entered as they circulated amongst the members of the Court circle, for Wiat had a great reputation as a "ballate-maker" at Anne Boleyn's Court. He himself set no store on his lighter verse, judging from the number of Court songs peculiar to the D. MS. For a detailed account of the Court songs, see *Study of Sir Thomas Wyatt*, Chap. X.

PART I

The first part consists of poems in the D. MS., ff. 1–68, which are not common to Wiat's MS. The chief feature of this group is the variety and beauty of the refrain song.

No. 1. **Take hede betyme.** This, in monorhymed triplets with refrain, is a gay little poem, and is the first entry in the D. MS. Its character and its gaiety mark it as an early poem. For other examples of this form see No. 7 and No. 27 ("Fforget not yet").

No. 2. This poem should be compared with the farewell to his lute, "My lute awake," for the same stanza setting and rhyme scheme. The idea is similar. Cf. the refrain, "My pen I prithee wryght no more" with "My lute, be still, for I have done."

No. 3. **I love lovyd and sodothe she.** This is a doubtful poem. No signature, but this is no guide, for several known to be Wiat's are unsigned. It is merely an adaptation of an older song. For another version see the Fairfax MS., "I love lovyd, and loved wold I be." The faint inscription at the foot of the poem, see p. 256, encourages the idea that it has some bearing upon the romantic attachment of Sir Thomas Howard for Lady Margaret.

l. 5. *O deadly yea.* Cf. the "deadly nay" of the lady in Sonnet, l. 14.

No. 4. **Suffryng in sorow.** The same stanza form as No. 2, with refrain fifth line, "Serve and suffer styll I must." The poem has a special interest on account of the remarks upon it made by Lady Margaret and Mary Shelton. See footnote, p. 258.

No. 5. A nine-line stanza in eights and sixes. The copyist has omitted the last rhyming word in l. 7, writing it at the beginning of l. 8, thus: "Sustayne Alas that dye wold faine." The word "Sustayne" is restored to its proper place at the end of l. 7.

No. 6. **To wette your Iye.** There is no signature to this song, but it is in Wiat's indignant style, and the tone is too bitter for artificiality. It is intended most probably for the same person as the "What no perdy" Rondeau and the "There was never ffile" Sonnet. Several times in the poems there is an accentuation of bitter feeling directed against *one* person. Wiat never writes invectives against the sex, although he constantly makes use of the stock phrase that women are changeable. Yet in his more serious moods he acknowledges the weakness of this saying by quoting the proverb, "Like to like."

No. 7. **What menythe thys.** Other poems in this mood are "The restful place" and "O restful place." It is in the same metre as No. 1.

No. 8. **The hart and servys to yow profferd.** This poem deserves a wider reputation. There is a freshness of feeling and simplicity of language which increases the lyrical charm of the setting, and adds beauty to a subject which is much more artificial in the translation of the Petrarchian Sonnet, "My hert I gave the not to do it payn."

l. 5. *And tho it be a small present.* The idea is repeated in the more ambitious and very fine poem, "To seke eche where," written in Spain about 1538.

Stanzas 4 and 5 may have suggested Herrick's song to Anthea, "Bid me to love and I will live." See ll. 15–16—

> Bid ye me go and strayte I glyde
> At your commandement humbly.

l. 16. *humbly* scans as three syllables. Cf. *gentylly*, l. 4. This poem has no signature, but it is obviously Wiat's diction and turn of expression.

No. 9. **Farewell all my welfare.** There is no signature to this poem. In Tottel's *Miscellany* it begins at the fourth stanza, "It is a grevous smart." It is marked by "Margaret Howard" as one of her favourites.

The poem is a woman's lament of a man's unfaithfulness, and belongs to the older class of French lyric known as the chanson-à-personages, where a woman laments her wrongs. See next poem for a later development in the lover's lament.

No. 10. **Alas poore ma** A doubtful poem. Without signature. Here the lover laments, cf. No. 9. Notice the conceit of the heart-less body in stanza 5. For the origin of Nos. 9–10 see *Study of Sir Thomas Wyatt*, Chap. X.

l. 28. *To love above my pore degre.* It was the rule rather than the exception for a poet to address his verses to a great lady, and pay her the homage of a lover. This custom was prevalent among the Provençal singers; two famous examples are Bernard de Ventodorn, and Chrestien de Troyes, the French poet. Nor had the custom died out in the sixteenth century. Margaret of Navarre, sister of Francis I, her cousin Renée, Duchess of Ferrara, and Vittoria Colonna, three noble women by birth and by character, received homage from, and were the patrons of, many poets in their day.

At Henry's Court the love of Thomas Howard for Margaret, the King's niece, was the cause of one of the tragic episodes of the reign. Wiat himself had a firm friend in Mary Fitzroy, Duchess of Richmond, and sister of Lord Surrey, the joint owners of the D. MS.

No. 11. **Ys yt possyble.** One of the elaborate experiments in verse combination. Wiat very successfully unites verses of five with those of eight and ten syllables. Different lengths of verse were first tried unsuccessfully in the Rondeau. This poem is one of the happiest achievements in stanza structure. I believe this is a deliberate experiment in combining odd syllable verses, as advocated by Dante, "De vulg. eloq.," II. xii. Trissino translated this treatise into Italian, and it was printed with his *Poetica*, which Wiat seems to have read and studied, judging from indications in his poems. Here we find fives in combination with eights and tens (corresponding with the sevens and elevens of Italian verse). The *Poetica* was a text-book for all sorts of lyrical forms; it was especially valuable as emphasizing Dante's remarks on metre, and giving copious examples from Provençal and Italian poets.

No. 12. **And wylt thow leve me thus.** The most beautiful little song in the collection. Wiat advanced from a knowledge of music to the musical quality of words, partly arrived at through his reading of Italian. The poem is copied in a very beautiful hand. See reproduction, p. 272. Note Lady Margaret's comment in the right-hand corner.

No. 13. **That tyme that myrthe dyd stere my shypp.** No signature. It is copied by the scribe who adds Wiat's name to his poems. It is therefore doubtful.

l. 1. An allusion to the early days at Court, further exemplified in l. 6; a possible reference to the friendship with Anne Boleyn. Another part of the album has a drawing of a hand, with the inscription "An" and "I am yowris." But it is futile to attach any deep signification to such trifles. "Yours" to-day is the most usual signature in the most matter-of-fact relations, and there is no ground for imagining any deep feeling between the parties concerned.

No. 14. **As power and wytt wyll me assyst,**
My wyll shall wyll evyn as ye lyst.

The introductory couplet is interesting; it forms the motif of the poem, and the whole or part serves as a refrain. In this example the last half-line of the couplet is repeated after every stanza; many Middle English songs have introductory couplets; for example—

I hold him wise and well y taught
Can bar a horn and blow it naught,

repeating the last line after every stanza.

There are numerous examples in the Percy Collection and other Middle English collections of songs. G. F. Nott erroneously attributes Wiat's poems of this description to a Spanish form of verse called Glosa.[1] The examples in

[1] Glosa, Sp. for "Commentary," used as a poetical term for the amplification of a verse.

the Percy Collection are English examples of a continental vogue, where a short verse or couplet is made the text of the following poem; Wiat is carrying on the English tradition in such examples. Had he imitated from the Spanish, these poems would have *certainly* been included in the E. MS.

As the opening couplet states, the poet uses his wit, after the Court fashion, to compose a song with similes and conceits drawn from the common stock, cf. stanza 2, and in consequence the poem exhibits a confused jumble of metaphors.

l. 9. The *lamb of humble kind* is singularly inappropriate where Wiat is concerned, and suggests another author.

l. 10. *byrd in cage.* Cf. the poem from the Parker MS., Corpus Christi, "Like as a byrde in the cage enclosed."

l. 18. *But as ye lede to follow the trace.* Cf. "Myne olde dere enmy," l. 25. "With the amourous dawnce have made me traced."

Stanzas 5–6 are literal examples of play upon words. There is no signature to this poem, but it is certainly Wiat's style.

No. 15. A lyric in happy vein. It is not signed, and is doubtful. There were at Court during the period 1533–6 many versifiers. Francis Brian, George Boleyn, Lord Vaux, could write graceful lyrics, and it is quite possible that Brian or Boleyn wrote the poems marked doubtful. Cf. the last stanza with the more elaborated sentiment of the poem to "seke eche where," imitated from C. Marot's Etrenne.

l. 20. *And never to change yow for no new.* This is as persistent a phrase on the part of the lover as "his complaint of change" on the lady's part, both equally artificial.

No. 16. **Pacyence of all my smart.** There are two songs in the E. MS. in the same short-lined Romance metre beginning with "Patience."

Wiat no doubt found his model in Serafino's Canzone "de la Patientia," [1] beginning

Patientia alla malora
Poi che vol cosi fortune.

The imitation ceases here, but such a couplet, like that in the Glósa songs, as Nott calls them, forms the burden of the ensuing poem. There are some very fine lines in the poem, and the elegiac form has the stamp of reality. Cf. stanza 4—

Pacyence to be content
With froward fortunes trayne
Pacyence to the intent
Sumwhat to slake my payne,

with the exceeding bitter cry of Lear—

You heavens give me that patience, patience I need.—II. iv. 268.

l. 26. *My chance is chawnsyd so.* Note the play upon words; this special instance is common in the songs.

l. 41. *Thys ys a strange dyssese.* Wiat's conversational style. The same phrases in the poems recur in the letters and dispatches.

l. 46. *To have the mate*, i. e. "checkmate."

No. 17. **In faythe methynkes yt ys no ryght.**

l. 3. *So fayre a face, so full of spyght.* Cf. the song, "Blame not my lute" (No. 30), evidently addressed to the same person, stanza 4, l. 1. *Spyght asketh spyght, and changing change*, and No. 6, ll. 1–2—

[1] Serafino, *Collezione di opere inedite.* Bologna. 1896.

for tho thou brake
My strynges in spight with grett desdayn.

l. 7. *I shall you leve and other prove.* Cf. "I shall anothr love obtaine."

l. 14. *Syns women use so muche to fayn.* The stock cry of the angry lover.

The poem is an example of Wiat's bitter mood, and is unfinished. Cf. Rondeau 9, "What no perdye," for the most striking example.

A poem by Sir Anthony Lee, Wiat's brother-in-law, follows in the D. MS., carrying on the same train of thought. An inspection of his verses proves him to be one of the many versifiers using the stock phrases, but in no sense a poet.

It is the exception rather than the rule for the poems in this section to be signed.

The definite group of poems beginning fol. 69e is a different matter; they were meant as a complete record of Wiat's poems, and were signed with his monogram.

No. 18. **The knot which fyrst my hert did strayn.** There are several varieties of this six-lined octosyllabic stanza with a tail rhyme. Here there are only two rhymes, $ababab^a$. In the next, No. 19, a new rhyme occurs at the fifth line, agreeing with the tail, with the metrical scheme $ababcb^c$. The tail forms the opening words of every following stanza.

No. 19. **It was my choyse.** This and the preceding example are two poems in another group in a new hand, *all of which are in the E. MS.*, except Nos. 18–19. The last poem of the group is signed "T. Wiat."

No. 20. **So unwarely was never no man cawght.** The poem turns on the favourite Provençal conceit of the power of the eye, like a stroke of lightning, to pierce through to the heart of the lover.

l. 5. *Thorow myn Iye.* So Chaucer, *Kt. T.* 1096—

> But I was hurt right now through-out myn yë
> Into myn hert.

Wiat collects conceits from Petrarch from stanza to stanza.

l. 9. *Like a man for woo amasyd.* Cf. Sonnet, "The lyvely sperkes," ll. 8–9—

> Dased ame I : muche like unto the gyse
> Of one y stricken with dynt of lightening.

l. 16. *Quakynd*, an archaic form.

l. 24. *Thys restles lyff.* Cf. the later poem written in Spain, "I lede a liff," Epigram No. 18—

> So chaungethe unrest that nought shall fade

And the Epigram, "Off Cartage he," l. 8—

> I restles rest in Spayne.

No. 21. **How shuld I.** A very popular style of song at Henry VIII's Court. Of French origin, their prototypes are found in the thirteenth and fourteenth century lyrics beginning "L'Autrier" (or "L'autre jor") "chevauchai."

The songs are examples of the "chanson-à-personages." The earlier songs voiced the complaint of the young wife, and later development made the speaker a man.

Both types exist in the sixteenth-century song-books.

King Henry's song-book, British Museum,[1] has this example, beginning—

> The other day
> I herd a *May* [2]
> Right grevously complayne.

A lover's complaint is found in the Royal Appendix, British Museum [3]—

[1] Add 31922. [2] *May*, young girl. [3] Royal Appendix 58.

This yonder nyght
I herd a *wyght*
Most grevously complayne.

Wiat's song continues—

I herd a man
That now and than
Himself thus did bemone.

The sixteenth-century songs were compiled from fragments of older songs; these older parts come in as refrains or as introductory and concluding stanzas, as here. For a more commonplace example in octosyllabic verse cf. No. 10, and for a combination of sixes and eights cf. No. 9. These songs, though of the same class, lack the out-of-doors element of No. 21 that gives it the air of a pastoral.

l. 45. *With selie boordes*, archaic language for foolish jests.

No. 22. **Full well yt maye be sene.** Troilus metre in a six-syllable verse. From the days of Chaucer to the sixteenth century, Troilus measure (or its apology) was the standard of verse. Among Wiat's poems there is a great variety of the seven-line stanza on the Troilus rhyme. In the miscellaneous group (Part I) of the E. MS. there are several examples in different length of verse.

ll. 31–32. *Than see the wyse, so ware, In love to be so blynd.*

This is an old saying. It is Wylly's "Emblem" in the "Shepherd's Calendar" for March—

To be wise and eke to love
Is grauntyd scarce to Gods above.

The idea is developed in the trilogy of poems, "Lo what it is to love."

The third stanza in each part turns on the idea of the impossible combination of love and wisdom.

No. 23. **Syns love ys suche.** This poem continues the argument of the preceding, granting that passion is a folly of youth, and the poet gives his own experience of reckless youth with no boundary to folly. Now his faith is anchored, and he is happy, "Knit fast, in lasting bonds of love." It is an interesting debate on passion and love; the one momentary and to be outworn, the other steadfast and lasting.

l. 23. *Thankyd be fortune.* Cf. "They fle from me," II. 1, for this expression.

l. 37. *The knott thereof.* Cf. Epigram 29, "And knyt agayne the knott that should not slide."

No. 24. **Lo how I seke and sew to have.**

l. 8. *To take that comes as well in worthe*, as of good omen, or important. Cf. "Myne olde dere enmy" for the expression "price that is *well worth*" (l. 140) (in the sense of a good bargain), and in the preceding verse, "that *wo worth thee*." The phrase is dialectal and north country, including Yorkshire, Wiat's native county.

No. 25. **Syns so ye please to here me playn.** A douzaine. Cf. with "Madame withouten eny wordes," which is a translation of Marot's douzaine without any attempt at a special scheme of rhyme. Here the first and second parts are united by a common rhyme, by the connection of the fourth and fifth lines, a common device of French verse.

No. 26. **Now must I lerne to lyve at rest.** A farewell song. It may refer to Wiat's parting from Anne Boleyn and his departure from the Court; see stanza 4—

> I may not sighe in sorows depe
> Nor wayle the want of love,
> Nor I may nother cruche nor crepe
> Wher hyt dothe not behove.

In 1526, and again in 1533, Wiat was dismissed from Court temporarily by the King. There is no other apparent reason why he should not wail loudly in lover's fashion, as many of the songs testify.

But the chief interest in this poem is that it is the prelude to the farewell beginning "Fforget not yet"; see ll. 19–20—

> And frome henceforthe must undertake
> Suche foly to *fforgett.*

No. 27. **Fforget not yet the tryde entent.** It is unnecessary to comment on the lyric, which has received the highest praise from great critics, and is the piece above all others which has appeared in anthologies. The crispness of setting, and the dignity of expression, with the underlying pathos and haunting music of the refrain are the chief points in its favour.

This song is the last of a series of poems which refers to an unhappy episode in Wiat's life.

No. 28. **O myserable sorow.** This poem is undoubtedly Wiat's: it is unsigned, and written on fol. 58 in a new (and very fine) hand, possibly that of Surrey's friend, Sir E. Knevet, who has also copied the Rondeau, "Goo burnyng sighes" (also without signature). At this part of the MS. there are entries by Mary Shelton, E. Knevet, and Lady Margaret, which appear to have been written between 1540–5.

No. 29. **Blame not my lute for he must sound.** There are several pages between this and the previous poem. It is the last casual entry, and comes after two important entries: a poem by Howard, Lord Surrey, "O happy dames," which is copied in Mary Shelton's handwriting, and was certainly not composed until about 1537, relating the tragic love of

Thomas Howard for Margaret Douglas, the King's niece, which resulted in his imprisonment and death. Surrey's poem expresses sympathy for Margaret and indignation at the treatment of his uncle. A second poem, in Lord Darnley's handwriting, and therefore not written until after 1560, is inserted between Nos. 29 and 30—a sufficient proof that this MS. is not in chronological order. See Appendix C.

"Blame not my lute" has neither the power of "My lute awake," nor the grace of the short-metred stanzas to his lute written in Spain. It commended itself in Wiat's day on account of the refrain. Music was one of the chief pastimes at Henry VIII's Court. Professional musicians, including Cornysshe, set various songs to music—see his setting of Wiat's "A Robyn, Joly Robyn," p. 62.

These poems endow the D. MS. with special interest. They represent the intimate part of Wiat's life, whereas the E. MS. is the outcome of his aspirations for literary art. The refrain songs, especially, carry us into the very atmosphere of the Court life of his day, and represent his actual contact with society.

PART II

THE second part of the D. MS. contains sixty-five poems entered continuously and in one hand, with Wiat's monogram signature "T. V." at the foot of every poem except one ("Patiens for I have wrong").

The poems included in Part II are those which are absent from the E. MS., and are with about two exceptions peculiar to the D. MS.

The first poem of the group is "Behold love," on fol. 69b,

the Rondeau which appears as the first entry in the E. MS. Two poems [1] on the preceding page, fol. 69a, are written in a different hand, while the initials, "T. V.," are appended, but written in a different style from the usual monogram signature.

Lyrical songs preponderate, a natural result, since the collector of the poems was undoubtedly Mary, Duchess of Richmond, whose initials "M. F." (*i. e.* Mary Fitzroy) are on the front cover of the album. She and her brother, as well as her husband, the Duke of Richmond, were equally interested in music and poetry. By their birth and station, they formed the centre of the Court group from 1533 to 1536, the time when these poems were entered.[2] See Appendix C for an account of the D. MS.

Many poems in this group are not inserted here, because they are common to the E. MS.

Certain poems written in graver mood, or with a more ambitious purpose, appear to have circulated in MS. amongst the members of the Court, and in this way have come down to us in the D. MS., as well as in Wiat's own MS. The last few entries, on the whole, are distinctly late (1540–1), although the last fragment is part of the second Satire, composed 1536–7. The position is this, I think: the songs written for the Court proceed from early to late, and are more or less chronological, since they were probably entered into the Court album as soon as they were composed. Other poems—which are found in the E. MS.—Epigrams, Sonnets, and such pieces, showing foreign influence or imitation, were copied into the MS. simply in the order of their

[1] These two poems are, "To cause accord," which is the last of the Miscellaneous Poems 1533–6, and the Epigram "All yn thi sight."

[2] As far as the song "Now all of chaunge." This poem is connected with the imprisonment of Mary's uncle, Sir Thomas Howard, in 1536. (See Appendix.) The last few poems of the MS. were later.

coming into the Duchess of Richmond's possession; in such cases no chronological order is discernible.

The poems show considerable variety. The lyrical gem is the short-lined "What shulde I saye" (No. 3), with the same pulsation of real feeling and freshness of utterance in dealing with love that enthralls us in some of the mediæval poets. Such lines, forged in the heart and soul of the writer, pulse and throb for evermore, because they are alive with the spirit of the poet who uttered them.

No. 1. **If with complaint the paine myght be exprest.** This poem is an example of Wiat's skill in combining different verse lengths, a feature of his mature style. The first two lines are decasyllables and introduce the two rhymes, ab, the third and fourth lines are octosyllables and rime on a, the fifth line is a six-syllable rhyming on b, and the stanza finishes with a decasyllable rhyming b. The pause at the fifth line caused by the short metre is very effective coming before the concluding five-foot verse.

For a similar treatment of stanza structure, though in reverse order, this poem should be compared with the lyric "Ys yt possyble," which is of peculiar interest because of the *five-syllable* verse, after the Italian manner, which alternates with verses of eights and tens. Cf. Milton's effective use of the short verse, to vary the metre, in the Horton Poems.

No. 2. **Sins you will nedes that I shall sing.** A five-line stanza, after the style of "My lute awake" and "My pen take payne," with a tail rhyme in stanzas 1 and 2 which is a partial repetition of the last verse, for example, ll. 5–6,

Boteles for boote, crying *to crave*,
To crave yn vayne.

Wiat uses the device of verbal repetition most effectively at times. Cf. "Hevyn and erth" for a better example.

ll. 7–8. *Suche hammers worke within my hed. That sounde nought els into my eris.*

The lines are reminiscent of Ariosto. The phrase occurs in the verse edition of "Gli Suppositi," a comedy first written in prose in 1509. Ariosto was persuaded to set it in verse form, and it was acted before Leo X in the presence of a great concourse of people in 1519. In this version, but absent from the prose edition, is the couplet—[1]

Tutto e tornato bizarro e fantastico
Tanto martello ha che creppo.

Gascoigne translated (ed. 1566): "*He hath so many hammers in his head* that his brains are ready to burst."

When Wiat visited Italy in 1527, Ariosto had lately settled at Ferrara; he built a house there and spent the last few years of his life in arranging the comedies for presenting before the Duke of Ferrara and his Court. Wiat stopped at Ferrara, and must have seen the comedy, "Gli Suppositi," acted. This striking phrase sank into his memory and came out later in this poem. It appealed to Surrey, and he quoted the phrase later in his appreciative Elegy on Wiat—

A head where wisdom mysteries did work,
Whose hammers beat still in that lively brain
As on a stithy. . . .

G. F. Nott considers these imitations of Wiat by Surrey as proofs of their "community of study." This position cannot be entertained, for Surrey was a mere lad in 1532, on his first appearance at Court as companion to the Duke of Richmond, whereas Wiat had not only passed his youth, but had written a considerable amount of poetry, and was, more-

[1] See "Gli Suppositi," ed. by Cunliffe, 1904, for the parallel versions of prose and verse.

over, a distinguished man of letters, an acute diplomatist and a witty courtier—facts which put Surrey into the position of a pupil before a great master. Again, Surrey wrote little, if anything, before the year 1537. Until the latter part of the year 1536, he was the constant companion of the Duke of Richmond, and was obliged to merge his interests in those of the young prince.

l. 19. *A brokin lute, untunid stringes.* References to the lute are numerous, and simply show how closely connected these songs are with music accompaniments.

No. 3. **What shulde I saye.** This lyric stands amongst the few rare poems which have earned for Wiat a place amongst the chief English lyrists; there is an airiness and lightness of touch about it which is amazing when we contrast it with some of the most conceited translations of the Sonnets. But combined with the lightness of structure there are depths of underlying feeling, culminating in the last line, "Farewell unkiste." Cf. with the little song in Part I, "And wylt thow leve me thus," for the same delicacy but sureness of touch, and for that intangible quality which we define as the poetic spirit, the manifestation of true creative genius.

No. 4. **Gyve place all ye that doth rejoyse.** A comparison between this and the preceding poem brings out the curious inequality of the poet. Here we have a purely artificial song, with the usual stock phrases of the woful lover, and the cruelty of the lady.

l. 34. *slip the knott.* This phrase often occurs in Wiat's verse. Cf. Epigram 29, l. 8, and elsewhere.

No. 5. **Me list no more to sing.** Personal touches are rare in Wiat's poems; here he differs from the continental fashion; French verse in particular is often a running commentary or biographical notice of the poet's life. Here we find a rather humorous allusion to traits in Wiat's poetry that were not approved by his contemporaries. For instance, l. 5—

> Men dede my songis mystake.

and ll. 9–10—

> Therefor me to excuse
> Theye shall be song more plaine.

The underlying element of pathos or satire, which is often to be found in Wiat's best work, evidently did not suit his audience. They liked the gay and the witty, the rather empty artificial compliments of the polite Court atmosphere. Wiat in his best vein eschewed this style.

> My songes ware to defuse
> Theye made folke to muse

Humanity in its light side and more careless aspect is the same whatever century we touch. The tendency is to cling to the moments as they pass and carefully refrain from thoughts that cause discomfort; to wilfully close the eyes to what is unjust and hurtful, or shameful. The consequence is that wrongs have accumulated from century to century until the task of unravelling the tangled threads of social evil is appalling.

Wiat sees and meditates upon many things in these later poems, concerning which the Third Satire is a fair summary.

l. 13. *For frute withouten tast.* The meaning is not savourless fruit, but fruit left untasted. Stanzas 4–7 present a certain ironical view, uttered in the same temper as—

> Praise Sir Topas for a noble tale.

Contrast with ll. 30–4 the lines—

> Of such a fruyte cometh fruyte fruytles

and

> I seke no longer rotten boughs to clime.

The sixth stanza is a very fresh rendering of one of the most constant recommendations to "Enjoy life while ye may," from the "Carpe diem" of Horace to Shelley's rendering, with the inevitable mournful note always struck by the early nineteenth-century romantic poets—

> Whilst skies are blue and bright
> Whilst flowers are gay,
> Whilst eyes that change ere night
> Make glad the day;
> Whilst yet the calm hours creep
> Dream thou—and from thy sleep
> Then wake to weep.

Herrick's "Gather ye rosebuds while ye may" is a graceful version of the same idea, and he possibly owes something to Wiat, besides Horace, for his lyric.

The last stanza is a delightful little challenge to those who have found the poet "difuse" or have mistaken his meaning. What do you think of these sentiments? Think what you will, "I reke not a bene." In these witty touches the personality of Wiat comes out, and herein lay the chief cause of his celebrity during his lifetime.

This jesting view of life for pleasure alone is more seriously attacked in Satire 3, for after commenting upon the vice of the age in satiric fashion, come the lines—

> Laughest thou at me? Why? do I speak in vain?
> No, not at thee, but at thy thrifty jest.
> Wouldest thou I shold, for any loss or gain
> Change that for gold, that I have tane for best,
> Next godly things, to have an honest name?

No. 6. **The Joye so short alas, the paine so nere.** The style of this elegy in rhythm and language suggest an early composition (1528–30), when he was learning how to write in ten-syllable verse. It should be compared with No. 15, Part I, for the idea.

Romance accents must be observed in "départúre" (l. 2), "sodaínelye" (l. 4), "rémaine" (l. 5). "furst" (l. 3) scans as two syllables.

l. 5. *The bodye gone yet remaine shall the hert.* This conceit is constantly recurring—see also l. 9.

No. 7. **Payne of all payne the most grevous paine.**
Ys to love hartelye and cannot be loved againe.

An example of the "glosa" poem. Cf. No. 1, Part I, "As power and wytt wyll me assyst," for the introductory couplet that forms the motif of the poem.

This poem has never been printed. Nott did not include it, perhaps on account of the difficulty of reading the MS. The poem is signed in the usual fashion with Wiat's monogram signature, but I strongly suspect that it has been *erroneously* included as Wiat's. It is not in his usual style. If compared with "Myne olde dere enmy," when he was consciously imitating Skelton, we still find characteristics that proclaim it to be Wiat's composition. But here there is the curious jog of the fifteenth-century Troilus Measure found in Skelton and other of Wiat's contemporaries. The best example is Henry Parker, Lord Morley, who was closely associated with Wiat's circle. His daughter Jane married G. Boleyn, and his second daughter married Sir John Shelton, father of the Mary Shelton of the D. MS. Compare the following verses, which bear a striking resemblance to the style of No. 7—

HENRY LORD MORLEY TO HYS POSTERITYE

Never was I lesse alone than being alone
Here in this chamber evill thought had I none,
But always I thought to bryng the mynd to rest,
And y[t] thought of all thoughts I juge it the beste,

Ffor yf my coffers hade ben full of perle and golde,
And Fortune hade favorde me then as y^t I wolde,
The mynde out of quyat, so sage Senek sethe,
It hade ben no felicitie, but a painfull dethe.
Love then whoo love wyll to stand in hye[1] degre
I blame hym not a whytte, so that he followe me ;
And take his losse as quietly as when y^t he doth wynne,
Then Fortune hath no maistre of that state he ys in.

Here, hobbling verse alternates with twelves and fourteens. Such references as "Cupido" (l. 8), "Recorde of Terence" (l. 22), "Lucrece the Romaine" (l. 29), "olde antiquitie" (l. 36), carry on a prevailing fashion among fifteenth-century poets, common in Wiat's day—particularly in Italian poets, but *not followed* by Wiat. When he is translating he always reduces classic example as far as possible. Cf. Satire 1, for example, where L. Alamanni draws several examples from classic passages. Wiat skips the passage.

No. 8. **Lament my losse, my labor, and my payne.** A rather dull complaint of mis-spent youth. It appears as if this poem were written especially for the Court album. It is certainly not a song. See l. 25, "And patientely, *O reader* . . .," and l. 28, "*this boke abrode ys sente.*" Does this refer to the change of hands of the D. MS., for it certainly left Mary's keeping after the death of her husband the Duke of Richmond, and as *certainly* came into the hands of Lady Margaret, the affianced wife of Sir Thomas Howard?

No. 9. **Spight hath no power to make me sadde.** Wiat had clearly incurred the wrath of some person, formerly a friend (l. 21), who constantly came across his path, and apparently worked him ill. There are several references to spite. See l. 13, "Blame not my lute," No. 30, Part I. Notice last stanza.

[1] MS. spelling *hyge*. Probably a misprint.

l. 31. *Yet . . . she hath no name.* Wiat protests that the person does not exist. The natural inference is that he had some one definite in view.

No. 10. **A! my herte, a! what aileth the.** A refrain song imitated from Serafino. Above this poem is a short-lined quatrain signed "T. V."—

Ffortune doth frowne
  What comedye
I ame downe
  By destinye.

No. 11. **Hate whom ye list for I kare not.** A poem without value—obviously a Court trifle. Poems with a like termination throughout were called *like loose* (*i. e.* like end), from a term in archery; they were subjected to criticism from later sixteenth-century writers. Puttenham, the sage critic of his time, while representing Wiat with Surrey "as the two chief lanternes of light," [1] severely censures such a poem as this. Says Puttenham, Lib. II., p. 185, "a rime of good simphonie should not conclude his concords with one and the same terminant sillable, as *less, less, less,*[2] but with divers and like terminants as *les, pres, mẹs* . . . yet many use it otherwise, neglecting the Poeticall harmonie and skill. And th' Earle of *Surrey* with Syr *Thomas Wyat*, the most excellent makers of their time, more peradventure respecting the fitnesse and ponderositie of their wordes then the true cadence or simphonie, were very licentious in this point."

No. 12. **Grudge me who liste, this ys my lott.** A "glosa" poem. Cf. Part I, No. 14.

1 This passage has been so frequently quoted that it is well known. See Puttenham, *Arte of Englishe Poesie*, I. p. 76. It is due to this special passage that Wiat and Surrey have been labelled under the same criticism, Surrey taking the lead.

2 In Wiat's poem "not, not, not."

There is a pleasant variety in this example both in the matter and the arrangement. The speaker is a young woman. Cf. ll. 1–4, 5–7, 17–20. Part of the introductory couplet, "If yt ware not," forms a refrain to every quatrain. And at the end of every two quatrains, the introductory couplet is sung. The tendency is for the refrain to occupy a more prominent place, in order that the audience may take up the burden of the song more frequently. *If it ware not* is repeated in the refrain of No. 26, but no two poems could be more unlike in their mood than these.

l. 22. *fewe wordes among the wise.* Cf. next poem, l. 29.

No. 13. **Greting to you both yn hertye wyse.** Like No. 8, this was written for an album of verse to be perused and not to be sung as a song, like the majority of pieces in this section. A very moral letter in rhyme, but it is very different to the doubtful poem ascribed to Lord Morley.

Throughout the poem phrase after phrase is in Wiat's characteristic style, and his quotations of old sayings in particular give substantial proof of his authorship. See ll. 5–7, 12–14, 15–21, 22–24, and 29. The poem is in humorous vein with general moral truths expressed; compare the sentiments in Shakespeare, *All's Well*, I. i. 76.

Love all, trust a few
Do wrong to none: be able for thine enemy
Rather in power than use: and keep thy friend
Under thy own life's key.

l. 36. *The manner place*, either Allington or W. Malling Manor.

l. 41. The letter is dated "the 20th of March." The tone of the letter, to be careful of friends (so-called), would place it as a late poem, but the latest date to be assigned is 1537. After this date he was abroad on March 20th until 1541.[1]

[1] March 20. The probable date of this epistolatory poem is March

Compare the sentiments of "Luckes my faire falcon," Epigram 30, ll. 3–5. The letter is in Wiat's easy conversational style, very different from the grip of thought, and the nervous tensity of his phrasing, that is so pronounced in his dramatic monologues.

No. 14. **Tanglid I was in loves snare.** An imitation of Serafino's First Barzaletto, ed. 1516.

l. 1. *loves* here and in l. 16 scans as two syllables.

I think this poem is out of place here. It belongs to the earlier poems of the Court group, 1532–5, and to the sentiment of the Epigram "Some tyme I fled." Cf. also Sonnet 7, l. 14, "Me lusteth no lenger rotten boughes to clyme," and the sestet of Sonnet 24.

The refrain

> But ha ! ha ! ha ! full well is me,
> For I am now at libertye.

is imitated from Serafino's refrain, as follows—

> Ha ! ha ! ha ! men rido tanto
> Chio son vivo and son di fore.

The only other actual translation is the first line, "Fui serrato nel dolore," "Tangled I was. . . ."

No. 15. **Longer to muse.** Contrast this with the following, No. 16.

A graceful little poem, built up on the common stock of phrases, oft repeated in Wiat's Court poems. The resignation of the lover to "leve" and "forget" since his mistress has no constancy, proves the artificiality. The aim of the poem is merely to produce a song to please; and the accom-

1536, or the following year. In 1537 he was busy preparing for his Embassy ; for he left England in April. On March 20, 1538 and 1539, he was in Spain, and in 1540 he was at Ghent. The following March he was in prison ; 1542 is too late to be considered.

paniment in these songs was the principal element. The Court poet often adapted a new poem to an old and popular tune. There are many examples in the Royal Appendix and sixteenth-century Song-Books. In the printed Miscellanies, as well as the Song-Books, various poems are assigned to certain well-known tunes.

No. 16. **Love doth againe.** Notice the tendency to express contrasting moods. Here, the lover remains faithful in spite of his mistress' coldness. Neither the preceding, nor this, poem suggest very serious thought or feeling; but rather set forth an account of the varying moods of a lover.

No. 17. **With serving still.** Another lute song, the only poem of this metre in short quatrains in the collection; No. 3 has a different stanza form.

No. 18. **Now all of change.** The rhyming scheme is unusual: abc, abc, with the metre 448, 448. It is written in eight lines, in the MS., but the third and fourth and seventh and eighth are bracketed. This poem appears to have been a favourite; the MS., here, is worn.

No. 19. **Dryven bye desire I dede this dede.** An obscure poem. Cf. the last two lines with the Epistolatory poem No. 13. It is also in Tottel.

No. 20. **Perdye I saide it not.** G. F. Nott says, ed. 1816, "This does not occur in any of the MSS. It is therefore taken from Tottel's Songs." It is strange that he should have overlooked it in the D. MS., fol. 70b.

A very old measure, but unusual with Wiat.

The song is a free translation of Petrarch's Canzone "S'il dissi mai," which is imitated in the Italian of Serafino—

Donna, se io dissi mai contra tuo onore
Te mostri a me crudel sempre e più bella.

Puttenham quotes this poem as an example of *Ecphonisis*, or outcry. He defines the class as poems that "do show any extreme, whether it is by way of exclamation, crying out, admiration or wondering, as Chaucer of the Lady Cresseida, by exclamation—

"O soppe of sorrow, soonken into care
O caytife Cresseid for now and evermare."

After quoting Gascoigne, he goes on, "Petrarch in a sonet, which Sir Thomas Wiat Englished excellently well, said in this figure by way of imprecation and obtestation: thus 'Perdie I said it not.'" The translation is free.

ll. 21–22. *Suche warre As they brought out of Troye.* Wiat's interpolation; Petrarch introduces a simile from Pharaoh pursuing the Hebrews—

Ma terribil procella
Qual Pharaone in perseguir li Hebrei.

ll. 45–48. *For Rachell have I servid.* Wiat's version misses the concluding poetic thought. The Italian runs—

Per Rachel ò servito et non per Lia;
Né con altra saprei
Viver; et sosterrei,
Quando'l ciel ne rappella,
Girmen con ella in sul carro de Helia.

No. 21. **Absens absenting causithe me to complaine.** This poem is probably a conscious imitation of the older style. The halting gait of Morley's verse, and of late fifteenth century, is discernible. It is not in the vigorous trisyllabic movement that Wiat adopts occasionally. The device of making the last few words in one stanza the opening of the following stanza is successfully tried by Wiat in the refrain song, Part I, No. 18, "The knot which fyrst," and in No. 23 of this section.

Nos. 22–26 are certainly late poems. They suggest the attitude of a man who looks back upon worldly pleasures and disappointments in the temper of the Hebrew poet, "Vanity of vanities, all is vanity." In No. 23, like Hamlet, he considers the question of escaping present trouble by putting an end to his life.

No. 22, **When that I call,** is reminiscent of Wiat's past.

l. 7. *slipper holde.* Cf. late poem, "Stand who so list upon the *slipper* top."

ll. 15–17. *Amiddes my welthe . . . weake.* Wiat here seems to touch upon the early heedless days, when he was suddenly recalled to the sternness of life by domestic troubles and by his removal from Court in 1526. From this time onwards Wiat is a man with a definite purpose, with his eyes open to the world, its requirements, its disappointments and its possibilities, retaining, however, the sunny temper and humour, which deepened into a richer vein differing from the earlier gaiety of the young courtier.

l. 28. *With patiens for remedye.* This phrase constantly recurs, and is the subject of several poems. It is Wiat's philosophic conclusion, as the only remedy of meeting trouble.

l. 29. *As . . . livith by restrainte.* A favourite construction, found in Chaucer.

No. 23 was probably written in 1540. In desperate mood, with possible disgrace and death before him, he deliberates upon suicide; but reason and noble courage always seem to prevail in Wiat's mental conflicts. Cf. "Most wretched hart," p. 174.

No. 24. All Wiat's later poems that touch on love are written in the vein of one who has not had his love consummated. Wiat's disposition was affectionate, even tender, and the loss in his life is apparent. He was not happily married. For reasons which are obscure, and equally culpable on both sides (by his own statements to his son), Wiat refused to live with his wife or even to support her. There is a pathetic absence in Wiat's poems of interest in child-life [1] and domestic affection in the writings that have come down to us. There is no word of his son beyond the letters "out of Spayne." Then, in 1537, these letters are written, for a definite purpose, whose tragic purport is easily discovered. His son is married, and Wiat is filled with the desire that his life shall not be wrecked on the domestic side as his was, by heedless entering of the marriage state, and by a want of understanding on either side. Wiat had full capacity for love in its gracious aspect, yet like so many men and women, had found when it was too late that the union was incompatible. The nobility of his character is thrown into greater relief by the knowledge of the public and private sorrows that he combated so manfully.

No. 25. There is a deliberate desire to be obscure here, as in the following; the whole poem is a quibble of words, but the thought underlying is the submitting to circumstance.

No. 26. **I am as I am.** Wiat intends to go on his own way, whatever others may think or say, living equably, inured to the fret of life, without overmuch leaning towards mirth. This is the spirit of the late poems, but the grace of Wiat's intimate style is very marked throughout. See stanzas 3–6 in particular. The old humour breaks out in stanza 8.

No. 27. **Patiens for I have wrong.** This short stanza is inserted in a strange hand and without signature; the only instance in this section.

[1] Contrast Surrey's delightful touches of conjugal love and paternal affection in this respect in the poem beginning "Good ladies."

POEMS ABSENT FROM THE E. AND D. MSS.

THIS section consists of poems which have survived in Tottel, in the *Court of Venus*, and in MSS. other than E. and D.

Sonnets and Epigrams absent from E. have already been inserted in their respective groups. The absence of important poems from E. is accounted for by many missing pages; for this reason the Harleian MS. and the Harrington MS. (known as P., and acquired by the British Museum in 1900) are of very great value, since they establish, by MS. evidence, the authorship of poems already ascribed to Wiat in Tottel's *Miscellany*.

Another interesting source for some of Wiat's songs is an early anthology called the *Courte of Venus*, which survives in two fragments—at Britwell Court and the Bodleian respectively.

The Britwell fragment consists of the first eight folio sheets; in this way the title [1] has fortunately been preserved. It contains a "Prologue to Venus," and eleven songs, including six which are known to be Wiat's, and one which is so characteristic of his style that it is inserted as the first poem of this group. The four remaining songs are bad imitations or adaptations of Wiat's songs. The "Prologue to Venus"

[1] "The *Courte of Venice* newly and diligently corrected with many proper Ballades newly amended, and also added therunto which have not before bene imprinted." This little book evidently consisted of songs new and old; the "Ballades not before imprinted," appear to have consisted mainly of Wiat's songs. It will be remembered that Wiat was called a "ballate-maker."—State Papers, May 1536.

is in the old style of the early fifteenth-century writer of Troilus verse. It begins thus—

In the month of May when the new tender grene
Hath smoothly covered the ground that was bare,
Poudted[1] with flours so wel be sene :
I would have brought my hart out of care :
And as I walked in the wood so fayre
Thycke of grasse among the floures swete
And many a holsome herbe fayre under the fete.

At the conclusion of the Prologue appears the following : "Thus endeth the Prologue and hereafter foloweth the new Court of Venus." Four songs by Wiat follow ; the next two pieces are bad copies of two of his songs ; the seventh is the popular song, "If fansy would favour" (found in E, D, and A. MSS.) ; the eighth and ninth are poor adaptations of Wiat's verse, the tenth piece is a version of a poem found only in the D. MS., and the last song contained in this fragment is the widely known lyric, "Marvail no more altho" (found in E, D, A, and T.). Wiat's songs are evidently intended to represent the "*New* Court of Venus" ; that is, the new fashion of love handled in the Petrarchan manner, and introduced by Wiat, in contrast to the old type after the style of the "Roman de la Rose." And to bring out the contrast the edition of the *Courte of Venus* began in the old manner with the Prologue.

The second fragment (Douce g. 3, Bodleian, Oxford) consists of fourteen folio sheets ; the date assigned is *c.* 1560. It contains a song, and a fragment of song, and a long, dull controversial poem on monastic life, called the "Pilgrim's Tale"[2] ; no poem by Wiat exists in this fragment.

1 "Poudted," *i. e.* "sprinkled."

2 The Bodleian fragment is of little interest in regard to Wiat's poems, but the question to be solved, is whether this fragment is part of a later edition of the Britwell *Courte of Venus.* The last poem (fol. xlv.) is similar to the *old style* of the Prologue in the Britwell fragment. Follow-

The earliest date assigned to the first publication of the *Court of Venus* is 1542, the year of Wiat's death. It is highly probable that the Britwell fragment is part of this 1542 edition. The poems were obtained from some one who knew the D. MS., or was connected with the Court, for five of Wiat's songs in the *Court of Venus* are contained in the D. MS., two of these being peculiar to that MS. The other two songs, inserted here, were evidently Court poems which were never inserted in the Court album.

The *Courte of Venus* followed a continental fashion prevalent in the fifth decade of the sixteenth century for printing anthologies.

No. 1. **To whom should I sue.** This follows "My pen take payne" and "My Lute awake," and precedes "Dysdaine me not." The phrasing and the repetition of the refrain are undoubtedly in Wiat's manner. Cf. also the sentiment expressed in ll. 16–20. The second stanza is incomplete, wanting l. 7.

l. 11. *Or els . . . complayne.* Cf. Rondeau "Help me to seke."

l. 13. *I fly . . . espyed.* Cf. "Take hede betyme," l. 1.

---

ing the Pilgrim's tale is "An exclamation of the Auctor agaynst Sathan, our old enemy," serving as an epilogue to the preceding tale. I insert it as a curiosity, showing how far from Wiat's "new style" the book had wandered, and how successfully the poetic muse had hidden herself in the quarter of a century between Wiat's death and the Elizabethan age.

O wycked worme to penaunce conjuryd,
And of God him selfe furst accorsyd,
Amongst all creatures most to be aborred
By whom in to this world came first
The fal of man, tell me how thou durst
Presum to ryse most ungraciouse beast !
And so by God imputed to crepe apon thy brest.

No. 2. **Dysdaine me not.** Tottel has probably omitted the refrain; there is no evidence to prove it, but it is known that Wiat was partial to refrains, and that Tottel in at least three cases omitted the refrain, and turned Wiat's Rondeaus into Sonnets. It is therefore probable that the *Courte of Venus* version of this song is the original.

ll. 14–15. *Nor hate me not til I swerve.* The text follows the *Courte of Venus*, which is incomplete here. Tottel reads—

Nor hate me not, tyll I offend.
Destroy me not, tyll that I swerve.

The printer has evidently begun l. 14, "Nor hate me not," and continued the line with the latter half of l. 15, "til I swerve."

The other pieces in the fragment are contained in D., or both D. and E. As a conclusion to the C. V. poems, I append the C. V. version of the poem found only in the D. MS., "Hate whom ye list for I kare not" (see Part II, No. 11).

Love whom you lyst and spare not
  Therwyth I am content,
Hate whom you lyst and spare not
  For I am in dyfferent.

Do what you lyst and dread not
  After your owne fantasye,
Thynke what you lyst and feare not
  For al is one with me.

For as for me I am not
  Wavering as the wind,
But even as one that reketh not
  Wych way you turne your mind.

For in your love I doubt not
  But as one that reketh not,[1]
Whether you hate or hate not
  Is least charge of my thought.

---

[1] *Not*, i. e. *nought.*

Wherfore I pray you forget not
  But that I am wel content,
To love whom you list and spare not
  For I am indifferent.

Cf. "Like as the swan" for the alternate rhyme throughout on *not(e)*.[1] The existence of this poem in the E. and D. MSS. is a reason for suggesting that "Love whom ye lyst" may have been Wiat's version, whereas the poem as it stands in the D. MS. may be the attenuated form, inserted, like many trifles in the D. MS., as a game. Notice that the poem inserted above does not betray the awkward hand of an ordinary mediocre versifier who has filled in Wiat's outline; it runs smoothly with the general phrasing of Wiat's style.

No. 3. **Lyke as the wynde.** From the Harleian MS., with title as in text. A similar poem is ascribed to Surrey in the P. MS.; Tottel printed it with two verses of the P. version omitted, and an extra verse, not found in P.

Professor Padelford, *Sixteenth-Century Lyrics*, p. 128, takes the version ascribed to Wiat as a corruption of Surrey's, "the fresh stanzas being contributed by some reviser." Of the seven stanzas in Wiat's version, five are found in Surrey's with slight alteration. The quality of the remaining stanzas (the first and third) is distinctly Wiat's. The introductory simile and the phrasing is an exact imitation of Wiat's style. Stanza 3 consists of familiar phrases often found in the Sonnets and elsewhere, and if the verses were indeed added by a later reviser, it was some one who knew Wiat's poems thoroughly, and could imitate his style exactly. Analyzing the poem, it will be seen that Wiat's is

[1] *Not(e)*, with a quibble of meaning, used twice in every quatrain, as a musical sound and negation respectively.

well knit together; it seems to me that Surrey, a good Italian scholar, took over the verses based on Petrarch, and added more verses derived from the Italian.

Again, the slight difference in the versions is that between the more correct verse of Surrey and the freer verse of Wiat. ll. 21–24, for example, when compared with Surrey's version, will be seen to follow Wiat's manner; the variants in Surrey disguise that manner.

Wiat.	*Surrey.*
Lyke as the *flye dothe seke* the flame, 21	Like as the *flee that seethe* the flame,
And *afterwarde playeth* in the fyer,	And *thinkes to plaie her* in the fier,
Who *findeth her woo and sekethe her game,*	That *fownd her woe* and *sowght her game,*
Whose greffe dothe growe of her owne desyer."	Whose grief did growe by her desire.

I consider, then, that Wiat's version proclaims his authorship. Such verbal differences as above prove in themselves that it is the earlier version.

Notice specially the construction of l. 21, with the omission of the relative, a form frequently found in Wiat, archaic in his day.

Finally, a close attention to the verse of Surrey proves in a very striking way how much he was indebted to Wiat for his language and his ideas. His following of Chaucer and Petrarch in his allegiance to external nature have gone far to disguise this fact.

No. 4. **Under this stone.** The epitaph on Sir Thomas Gravener is taken from the Harleian MS. Wiat's estimation of his friend answers to the character of the poet. The third stanza is peculiarly applicable, especially the last line, which, coming from Wiat's pen, has a tragic import.

No. 5. **Like as the byrde.** From the Parker MS., Corpus Christi, Cambridge. It is difficult to place this poem; but it belongs, probably, to the later period. The thought may apply to any one of Wiat's imprisonments. The metre, in the fifteenth-century accentual style, is deliberately employed by Wiat on rare occasions, in contradistinction to the decasyllable line learnt from the Italian. This post-Chaucerian metre is employed for an epistolatory or familiar style, when he is writing a short poem which is not intended for a song. At such times he follows to a certain degree the older poet Skelton, and reverts to a popular form.

The first poem in this style was probably the Canzone "Myne olde dere enmy." Although a translation, it appears to have been written in the English style as a tribute to Skelton, lately dead; this is the obvious reason for its inclusion at that particular time (*c.* 1529) among the Sonnets and Rondeaus.

One or two other examples in the same metre in the D. MS. are clearly late. The tenor of this poem may be compared with one of the last entries in the D. MS., No. 23, Part II, where Wiat deliberates on the question of taking his life.

No. 6. **Stond who so list.** From the A. MS., fol. 143. Tottel differs considerably. The poem is taken from a passage of Seneca's *Thyestes*,[1] an author much read by Wiat in his later years.

[1] *Thyestes*, v. 391, *et seq.*

Stet quicunque volet potens
Aulæ culmine lubrico :
Medulcis saturet quies
Obscuro positus loco
Leni perfruar otio.
Nulla nota Quiritibus
Ætas per tacitum fluat

l. 8. *greep'the.* A. MS. spelling, for *greepeth*, i. e. *grips.*

ll. 8–10. Wiat's involved style. He translates Seneca's statement, so fatally true in the reign of Henry VIII, that the public man is in danger of being cut off suddenly by death. The practice, common in Seneca's day, of removing rivals by poison or otherwise, was not unknown in the sixteenth century. Tottel has considerately altered the passage.

Sic cum transierint mei
Nullo cum strepitu dies
Plebeius moriar senex,
Illi mors gravis incubat,
Qui notus nimis omnibus.
Ignotus moritur sibi.

FROM TOTTEL'S "SONGES AND SONETTES"

No. 1. **Accused though I be.** This poem has the appearance of being intended as a Sonnet, in the three-quatrain and final couplet form. There is a break in the thought in the last stanza, after ll. 9–10. I believe that two lines have been omitted here, and the final couplet is intended for ll. 13–14.

Nos. 2–4 are Court songs of the middle period.

Notice a favourite refrain in No. 4, "To serve and suffer paciently," derived from Seneca, "Dolor patientia vincetur."

No. 5. **For want of will.** There are traces of Tottel's alterations to be seen in "sweltyng," l. 7.

l. 15. *As hounde.* References to animal life are rare. The notable instance is the Epigram to the falcon.

No. 6 is a Song to Fortune. It is influenced by the passage in "Troilus and Cressida," I. 836–53.

l. 25. *For she hath turned so her whele.* Cf. "Troilus and Cressida," 837.

> For wel finde I that Fortune is my fo
> Ne alle the men that ryden conne or go
> May of hir cruell wheel the harm withstonde.

And "Troilus and Cressida," IV. 323.

> O ye lovers that heighe upon the wheel
> Ben set of Fortune.

ll. 39–40. Wiat's resignation follows out the spirit of the passage in Chaucer, where Pandarus assures Troilus—

> That as hir Joyes moten overgoon
> So mote hir sorowes passen everichoon.

No. 8. A late poem, possibly refers to the false accusations made concerning Wiat by Bonner in 1538, and taken up by his enemies after Cromwell's fall in 1540.

The dominant motive of Wiat's morality is clearly expressed, that truth must win in the end, ll. 3–4. Cf. another passage, "Tyme trieth troth."

No. 10. A six-lined stanza with epigrammatic force.

l. 3. *good chepe*, i. e. "good bargain." "Chepe" ("cheap," < O.E. "ceap") has survived its original meaning in *Cheapside*.

No. 11. **It burneth yet.** This dialogue is one of the finest achievements in a short poem. It brings out Wiat's sympathetic knowledge of human nature, and the consequent ability to set forth different points of view. A subject, difficult to handle, has been made beautiful through restraint, purity of attitude, and intense feeling. It is the best example for gauging what Wiat's attitude was towards women, and in this dramatic poem the distinctive characteristic pourtrayed by the "Lady" is sympathy, and what we may call the maternal instinct that every woman possesses for those whom she loves. And here, unconsciously or not, is the suggestion of the tragedy; the other side of the situation is given in the little poem, "Farewell! all my welfare."

The poem is of real dramatic value. The intense feeling, and the sympathetic element, is expressed in the brief, tense dialogue. The last line forms an epilogue to the poem.

No. 12. **Speake thou and spede.** This sestet in the classical couplet is remarkable for its finish. Starting as he did with no knowledge, and no regular example, of decasyllabic verse, Wiat's achievement is very great.

This late poem sufficiently answers the standpoint that Wiat was irregular from inability to understand correctness in verse. The change of verse denotes the change in the attitude of the man. His outlook is calm and controlled; the virile force, the fire and intellectual strength are all there, but in abeyance, and the few words contain depths of thought, showing how strong the current is beneath the unruffled surface.

No. 13. The preceding poem reaches the high-water mark of Wiat's attainment in metrical form. This last example is in his normal style, and is an imitation of the Boethius. See the *Study*, "Chaucerian Influence." There is an intense earnestness about Wiat's late poems, of which the Penitential Psalms is the great example. Wiat's attitude, though a man of the world, is similar to that of Donne in his later years. Both desired to lead men to a higher outlook of life. Donne by his impassioned utterances and his presentment of death, Wiat by the steady, convincing sincerity of his temperament, and by his wide knowledge and deepened sympathy with human nature. Wiat is infinitely the greater character, because his course was always clear, his faith steady, and his face ever towards "the morning," in spite of the rough winds that blew.

APPENDIX A

ITALIAN SOURCES

Rondeau No. 1.—Behold love.

Petrarch. Madrigale.

Or vedi amor, che giovenetta donna
Tuo regno sprezza et del mio mal non cura,
Et tra dui ta'nemici è si secura.
Tu se'armato, et ella in treccie e'n gonna
Si siede, et scalza in mezzo i fiori et l'erba,
Ver me spietate e'n contra te superba :
I son pregion; ma, se pietà anchor serba
L'arco tuo saldo et qualchuna saette
Fa'di te; e di me, signor, vendetta.

RONDEAU No. 5.—Yf it be so.

The refrain and *general idea* is to be found in Marot's rondeau "S'il est ainsy," but the borrowing is to be set down to remembrance of the music, and not to studied reproduction.

The following sonnet is the probable source ; it occurs among the group of *doubtful* sonnets attributed to Serafino. Ed. Bologna, 1896. "Collezione di opere inedite o rare."

Se questo miser corpo t'abandona,
Inclita mia madonna, el cor ti resta
In cambio di mia fé, che è cosa onesta
De non ritor quel ch'un tratto se dona
Amor mi tien, necesita mi sprona
Lo star mi piace, el partir mi molesta,
Ma sia che vuol, se'l ciel vita mi presta
Lontan da te non amerò persona.
I'me ne vo se tu m'amasti mai,
Te raccomando el cor che riman teco.
Forse che'l corpo piu non revedrai
E s'alcun te dicesse : l'amor cieco
Se ha fatto en altro amar, risponderai :
Come amar può, che non ha el cor non seco ?

APPENDIX A

RONDEAU NO. 7.—Goo burnyng sighes.

PETRARCH. Sonnet cliii.[1] (f. 69a.)

Ite, caldi sospiri, al freddo core;
  Rompete il ghiaccio che pietà contende;
  Et se prego mortale al ciel s'intende,
  Morte o merce sia fine al mio dolore.
Ite, dòlci pensier, parlando fore
  Di quello ove'l bel guardo non s'estende:
  Se pur sua asprezza, o mia stella n'offende,
  Sarem fuor di speranza et fuor d'errore.
Dir si po ben per voi, non forse a pieno,
  Che'l nostro stato è inquieto et fosco,
  Sí come'l suo pacifico et sereno.
Gite securi homai: ch'Amor ven vosco:
  Et ria fortuna po ben venir meno,
  S'ai segni del mio sol l'aere conosco.

1 The editions of Petrarch used.—The 1514 Aldine edition, "Il Petrarca," with colophon "Impresso in Vinegia nelle case d'Aldo Romano, nel'anno M.DXIIII del mese di Agosto. The Illuminated edition, Venice, 1470; Florence, 1904.

THE POEMS OF SIR THOMAS WIAT

SONNET No. 1.—Cesar, when that the traytor of Egipt.

PETRARCH cxii. (f. 44b).

Cesare, poi che'l traditor d' Egitto
Li fece il don de l'honorata testa,
Celando l'allegrezza manifesta,
Pianse per gli occhi fuor, si come è scritto;
Et Hanibal, quando a l'imperio afflitto
Vide farsi fortuna sí molesta,
Rise fra gente lagrimosa et mesta,
Per isfogare il suo acerbo despitto;
Et cosi aven, che l'animo ciascuna
Sua passion sotto'l contrario manto
Ricopre co la vista hor chiara hor bruna.
Però s'alcuna volta io rido o canto,
Facciol perch'i non ho se non quest'una
Via da celare il mio angoscioso pianto.

APPENDIX A

SONNET NO. 2.—The longe love.

PETRARCH cxl.

Amor che nel pensier mio vive et regna,
Et'l suo seggio maggior nel mio cor tene
Talor armato ne la fronte vene :
Ivi si loca et ivi pon sua insegna. 4
Quella ch'amare et sofferir ne'nsegna,
E vol che'l gran desio, l'accesa spene,
Ragion, vergogna et reverenza affrene,
Di nostro ardir fra sé stessa si sdegna 8
Onde Amor paventoso fugge al core,
Lasciando ogni sua impresa, et piange et trema :
Ivi s'asconde et non appar piú fore. 11
Che poss'io far, temendo il mio Signore.
Se non star seco infin a l'ora estrema ?
Ché bel fin fa chi ben amando more. 14

SONNET No. 3.—Who so list to hount.

PETRARCH CXC.

Una candida cerva sopra l'erba
Verde m'apparve, con duo corna d'oro,
Fra due rivere, all'ombra d'un alloro.
Levando'l sole, a la stagione acerba.
Era sua vista si dolce superba
Ch'i lasciai per seguirla ogni lavoro;
Come l'avaro che'n cercar tesoro
Con diletto l'affanno disacerba.
" Nessun mi tocchi," al bel collo dintorno
Scritto avea di diamanti et di topazi;
" Libera farmi al mio Cesare parve."
Et era'l sol già volto al mezzogiorno;
Gli occhi miei stanchi di mirar, non sazi,
Quand'io caddi ne l'acqua, et ella sparve.

Cf ROMANELLO. Sonetto 3.

Una cerva gentil, che intorno avolto
Al suo bel collo haveva un cerchio doro,
A me se offerse, a pe de un sacro aloro,
Mentre era a contemplar ne lumbra accolto.
Tanto piacer mi porse el suo bel volto,
Che abandonai el mio digno lavoro
Spreciando lumbra, et ogni altro restoro,
Col cor dogni pensier spogliato e solto.
Et qual falcon po la silvaggia fera
Volando corsi, et quando a lei fu gionto
Si volse indietro et disse in voce altera,
Tocar non lice la mia carna intera
Caesaris enim sum, et a quel punto
La cerva sparve, e fece el giorno sera.

APPENDIX A

SONNET NO. 4.—Was I never yet.

PETRARCH lxxxii.

Io non fu d'amar voi lassato unquancho,
  Madonna, né sarò mentre ch'io viva :
  Ma d'odiar me medesmo giunto a riva
  Et del continuo lagrimar so stancho; 4
Et voglio anzi un sepolcro bello et biancho,
  Che'l vostro nome a mio danno si scriva
  In alcun marmo, ove di spirto priva
  Sia la mia carne, che po star seco ancho. 8
Però, s'un cor pien d'amorosa fede
  Può contentarve, senza farne stracio,
  Piacciavi omai di questo aver mercede. 11
Se'n altro modo cerca d'esser sacio
  Vostro sdegno, erra; et non fia quel che crede;
  Di che Amor et me stesso assai ringracio. 14

Sonnet No. 6.—If amours faith.

Petrarch ccxxiv.

S'una fede amorosa, un cor non finto,
Un languir dolce, un desiar cortese;
S'oneste voglie in gentil foco accese,
S'un lungo error in cieco laberinto; 4
Se ne la fronte ogni pensier depinto,
Od in voci interotte a pena intese,
Or da paura or da vergogna offese;
S'un pallor di viola et d'amor tinto; 8
S'aver altrui piú caro che sé stesso;
Se sospirare et lagrimar mai sempre,
Pascendosi di duol, d'ira et d'affanno; 11
S'arder de lunge et agghiacciar da presso
Son le cagion ch'amando i mi distempre:
Vostro, Donna, 'l peccato et mio fia'l danno. 14

APPENDIX A

Sonnet No. 8.—My hert I gave the.

Serafino. Strambotti, f. 161. Ed. Firenze, 1516.

El cor ti diedi non che el tormentassi
  Ma che fosse da te ben conservato
  Servo ti fui non che me abandonassi
  Ma che fusse da te remeritato,
Contento fui che schiavo me acchatassi
  Ma non di tal moneta esser pagato,
  Hor poi che regna in te poco pietate
  Non si spiaccia fio torno in libertate.
La donna di natura mai si satia
  Di dar effecto à ogni suo desyderio,
  E sempre ti stá sopra con audatia
  Del tuo martyr pigliando refrigerio,
Quanto piú humil li vai tanto piú stratia
  Perfin che thá sepulto in cymiterio,
  Perche chi pone la suo amor in femina
  Zappa nel acqua et nella harena semina.

SONNET NO. 10.—Som fowles there be.

PETRARCH xix.

Son animali al mondo de si altera
Vista, che'ncontra'l sol pur si difende :
Altri, però che'l gran lume gli offende,
Non escon fuor se non verso la sera : 4
Et altri, co'l desio folle che spera
Gioir forse nel foco perché splende,
Provan l'altra vertú, quella che'ncende.
Lasso, il mio loco è'n questa ultima schera ! 8
Ch'i'non son forte ad aspectar la luce
Di questa Donna, et non so fare schermi
Di luoghi tenebrosi o d'ore tarde. 11
Però con gli occhi lagrimosi e'nfermi
Mio destino a vederla mi conduce :
Et so ben ch'i vo dietro a quel che m'arde. 14

APPENDIX A

SONNET NO. 11.—Bicause I have.

PETRARCH xlix.

Perch'io t'abbia guardato di menzogna
A mio podere et honorato assai,
Ingrata lingua, già pero non m'aì
Redduto honor, ma facto ira et vergogna.
Chè quanto piú'l tuo aiuto mi bisogna
Per dimandar mercede, allor ti stai
Sémpne piú fredde; et se parole fai
Son imperfecte et quasi d'uom che sogna:
Lagrime triste, et voi tutti le notti
Mi accompagnate ov'io vorrei star solo;
Poi fuggite dinanzi a la mia pace
Et voi, sì pronti a darmi angoscia et duolo,
Sospiri, allor traete lenti et rotti.
Sola la vista mia del cor non tace.

SONNET No. 12.—I fynde no peace.

PETRARCH cxxxiv.

Pace non trovo et non ò da far guerra;
Et temo et spero, et ardo et son un ghiaccio;
Et volo sopra'l cielo, et giaccio in terra;
Et nulla stringo et tutto'l mondo abbraccio. 4
Tal m'a in pregion, che non m'apre né serra;
Né per suo mi riten né scioglie il laccio;
Et non m'ancide Amore et non mi sferra;
Né mi vuol vivo né mi trae d'impaccio. 8
Veggio sezza occhi at non ò lingua et grido;
Et bramo di perir et cheggio aita;
Et ò in odio me stésso et amo altrui. 11
Pascomi di dolor, piangendo rido;
Egualmente mi spiace morte et vita,
In questo stato son, Donna, per vui. 14

APPENDIX A

SONNET No. 14.—My galy.

PETRARCH clxxxix.

"Passa la nave mia colma d'oblio
Per aspro mare, a mezza notte, il verno
Enfra Scilla et Caribdi; et al governo
Siede'l Signor, anzi'l nemico mio 4
"A ciascun remo un penser pronto et rio,
Che la tempesta e'l fin par ch'abbi a scherno:
La vela rompe un vento humido, eterno
Di sospir, di speranze et de desio 8
"Pioggia di lagrimar, nebbia di sdegni
Bagna et rallenta le già stanche sarte,
Che son d'error con ignorantia attorto. 11
"Celansi i duo miei dolci usati segni;
Morta fra l'onde è la ragion et l'arte:
Tal ch'i'ncomincio a desperar del porto." 14

Cf. *also Filosseno*, ed. 1507. Sopra una nove cosa de pensieri. *Scvofino Aquilano*, le rime Bologna 1896, p. 164. "Vanne, miscor, in la infelice barca de dolor fatte . . ." Sonnet attributed to *B. A.*

SONNET NO. 15.—Avysing the bright bemes.

PETRARCH clxxiii.

Mirando'l sol de begli occhi sereno
Ov'e chi spesso i miei depinge et bagna,
Dal cor l'anima stanca si scompagna
Per gir nel paradiso suo terreno. 4
Poi trovandol di dolce, et d'amar pieno,
Quanto al mondo si tesse, opra d'aragna
Vede, onde seco et con Amor, si lagua
Ch'à si caldi gli spron, si duro il freno. 8
Per questi extremi duo contrari et misti
Or con voglie gelate or con accese
Stassi cosi fra misera et felice. 11
M'à pochi lieti et molti penser tristi;
E'l piú si pente de l'ardite imprese:
Tal frutto nasce di cotal radice. 14

APPENDIX A

SONNET NO. 16.—Ever myn happ.

PETRARCH lvii.

Mie venture al venir son tarde et pigre
La speme incerta, e'l desir monta et cresce,
Onde e'l lassar et l'aspectar m'incresce;
Et poi al partir son piú levi che tigre. 4
Lasso, le nevi fien tepide et nigre,
E'l mar senz'onda, et per l'alpe ogni pesce,
Et corcherassi il sol là oltre ond'esce
D'un medesimo fonte Eugrate et Tigre : 8
Prima ch'i trovi in ciò pace né tregua,
O Amor, o Madonna altr'uso impari
Che m'anno congiurato a torto incontra; 11
Et s'i ò alcun dolce è dopo tanti amari.
Che per disdegno il gusto si dilegua.
Altri mai di lor gratie non m'incontra. 14

SONNET No. 17.—Love and fortune.

PETRARCH CXXIV.

Amor, fortuna et la mia mente schiva
  Di quel che vede, e nel passato volta.
  M'affligon si ch'io porto alcuna volta
  Invidia a quei che son su l'altra riva.
Amor mi strugge'l cor, fortuna il priva
  D'ogni conforto; onde la mente stolta
  S'adira et piange; et cosi in pena molta
  Sempre couven che combattendo viva
Ne'spero i dolci dí tornino in dietro,
  Ma pur di male in peggio quel ch'avanza;
  Et di mio corso ò giá passato'l mezzo.
Lasso, non di diamente, ma d'un vetro
  Veggio di man cadermi ogni speranza.
  Et tutt'i miei pensier romper nel mezzo.

APPENDIX A

Sonnet No. 18.—How oft have I.

Petrarch xxi.

Mille fiate, a dolce mia guerrera
Per aver co begli occhi vostri pace,
V'aggio proferto il cor; ma voi non piace
Mirar si basso colla mente altera.
Et se di lui fors'altra donna spera,
Vive en speranza debile et fallace:
Mio, perché sdegno ciò ch'a voi dispiace,
Esser non può già mai cosi com'era.
Or s'io lo scaccio, et e'non trova in voi
Nel'exilio infelice alcun soccorso,
Né sa star sol, né gire ov'altri il chiama,
Poria smarrire il suo natural corso:
Che grave colpa fia d'ambeduo noi,
Et tanto piú de voi, quanto piú v'ama.

SONNET No. 19.—Like to these.

SANNAZARO. Rime, Part iii. Sonetto iii.

Simile a questi smisurati monti
E l'aspra vita mia colma di doglie
Alti son questi, et alte le mie voglie
Di lagrime ambedui, questi di fonti. 4
Lor han, di scogli, li superbi fronti
In me duri pensier, l'anima coglie
Lor son di pochi frutti, e molte foglie
Io pochi affetti a gran speranza aggiunti. 8
Soffian sempre fra lor rabbiosi venti
In me gravi suspiri, esito fanno
In me se pasce Amor : in lor armenti 11
Immobile son io, lor fermi stanno
Lor, han d'uccelli, liquidi accenti
Et io la mente, di superchio affanno. 14

Ed. 1531, by Nicolo d'Arstotele, *called the "Lame,"* in fol., detto Zoppino, contains 5 sonnets, 1 capitolane, 2 canzone, unpublished in previous ed., added as Part iii.

APPENDIX A

SONNET NO. 20.—The lyvely sperkes.

PETRARCH cclviii.

Vive faville uscian de'duo bei lumi
Ver me sí dolcemente folgorando,
Et parte d'un cor saggio sospirando
D'alta eloquentia sí soavi fiumi,
Che pur il rimembrar par mi consumi
Qualor a quel di torno, ripensando
Come venieno a miei spirti mancando
Al variar de'suoi duri costumi.
L'alma nudrita sempre in doglia e'n pene
(Quanto è'l poder d'una prescritta usanza !)
Contra'l doppio piacer si'nferma fue,
Ch'al gusto sol del disusato bene
Tremando or di paura or di speranza
D'abandonarme fu spesso intra due.

SONNET No. 21.—Such vayn thought.

PETRARCH clxix.

Pien d'un vago penser che me desvia
Da tutti gli altri et fammi al mondo ir solo,
Ad or ad or a me stesso m'involo,
Pur lei cercando che fuggir devria;
Et veggiola passor si dolce et ria,
Che l'alma trema per levarsi a volo,
Tal d'armati sospir conduce stuolo
Questa bella d'Amor nemica et mia!
Ben, s'io non erro, di pietate un raggio
Scorgo fra'l nubiloso altera ciglio,
Che'n parte rasserena il cor doglioso:
Allor raccolgo l'alma; et poi ch'i aggio
Di scovrirle il mio mal preso consiglio,
Tanto gli ò a dir che'ncominciar non oso.

APPENDIX A

SONNET No. 22.—I abide and abide.

Lasso oimè.

Le Rime di Serafino de Ciminelli dall' Aquila, Introd. xxvi.
Brit. Mus. 12225, i. 10.

Lasso oimè, che gli è gran tempo
Che in tuo man posi el mio core
Ma s'io narro el mio dolore
Tu rispondi ch'i ò bon tempo.
Si è con Dio s'io ho bon tempo
E l'o sol quando tu voi
El tuo aiuto sie per tempo
Mentre che sanar mi puoi
Non tarder per dir da poi
Io comessi un gran errore
(*Refrain*) Ma . . .
Questi tempo mai non vene
Lo sperando pur l'aspecto
Sarà ben si fuor de pene
Ch'averai un tuo suzeto
Tu me struggi el cor nel pecto
Perché io vivo in tanto ardore
(*Refrain*) Ma . . .
De crudele, habbi mercede
Di una acta acerba e dura
E risquarda la mia fede
Quanto ell'è perfecta e pura
In servirti ogna mia cura
Fachè me'l comanda amore
(*Refrain*) Ma . . .

Io ho ben tempo in la tuo mano
E ne'dolce sguardi acorti
Se'l servir non sarà vano
Ne fien tardi i tuoi conforti,
Non pigliare e'camin torti
Questi è quel che vòl amore

(*Refrain*) Lasso, oimè, che gli è gran tempo
Che in tuo man posi el mio core
Ma s'io narro el mio dolore
Tu respondi ch'i ò bon tempo

NOTE.—Wiat has imitated the refrain only. The style of the Italian lyric is similar to certain poems in the D. MS., with initial couplets and refrains. Cf. Part I, No. 14, and Part II, No. 12.

APPENDIX A

SONNET No. 26.—Unstable dreme.

FILOSSENO MARCELLO.* Strammoto i. ii.

Pareami in questa nocte esser contento
Che teco junxi al disiato effecto,
Deh fossio sempre in tal dormir attento,
Poi che il ciel non mi porge altro dilecto.
Ma il gran piacer mutosse i gran tormento
Quando che solo, me trovai nel lecto,
Ne duolmi gia chel son m ha inganato
Ma duolmi sol che sonno sogno e stato

* Ed. Venice, 1507. Sylve de Marcello Philoseno Tarvisino poeta Clarissimi Capitoli Juvenili, Capitoli Senili, Stramotti Senili, Disperatte, Sonetti Senili, Satyre. Colophon, MDVII, a di primo junio.

SONNET No. 28.—If waker care.

PETRARCH. Sonetto ccxxiv.

S'una fede amorosa, un cor non finto
Un languir dolce, un desiar cortese;
S'oneste voglie in gentil foco accese
Un lungo error in cieco laberinto

These lines supply the *idea* of No. 27.

SONNET NO. 29.—The piller pearishd is.

PETRARCH. Sonetto, cclxix.

Rotta è l'alta colonna e'l verde lauro
Che facean ombra al mio stanco pensero;
Perduto ò quel che ritrovar non spero
Dal Borea a l'Austro o dal mar indo al mauro. 4
Tolto m'aì, morte, il mio doppio thesauro
Che mi fea viver lieto et gire altero;
Et ristorar nol po terra né impero,
Né gemma oriental, né forza d'auro. 8
Ma se consentimento è di destino,
Che posso io puì se no aver l'alma trista,
Humidi gli occhi sempre e'l viso chino? 11
O! nostra vita ch'è si bella in vista,
Com'perde agevolmente in un matino
Quel che'n molti anni a gran pena s'acquista! 14

APPENDIX A

MISCELLANEOUS POEMS

No. 2.—O restfull place.

PETRARCH, Sonetto ccxxxiv.

O cameretta che gia fosti un porto
A le gravi tempeste mie diurne,
Fonte se'or di lagrime nocturne
Che'l di'celate per vergogna porto 4
O letticiuol, che requie eri et conforto
In tanti affanni, di che dogliose urne
Ti bagna Amor con quelle mani eburne,
Solo ver me crudeli a si'gran torto. 8
Né pur il mio secreto e'l mio riposo
Fuggo, ma piú mi stesso él mio pensero.
Che, seguendol, talor levommi a volo; 11
Il vulgo, a me nemico et odioso,
Chi'l pensó mai? per mio refugio chero
Tal paura ò di ritrovarmi solo. 14

This Sonnet gives the *idea.* Cf. l. 5 *et seq.*

No. 4.—Myne olde dere enmy.

PETRARCH. Canzone. Torin No. ccclx. Edition 1904. Firenze.

Quel antiquo mio dolce empio Signore
Fatto citar dinanzi a la reina
Che la parte divina
Lien di nostra natura e'n cima sede;
Ivi, com'oro che nel foca affina.
Mi rappresento carco di dolore,
Di paura et d'orrore,
Quasi huom che teme morte et ragion chiede
E'ncomincio: " Madonna, il manco piede
Giovenetto pos'io nel costui regno:
Ond'altro ch'ira et sdegno
Non ebbi mai; et tanti et sí diversi
Tormenti ivi, soffersi,
Ch'alfine vinta fu quell'infinita
Mia patientia, e'n odio ebbi la vita.

Cosi'l mio tempo infin qui trapassato
E in fiamma e'n pene; et quante utili honeste
Vie sprezzai, quante feste:
Per servir questo lusinghier crudele!
Et qual ingegno à sí parole preste
Che stringer possa'l mio infelice stato,
Et le mie d'esto ingrato
Tante et sí gravi et sí giuste querele?
O poco mel, molto aloè con fele!

In quanto amaro à la mia vita avezza
Con sua falsa dolcezza,
La qual m'atrasse a l'amorosa schiera
Che, s'i'non m'inganno, era
Disposto a sollevarmi alto da terrà
E'mi tolse di pace, et pose in guerra.

Questi m'à fatto men amare Dio
Ch'i non deveva et men curar me stesso:
Per una Donna ò messo
Egualmente in non cale ogni pensero.
Di ciò m'è stato consiglier sol esso,
Sempr'aguzzando il giovenil desio
A l'empia cote, ond'io
Sperai riposo al suo giogo aspro et fero.
Misero! a che quel caro ingegno altero.
Et l'altre doti a me date dal cielo?
Ché vo cangiando'l pelo
Né cangiar posso l'ostinata voglia:
Cosí in tutto mi spoglia
Di libertà questo crudel ch'i'accuso
Ch'amaro viver m'a'volto in dolce uso.

Cercar m'a fatto deserti paesi
Fieri et ladri rapaci, hispidi dumi,
Dure genti et costumi
Et ogni error ch'e pellegrini intrica
Monti, valli, paludi et mari et fiumi:
Mille lacciuoli in ogni parte tesi;
E'l verno in strani mesi,

Con pericol presente et con fatica :
Né costui né quell'altra mia nemica,
Ch'i'fuggia mi lasciavan sol un punto.
Onde, s'i'non son giunto
Anzi tempo da morte acerba et dura,
Pietà celeste à cura
Di mia salute, non queste tiranno,
Che del mio duol si pasce et del mio danno.

Poi che suo fui, non ebbi hora tranquilla
Né spero aver; et le mie notti il sonno
Sbandiro, et piú non ponno,
Per herbe o per incanti a se ritrarlo.
Per inganni et per forza è fatto donno
Sovra miei spirti; et non sonó poi squilla,
Ov'io sia in qualche villa,
Ch'l'non l'udisse. Ei sa che'l vero parlo;
Ché legno vecchio mai non rose tarlo,
Come questi'l mio core, in che s'annida
Et di morte lo sfida.
Quinci nascon le lagrime e i,martiri,
Le parole e i sospiri,
Di ch'io mi vo stancando, et forge altrui,
Giudica te, che me conosci et lui.,,

Il mio adversario, con agre rampogne
Comincia : "O Donna, intendi l'altra parte;
Che'l vero, onde si parte
Quest'ingrato, dirà senza defecto.
Questi in sua prima età fu dato a l'arte

Da vender parolette, anzi menzogne:
Né par che si vergogne,
Tolto da quella noia al mio dilecto
Lamentarsi di me, che puro et netto
Contra'l desio che spesso il suo mal vole,
Lui tenni, ond'or si dole,
In dolce vita ch'ei misera chiama
Salito in qualche fama
Solo per me, che'l suo intellecto alzai
Ov'alzato per sé non fora mai.

Ei sa che'l grande Atride et l'alto Achille
Et Hannibal al terren vostro amaro,
Et di tutta il piú chiaro
Un altro et di vertute et di fortuna
Com'a ciascun le sue stelle ordinaro,
Lascai cader in vil amor d'ancille
Et a costui di mille
Donne electe excellenti n'elessi una
Qual non si vedra mai sotto la luna
Benché Lucretia ritornasse a Roma;
Et si dolce ydioma
Le diedi et un cantar tanto soave,
Che penser basso o grave
Non poté mai durar dinanzi a lei.
Questi fur con costui l'inganni mei.

Questo fu il fel, questi li sdegni et l'ire
Piú dolci assai che de null'altra il tutto.

Di bon seme mal frutto
Mieto : et tal merito à chi'ngrato serve.
Si l'avea sotto l'ali mie condutto,
Ch'a donne et cavalier piacea il suo dire;
Et si alto salire
Il feci, che tra caldi ingegni ferve
Il suo nome, et de'suoi detti conserve
Si fanno condiletto in alcun loco,
Ch'or saria forse un roco
Mormorador di corti, un huom del vulgo
E'l'exalto et divulgo
Per quel ch'elli'mparò ne la mia scola
Et do colai che fu nel mondo sola

Et per dir a l'extremo il gran servigio
Da mille acti inhonesti l'ò ritratto
Ché mai per alcun pacto
A lui piacer non poteo cosa vile
Giovene schivo et vergognoso in acto
Et in penser, poi che fatto era huom ligio
Di lei ch'alto vestigio
L'impresse al core et fecel suo simile.
Quanto à del pellegrino et del gentile,
Da lei tene et da me di cui si biasma.
Mai nocturno fantasma
D'error non fu sí pien, com'ei ver noi;
Ch'e in gratia, da poi
Che ne conobbe, a Dio et a la gente;
Di ciò il superbo si lamenta et pente.

APPENDIX A

Anchor, et questo è quel che tutto avanza,
Da volar sopra'l ciel li avea dat'ali
Per le cose mortali
Che son scala al Fattor, chi ben l'estima;
Che, mirando ei ben fiso quante et quali
Eran vertuti in quella sua speranza,
D'una in altra sembianza
Potea levarsi a l'alta cagion prima:
Et ei l'à detto alcuna volta in rima
Or m'à posto in oblio con quella Donna
Ch'i'li die'per colonna
De la sua frale vita.,, A questo, un strido
Lagrimoso alzo, et grido:
" Ben me la diè, ma tosto la ritolse."
Responde: " Io no, ma chi per se la volse."
Alfin ambo conversi al giusto seggio
I'con tremanti, ei con voci alte et crude
Ciascun per sé conclude:
" Nobile donna, tua sententia attendo"
Ella allor sorridendo:
" Piacemi aver vostro questioni udite;
Mia piú tempo bisogna a tanta lite."

EPIGRAMS

No. 3.—Alas madame.

SERAFINO. Opera edition, Finenze, 1516. Strambotta, f. 179b.

Incolpa donna amor se troppo io volsi
Aggiungendo alla tua la bocca mia
Se pur punir mi voi di quel chio tolsi
Fa che concesso replicar mi sia.
Che tal dolceza in quelli labri accorsi,
Chel spirto mio fú per fugirsi via
Só che al secondo tocco uscira fora
Bastar ti dé, che per tal fallo io mora.

APPENDIX A

No. 5.—What nedeth these threning wordes.

SERAFINO. Strambotta, f. 170.

A che minacci, à che tanta ira e orgoglio,
Per questo non farai chel furto renda,
Non senza causa la tua man dispoglio
Rapir quel daltri non fu'mai mi amenda
Famme citar davanti amor chio voglio,
Che la ragion de luno e l'altro intenda.
Lei il cor mi tolse et io gli tolto un guanto
Vorro saper da te se un cor val tanto.

No. 10.—He is not ded.

SERAFINO. Strambotta, f. 120a.

S io son caduto interra inon son morto
Ritorna el sol benche talhor si cele,
Spero mi dara'el ciel quelche conforto
Poi che fortuna har á sfocato el fele,
Chi ho'visto nave ritornarsi in porto,
Dapoi che rotte há in mai tutte soe vele
El salce anchora el vento abassa et piega
Poi se ridriza et glialtri legni lega.

No. 11.—The furyous gonne.

SERAFINO. Strambotta, f. 145b.

Se una bombarda è dal gran foco mossa
Spirando, ció che trova aterra presto.
Ma segli advien chella spirar non possa
Se stessa rompe et poco offende el resto,
Cosi io dentro ardo, et foco è giunto à lossa
Sel taccio imor, sel dico altrui molesto.
Sospeso vivo, amor mi da tal sorte,
Che altro non è che una confusa morte.

APPENDIX A

No. 15.—Venemus thornes.

SERAFINO. Strambotta, f. 117a.

Ogni pungenta e venenosa spina
Se vede à qualche tempo esser fiorita,
Crudel veneno posto in medicina,
Piu volte torna lhom da morte vita
El foco che ogni cosa arde & ruina,
Spesso risana una mortel ferita
Cosi spero el mio mal me fia salute
Ch'ogni cosi che noce ha pur virtute.

No. 17.—Off Cartage he.

PETRARCH. Sonnet ciii.

Vinse Hanibal et non seppe usar poi
Ben la rittoriosa sua ventura
Però, signor mio caro, aggiate cura
Che similmente non avegna a voi.

The opening lines of this Sonnet give the idea for the first line of Wiat's Epigrams. He continues in a personal strain. This is one of the biographical poems.

No. 19.—From thes hye hilles.

ARIOSTO. Orlando Furioso. Canto xxxvii, 110.

Come torrento che superbo faccia
Lunga pioggia tal volta o nievi sciolte
Va ruinoso, e guí da'monti caccia
Gli arbori e i sassi e i campi e le ricolte :
Vien tempo poi, che l'orgogliosa faccia
Gli cade, e si le forze gli son tolte,
Ch'un fanciullo, uno femina per tutta
Passa lo puote, e spesso a piede asciutto.

ODE.

No. 7.—Resound my voyse, ye wodes that here me plain.

G. F. Nott considers this ode to be based on the following Strambotta f. 125b, of Serafino.

"L'aer che sente el mesto e gran clamore,
Diuulga in ogni parte in mia doglia,
Tal che, pi compassione del mio dolore.
Par che ne treme in arbore ogni foglia.
Ogni fiero animal posa el furore.
Che daiintarmi ognum par ch abbia voglia,
Et con mugito stran uoglion le carmi,
Et uorrian sol parlar per consolarmi,

APPENDIX A

Payne of all payne. D. MS.

FILOSSENO.* Strammoti Juvenili, b. vi.

Tre gran dolori ho nel mondo prouato
Di qual non credo un sia maior tra noi
Primo amar forte e nai esser amato
Lo son in questo e gia gran tempo fui.

* Filosseno Edition, Venice, 1507.

Lyk as the swanne.

I voirei ben cantar come fa el cygno
Che doppo il canto morto se ritrova
Ma il fato mio non e tanto benigno
E vol che sempre il pianto mio rinova
È canto come fa il corvo maligno
Quando denuncia la stagion, che piova
E cone il gal fuer de stagion io Canto
Che añuncio la gran piogia dil mio pianto.

Filosseno. Strammoto, d. iii^{b}.

Hevyn and erth.

FILOSSENO. Strammoto, b. v.

Gridato ho nocte e giorno tanto forte
Che tutto il ciel e offeso da mia voce
Ho tanto suspirato e con tal sorte
Che l'aere dal mio foca se arde e coce
Ho pianto tanto ognor chiamādo morte
Chel troppo humor a tutta terra noce
Hor tacer voglio e toler ar mia guerra
Per nō turbar piu il ciel l'aer ne terra.

Cf. *also Strammoto d. iiii.*

Il ciel contra me intona guerra guerra
Et ío fugendo vo de sasso in sasso
Ma la fortuna exclama serra serra
Unde preso i me ritrovo a passo a passo
Amor sta inanti e dice a terra a terra
E la morte risponde al basso al basso
Cosi il ciel e fortune dhora in hora
E amor e morte gridan mora mora.

APPENDIX A

So feble is the thread.

PETRARCH. Canzone. Poem xxxvii. Edition Firenze, 1904.

Si è debile il filo a cui s'attene
La gravosa mia vita,
Che s'altri non l'aita,
Ella fia tosto di suo corso a riva;
Però che dopo l'empia dipartita
Che dal dolce mio bene
Feci, sol una spene
È stato in fin a qui cagion ch'io viva;
Dicendo: Perché priva
Sia de l'amata vista,
Mantienti anima trista.
Che sai s'a miglior tempo ancho ritorni?
Et a piú lieti giorni?
O se'l pesduto ben mai si racquista?
Questa speranza mi sostenne un tempo:
Or vien mancando, et troppo in lei m'attempo.

Il tempo passa, et l'ore son si pronte
A fornire il viaggio,
Ch'assai spacio non aggio
Pur a pensar com io corro a la morte.
A pena spunta in oriente un raggio
Di sol, ch'a l'altro monte
De l'adverso orizonte
Giunto il vedrai per vie lunghe et distorte.
Le vite son si corte,

Sí gravi i corpi et frali
Degli uomini mortali,
Che quando io mi ritrovo dal bel viso
Cotanto esser diviso,
Col desio non possendo mover l'ali,
Poco m'avanza del conforto usato;
Né so quant'io mi viva in questo stato.

Ogni loco m'attrista, ov io non veggio
Quei begli occhi soavi
Che portaron le chiavi
De' miei dolci pensier, mentre a Dio piacque
Et perche'l duro exilio piú m'aggravi,
S'io dormo ovado o seggio,
Altro già mai non cheggio,
Et ciò ch'i vidi dopo lor mi spiacque.
Quante montagne et acque
Quanto mar, quanti fiumi
M'ascondon que'duo lumi.
Che quasi un bel sereno a mezzo'l die
Fer le tenebre mie,
A ciò que'l rimembrar piú mi consumi,
Et quanto era mia vita allor gioiosa,
M'insegni la presente aspra et noiosa!

Lasso, se ragionando si rinfresca
Quel ardente desio
Che nacque il giorno ch'io
Lassai di me la miglior parte a dietro

Et s'Amor se ne va per lungo oblio,
Chi mi conduce a l'esca
Onde'l mio dolor cresca?
Et perche'pria, tacendo, non m'impetro?
Cero, cristallo e vetro
Non mostrò mai di fore
Nascosto altro colore,
Che l'alma sconsolata assai non mostri
Piú chiari i pensier nostri,
Et la fera dolcezza ch'è nel core,
Per gli occhi, che disempre pianger vaghi
Cercan dí et nocte pur chi gle n'appaghi.

Novo piacer che negli umani ingegni
Spesse volte si trova
D'amar qual cosa nova,
Piú folta schiera di sospiri accoglia,
Et io son un di quei che'l pianger giova;
Et pas ben ch'io m'ingegni
Che di lagrime pregni
Sien gli occhi miei, si come'l cor di goglia,
Et perché a cciò m'invoglia
Ragionar de'begli occhi
(Ne cosa è che mi tocchi,
O sentir mi si faccia cosi a dentro,)
Corro spesso et rientro
Colà donde piú largo il duol trabocchi,
Et sien col cor punite ambe le luci
Ch'a la strada d'Amor mi furon duci

Le treccie d'or che devrien fare il sole
D'invidia molta ir pieno,
E'l bel guardo sereno,
Ove i raggi d'Amor si caldi sono
Che mi fanno anzi tempo venis meno,
Et l'accorte parole,
Rade nel mondo o sole,
Che mi fer già di sé cortese dono,
Mi son tolte; et perdono
Piú lieve ogni altra offesa,
Che l'essermi contesa
Quella benigna angelica salute,
Che'l mio cor a vertute
Destar solea con una voglia accesa:
Tal ch'io non penso udir cosa già mai
Che mi conforte ad altro ch'a trar guai.

Et per pianger anchor con piú diletto
Le man bian che sottili
Et le braccià gentili
Et gli atti saoi soavemente alteri
E i dolci sdegni alteramente humili,
E'l bel giovenil petto
Torre d'alto intellecto
Mi celan questi luoghi alpestri e feri;
Et non so s'io mi speri
Vederla anzi ch'io mora;
Pero ch'ad ora ad ora
S'erge la speme et poi non sa star ferma;

Ma ricadendo afferma
Di mai non veder lei che'l ciel honora,
Ov' alberga honestate et cortesia,
Et dov'io prego che'l mio albergo sia,

Canzon, s'al dolce loco
La Donna nostra vedi,
Credo ben che tu credi
Ch'ella ti porgerà la bella mano
Ond'io son sí lontàno.
Non la tocchar, ma reverente ai piedi
Le di ch'io saró là tosto ch'io possa,
O spirto ignudo od nom di carne et d'ossa.

THE POEMS OF SIR THOMAS WIAT

SATIRES.

No. 1.—Myn owne John Poynz.

LUIGI ALAMANNI. Satira x.
A Tommaso Sertini.*

Io vi dirò, poi che d'udir vi cale,
Tommaso mio gentil, perch'amo e colo
Piú di tutti altri il lito provenzale;

E perchè qui cosi povero e solo
Piu tosto che seguir popoli e regi,
Vivo temprando il mio infinito duolo.

Nè ció mi vien perch'io fra me dispregi
Quei ch'han dalla Fortuna in mano il freno
Di noi, per sangue e per ricchezze egregi.

Ma ben è ver, ch'assai gli estimo meno
Che'l vulgo, e quei ch'a ciò che appar di fuore
Guardan, senza veder che chiugga il seno.

Non dico già che non mi scaldi amore
Talor di gloria, ch'io non vo mentire
Con chi, biasmando onor, sol cerca onore.

* Tommaso Sertini, a merchant at Lyons, to whom Alamanni addressed this satire. He addressed Satire ix to another Lyonese merchant, Thomas Gadayne.

Ma con qual piè potrei color sequire 16
Che'l mondo pregia? ch' io non so quell'arte
Di che le scale altrui convien salire.

Io non saprei, Sertin, porre in disparte 19
La verita, colui lodando ogni hora
Che con più danno altrui dal ben si parte.

Non saprei reverir chi soli adora 22
Venere e Bacco, nè tacer saprei
Di quei che'l vulgo falsamente onora,

Non saprei più che agl'immortali Dei 25
Rendere onor colle ginocchia inchine
A più ingiusti che sian, fallaci e rei.

Non saprei nel parlar covrir le spine 28
Con simulati fior, nell'opre avendo
Mele al principio, e tristo assenzio al fine.

Non saprei, no, dove il contrario intendo, 31
I malvagi consigli usar per buoni
Davanti al vero onor l'util ponendo.

Non trovare ad ognor false cagioni 34
Per abbassar i giusti, alzando i pravi,
D'avarizia e di'nvidia avendo sproni.

Non saprei dar de'miei pensier le chiavi 37
All'ambizion, che mi portasse in alto
Alla fucina delle colpe gravi.

Non saprei il core aver di freddo smalto 40
Contro á pieta, talor nocendo a tale
Ch'io più di tutti nella mente esalto.

Non di loda onorar chiara immortale 43
Cesare e Silla, condannando a torto
Bruto e la schiera che più d'altra vale.

Non saprei camminar nel sentier corto 46
Dell'empia inquità, lasciando quello
Che reca pace al vivo, e gloria al morto.

Io non saprei chiamar cortese e bello 49
Chi sia Tersite, nè figliuol d'Anchise
Chi sia di senno e di pieta rubello.

Non saprei chi più'l cor nell'oro mise 52
Dirgli Alessandro, e'l paüroso e vile
Chiamarlo il sorte ch'i Centauri ancise

Dir non saprei poeta alto e gentile 55
Mevio, giurando poi che tal non ride
Smirna, Manto e Fiorenza ornato stile.

Non saprei dentro all'alte soglie infidè 58
Per più mostrar amor, contr'a mia voglia,
Imitar sempre altrui se piange o ride.

Non saprei indivinar quel ch'altri voglia, 61
Nè conoscer saprei quel che più piace
Tacendo il ver che le più volte addoglia.

L'amico lusìnghier doppio e fallace 64
Dir non saprei gentil, nè aperto e vero
Chi sempre parli quel che più dispiace.

Non saprei l'uom crudel chiamar severo, 67
Nè chi lascia peccàr chiamarlo pio,
Nè che èl tiranneggiar sia giusto impero.

Io non saprei ingannar gli uomini e Dio 70
Con giuramenti e con promesse false,
Nè far saprei, quel ch'è d'un altro, mio.

Questo è cagion che non mi cal ne calse 73
Ancor giammai di seguitar coloro
Nè quai Fortuna più che il senno valse.

Questo fa che il mio regno e'l mio tesoro 76
Son gl'inchiostri e le carte, e più che altrove
Oggi in Provenza volentier dimoro.

Qui non ho alcun che mi domandi dove 79
Mi star o vada, e non mi sforza alcuno.
A gir pel mondo quando agghiaccia o piove.

Quando gli è il ciel seren, quando gli è bruno 82
Son quel medesmo, e non mi prendo affanno,
Colmo di pace, e di dolor digiuno.

Non sono in Francia, ove abbia scorno e danno 85
S'io non conosco i vin, s'io non bene
Qual vivenda è miglior di tutto l'anno;

Non nella Spagna, ove studiar conviene 88
Più che nell'esser poi, nel ben parere
Ove frode e menzogna il seggio tiene;

Non in Germania, ove il mangiare'l bere 90
M'abbia a tor l'intelletto, e darlo in predo
Al senso, in guisa di selvagge fere.

Non sono in Roma, ove chi in Cristo creda, 94
E non sappia falsar nè far veneni
Convien che a casa con suo danno rieda.

Sono in Provenza, ove quantunque pieni
Di malvagio voler ci sian gl'ingegni
L'ignoranza e il timor pon loro i freni.

Benchè d'invidia e d'odio ognor sian pregni
Contro i miglior, per non veder più innante,
Restan troncati a mezzo i lor disegni.

Ma sia pur com può, l'alma igrorante
Se ben torto vorria, può nuocer poco.
Come su chi ben n'ha provate alquante.

Or qui dunque mi sto prendendo in gioco
Il lor breve saver, le lunghe voglie,
Con le mie muse in solitario loco.

Non le gran corti, non l'eccelse soglie
Mi vedran gir coi lor seguaci a schiera,
Nè dir me avran troppo onorate spoglie
Avarizia e livor, ma pace vera.

ll. 100–6 appear in later editions. The first edition reads, ll. 100–2 (and omits ll. 103–6)—

"Che benche sian d'invidia & d'odio pregni
Sempre contro i miglior per veder poco
Son nel mezzo troncati i lor disegni."

NAENIAE

in mortem Thomæ
Viati equitis
incom
parabilis.

IOANNE LELANDO
ANTIQVARIO.
AVTORE.

Londini.
ANNO. M. D. XLII.

FACSIMILE TITLE-PAGE "NÆNIÆ"

APPENDIX B

Brit. Mus. 1075. m. 16 (4).

In effigiem Thomæ Viati

Holbenus nitida pingendi maximus arte
Effigiem expressit graphice; sed nullus Apelles
Exprimet ingenium felix animumque Viati.

Ætas Viati

Syderei peteret cum cœli regna Viatus
Tempora lustrorū non dum conpleuerat octo.

Johannis Lelandi Antiquaræ carmen ad Henricum Howardum Regnorum Comitem juuenem tum nobiliss. tum doctissimum

Accipe Regnorum comes illustrissime carmen,
Quo mea Musa tuum laudauit mœsta Viatum
Non expectato sublatum funere terris
Nominis ille tui dum vixit magnus amator.
Tu modo non viuum coluisti candidus illum,
Verum etiam vita defunctum carmine tali
Collaudasti, quale suum Chaucerus auitæ
Dulce decus linguæ vel juste agnosceret esse
Perge Howarde precor virtute referre Viatum
Dicêrisque tuæ clarissima gloria stirpis.

Clarus fons

Cæsaris orator Maurentius ostia Falæ
  Fluminis intravit vela secunda ferens.
Est data ducendi legatum cura Viato
  Hispanis nullus notior Anglus erat.
Urbs antiqua tenet regum monumenta duorum
  Clarus fons, sedes pontificumque fuit
Hic per dispositos properantem currere mannos
  Inuasit Thomam pestis et atra febris.
Nobilis Horsæus morienti lumina clausit,
  Quem Durotrigum gens colit, ornat, amat
Æternum peperit Clarus fons morte Viati
  Nomen, et illustris sit magis inde locus.

APPENDIX B

Officium pietatis

Sint mœste Charites, lubentiæque.
Et tristes sileant sales, lepôresque.
Extinctus jacet en Viatus ille
Ille inquam decus unicum Britannæ
Gentis, cuius ab ore profluebant
Musarum numeri rotundiores.
Vos cygni pia turba concinentes
Sublimem medio locate cœlo
Vestrum pro meritis suis poetam,
Et famam dare candidi perennem.

Conjunctio Animorum

Me tibi conjunxit comitem gratissima Granta
  Granta Camœnarum gloria, fama, decus,
Diuidet illa animos mors ingratissima nostros
  Non faciet : longum chare Viate vale.

Comparatio

Qualis erat clypei dominus septemplicis Aiax.
  Qualis et in bello Troicus Hector erat.
Qualis erat curru celeri conuectus Achilles
  Nostra quidem talis palma Viatus eques.

Immortalis Viatus

Ante suos Titan radios ostendere mundo
  Desinet, et nitidas Cynthia pulchra faces.
Desinet ante nouos flores producere tellus
  Quam pereat nomen clare Viate tuum.

Delectus amicorum.

Candido amicorum numerum dedit aula Viato
Sed tres præcipuæ selegit amicus amicos
Excoluit largi Poyningi [1] nobile pectus
Ingenio Blagi delectabatur acuto.
Doctrinæ titulo gratus Masonius [2] albo.
Hi nunc defunctum lachrimarum flumine lugent
Ter gemina charum resonantes voce Viatum.

Apotheôsis

Inter cœlicolas nuper certamen obortum
  Dissidiæ vera caussa Viatus erat.
Mars ait est noster juvenum fortissimus ille,
  Phœbus at ingenii flos ait ille meus
Mercurius virga litem dissolvit; et altis
  Intulet exutum corpore syderibus.

Communis Dolor

Tristi carmine passerem Catullus
Extinctum queritur parum pudicus
Deflet Stella suæ vices Columbæ
Vates molliculus, tener, cinædus.
At nos qui colimus severiora
Et musas sequimur sacratiores
Lumen iudicii boni Viatum
Abreptum querimur dolore qusto.

[1] John Poynz, to whom Satires I. and II. are written.
[2] Mason, Wiat's Secretary in Spain.

APPENDIX B

Anglus par Italis

Bella suum merito jactet florentia Dantem
Regia Petrarchæ carmina Roma probet.
His non inferior patrio sermone Viatus
Eloquii secum qui decus omne tulit. 4

Gemitus turturis

Æeria turtur gemitus tunc fudit ab ulmo
E medio raperent cum tristia fata Viatum. 2

Mors Victrix

Tu bellatorum vicisti tela Viate
Nulla manus mortis vincere tela potest. 2

Unicus phœnix

Una dies geminos phœnices non dedit orbi
Mors erit unius vita sed alterius
Rara avis in terris confectus morte Viatus
Houardum heredem scripserat ante suum. 4

Vita post cineres

Dicere nemo potest recte periisse Viatum
Ingenii cuius tot monumenta vigent. 2

Querela philomelæ

Tempore non solito cecinit Philomela canora
Virtutis caderet cum prima corona Viatus.
Cantrix cantorem merito lugebat ademptum
Officii memor adsonuit nemus omne canenti. 4

Mons acutus

Loqueri burgus, quē nomine Montis acuti
Ætas nostra vocat, dominum, gratumque patronū
Solicitis votis optabat habere Viatum.
Unde suas cœpit paulatim expandere cristas
Ast animis nunc spe sublata concidit omni,
Ingentem totis tectis patiturque ruinam.
Hinc Murotriges crudelia fata vocare
Non cessant, subito quæ subtraxere Viatum.

Cantii desyderium

Extinctum perluge tuum generosa Viatum
    Cantia, quo vivo lumine maior eras.

Vaga Fluuius

Nuper clara Vagæ facies : nunc fuscula nympha
Est luteis turbata vadis dominumque Viatum
Sublatum queritur salebroso murmure tristis
Quid, quod & infelix lachrimis indulget obortis,
Verberat & curuas violento gurgite ripas.

Alaunodunum

Magnanimus dum vixit Alaunia castra Viatus
In pretio stabant : sed nunc tutore remoto
Deponunt animos, & culmina celsa reclinant.

Clades eloquentiæ

Eloquii flumen, lumen, fulmenque Viatus
    Concidit, argutum nunc silet omne velos.

APPENDIX B

Lima Viati

Anglica lingua fuit rudis & sine nomine rhythmus
  Nunc limam agnoscit docte Viate tuam.

Nobilitas debet Viato

Nobilitas didicit te præceptore Britanna
  Carmina per varios scribere posse modos.

Viatus psaltes.

Transtulit in nostram Davidis carmina linguam
  Et numeros magna reddidit arte pares
Non morietur opus tersum, spectabile, sacrum
  Clarior hac fama parte Viatus erit.

Elementorum luctus

Non facit officium solitum vis ignea cœli
  Irriguas aer soluitur in lachrimas.
Turbine ventorum montes consurgit in altos
  Pontus : terra macram tristitiamque refert,
Caussa quidem justa est, sensere elementa Viatum
  Delicias orbis deperiisse meras.

Calculus Cæsaris

Carolus eximias vires laudare Viati
Cæsar, & eloquium est solitus laudare Viati
Ingenuos mores Cæsar laudare Viati
Ingeniumque probum solitus laudare Viati
Cæsaris unius multorum calculus instar.

Prosopographia.

Si quis in hac nostra non vidit gente Viatum
Hæc legat, atque viri formam sibi colligat omnem.
Corpore procerum finxit natura Viatum
Eius & inuectis nervos dedit illa lacertis.
Addidit hinc faciem, qua non formosior altra.
Læta serenatæ subfixit lumina fronti
Lumina fulgenteis radiis imitantia stellas.
Cæsariem iuueni subflauam contulit : inde
Defluxit sensim crinis, caluumque reliquit
Sylva sed excreuit promissæ densula barbæ.
Quisquis erit posthac syncerus cultor honesti
Laudibus emeritis felicem tollat ad astra
Nobile solertis naturæ plasma Viatum.

Viatus Aquila

Summa petit magni Jouis ales & ardua tentat
  Talis naturæ dote Viatus erat

Viatus ornamentum patriæ

Cedrinæ decori sunt celsis montibus umbræ,
Malaque solicite paradiso punica culto.
Sunt teretes decori fœcundis vitibus vuae
Purpureæque rosæ, violæque nitentibus hortis.
Ingenuis decori cunctis patriaque Viatus
  Vivus erat, patriæ mortuus ille decus.

APPENDIX B

Corona Viati

Castalii fontis cum margine forte sederent
Ex hedera Musæ nuper texere corollam,
Auro pingentes solito de more corymbos.
Circulus & postquam justum coniisset in orbem
Quæstio Cyrrheas est inter oborta sorores
Festa poetarum quis tandem præmia ferret.
Virginei quæ prima chori sic ora resoluit
Calliope : docto sunt munera digna Viato
Dixerat, & placuit reliquis sententia nymphis.
Atropos has illa laudes inuidit acerba,
Infestaque manu vitalia stamina rupit.
Confectum Musæ crudeli vulnere mystam
Eluxere suum lachrimis gemitusque dedere
Talia dicentes : potuit mors tollere corpus
Vivet at ingenium nostri sine fine Viati.

Nobilitas animi.

Intumuit nunquam fortunæ dotibus amplis
Nec se felicem duxit splendore Viatus
Aulæ, nec strepitu rerum, procerumve favore
Rectius ille animum studiis cordatus avebat
Exornare bonis, cœloque reponere curam.
Nobilitas hęc est animi verissima magni.
Est hic thesaurus longe pretiosior auro
Nomine quo mundo distractus in æthere viuit
Quid iuuat immenso nunc indulgere dolori,
Aut desyderio rapti languere Viati.

Curemus potius studiis imitarier illum
Sanctis, inque viros forteis euadere. Tandem
Sic nos efficiet quoque gloria vera Viatos.

Annulus Viati

Annulus in digito solitus radiare Viati
Fabre factus erat gemmaque superbus achate
Cæsaris effigies in qua verissima Juli,
Sculpta, occludendis signum spectabile chartis
Cæsaris ad summam virtutem calcar imago
Ingenitas auxit vires animosque Viati.

Epitaphium

Urna tenet cineres ter magni parva Viati
Fama per immensas sed volat alta plagas.

LONDINI

Ad signum ænei Serpentis

APPENDIX C

The history and the ownership of the D. MS. has been dealt with at some length in the *Study*, Appendix A, pp. 125–35. The theory of the successive owners has been based upon evidence derived from the fragment of fly-leaf, from facts obtained from various documents and State Papers, and from internal evidence.

The two clues followed are, first, the fragmentary signatures of the first owners; and, secondly, the solution of the initials "M. F." and "S. E." on the central panel of the front and back covers respectively, the binding of which is early sixteenth century.

The initials on the front panel are worn, those on the back are well preserved. The arrangement of lettering differs. Those on the front are placed one above the other; those on the back are side by side.

A facsimile of the fragment of fly-leaf is produced for this volume, since the names of those who were largely concerned in the MS. can be seen thereon.[1] The partial signatures enclosed within the flourishes on the right-hand upper part of the fragment are "H. Ho" for Henry Howard, Earl of Surrey, and the letters "Hen," and part of the downward stroke of a "y," stand for Henry Rychemond.[2]

Above these signatures is another flourish enclosing a word which resembles "marayge." This word suggests a clue to the initials on the front cover, "M. F." They probably

[1] See Vol. i. p. 251.

[2] The usual signature of Henry Fitzroy, natural son of Henry VIII by Elizabeth Blount, widow of Lord Talboys, and later, wife of Lord Clinton.

stand for Mary Fitzroy, or Mary and Fitzroy; for the book certainly passed into the possession of Mary, *née* Howard, sister of Henry Howard and wife of Henry Fitzroy, Duke of Richmond, and in all probability it was one of the marriage gifts from her brother and husband jointly. In the space torn away at the top of the fly-leaf, above and to the right of the word "marayge," Mary's name was most probably inserted.

On the lower portion of the fragment the very clear signature of Mary Shelton appears, and about an inch above is the partial name (almost obscured but still discernible in the original MS.) of Margaret How. (for Margaret Howard, *née* Douglas, daughter of Margaret Queen of Scotland, the sister of Henry VIII).

Between the names of Mary Shelton and Margaret Howard is that of Ryche,[1] and is probably the Mistress Ryche who is included among the Holbein portraits, but no definite part in the MS. has been discovered in regard to this name.

It has been possible to arrive at some definite conclusions concerning the part that these men and women played in the history of the MS.

The ownership of the volume by Henry Howard[2] was before 1529. In that year he became the companion to young Henry Fitzroy, then eleven[3] years of age. They

1 A certain Richard Riche was Solicitor-General and Chancellor of the Augmentations. His name and that of Elizabeth his wife occur frequently in the State Papers from 1530 and onwards.

2 It is quite possible that the volume had already been employed for copying Wiat's early songs, before it came into Henry Howard's possession. His father was constantly at Court, and when Wiat went to Calais in 1528 this record of the early songs may have been presented to Henry by his father in order that he might learn to sing and play them, as part of his education for a courtier's life.

3 Letters to the King in the Record Office witness the precocity of Henry Fitzroy. He writes in 1526, in a beautiful hand, to "make a

became singularly attached to one another, and shared everything in common, living at Windsor until 1532, and completing their education in the "sciences and seates of lernynge"[1] as well as in knightly accomplishments, including lute-playing, singing and composing verses. Amongst other possessions the volume was shared, and the lyrics (1524–6) were either inserted now or on an earlier date. In 1533 Henry Howard and Henry Richmond took their places at Court, on the occasion of the Coronation of Anne Boleyn. Shortly afterwards, Henry Richmond married Mary, his friend's sister, and Henry Howard married Frances de Vere.

The D. MS. appears to have been the Court album for the three years 1533–6. Mary shared her brother's tastes in music and poetry. The entry of the poems, singly or in small groups, continued, and the long group of poems, begun and never finished, was destined to include all Wiat's poems.

The Lady Margaret Douglas had a large share in the volume. Intimate with Mary, and secretly in love with her friend's young uncle, Sir Thomas Howard, her rank made her the chief figure among the younger members of the Court circle, and gave her the right to take an active interest in the poems.

On fol. 68 is an inscription to Madame Margaret and Madame de Richemont; on another leaf is the handwriting of Anne Boleyn and the inscription, "I am yowres. An."

In 1536 the smooth tenor of life was suddenly brought

---

demonstatione of thys my procedinge in writinge," and in April 1527, he asks the king "taccept thys my wrytyng pennyd with myne owne hand."

[1] "I effectialy give myne hole endevor, mynde, study and pleasure to the diligent appliance of all such sciences and seates of learnynge . . . as I am daylye advertysed."—Letter from Henry Rychemont to the King, January 1528.

to an end by a series of disasters. The trial and execution of George and Anne Boleyn, in May, was followed by the death of the Duke of Richmond in July, and the discovery that Sir Thomas Howard and the Lady Margaret were secretly affianced.

The king was furious; both were imprisoned, and a few months later Sir Thomas Howard died[1] in the Tower. Cromwell had endeavoured to obtain the release of Margaret by declaring that "she ceseth to have feelings for the gentleman," but both were obdurate and refused, under cajolery and threatenings, to break their plighted word.

Margaret Howard, released on her husband's death, took her place at Court as the chief mourner at Jane Seymour's funeral.

Meanwhile, the D. MS. had received the record of the last months of Howard's life. Verses of his experiences in prison and of never-failing devotion to his wife are in his handwriting and signed with his initials. Verses in Margaret's handwriting bear record of her bitter grief. These facts prove that both Margaret and Thomas Howard handled the volume during their imprisonment, which was evidently sent by the Duchess of Richmond as a solace to them in their misfortune.

The history of the D. MS. as a Court album ceased after about 1537. Mary went back to her father at Kenninghall; Margaret obtained leave to join her there, and until 1544 the records in the volume, other than Wiat's poems, commemorate the life at Kenninghall, Norfolk. Poems by E. Knevet,[2] verses by Mary Shelton, who was beloved of

[1] On All Hallowes Eve, 1537 (State Papers and Wriothesley's *Chronicle*).

[2] E. Knevet and T. Clere are not mentioned in the State Papers before 1541. They were intimate with Surrey 1540–5. The records in the MS. relate to these years.

Sir John Clere, companion to Surrey, and the sole example in the MS. of Surrey's poems (inserted by Mary Shelton), belong to the years 1541–4. In 1545, Surrey, writing verses on Sir John Clere's [1] death, says—

Shelton for love, Surrey for Lorde thou chase.

The group of Wiat's poems continued, and were entered in the MS. in the order that they were obtained. Amongst them is the poem, "So feble is the threde," written in Spain about 1538, and the last fragment is part of a satire. In 1544 Margaret was affianced to the Earl of Lennox, and went back to Scotland. She *took the volume of verses with her*, for, many years later, a poem was inserted in the handwriting of her son, Lord Darnley, the husband of Mary Queen of Scots. Wishing to please Mary Stuart, nothing could have been more appropriate than a presentation of verses collected at the English Court to one whose great ambition was to become Queen of England. In all probability the D. MS. came into Mary Stuart's possession in this manner.

There is a connected chain of evidence which follows the history of the D. MS., until it apparently came into the hands of Mary Stuart. The initials "S. E." and the presence of the MS. in the Devonshire library, still remain to be accounted for.

Now, though the case is "not proven," a curious bit of evidence provides a clue for the final history of the MS. For many years Mary was under the care of the Earl of Shrewsbury; he was known to have kindly feelings towards her, and he was eventually ordered to give up his charge to a sterner guardian. It is probable that when Mary parted from him, for whom she had a sincere attachment, she gave

[1] The names of Howard, Clere, Knevet, and Shelton include the most well-known families in Norfolk, fifteenth to sixteenth centuries. See Paston Letters.

him the volume of verses. The initials stand, in this case, for Shrewsbury and Elizabeth his wife.

Elizabeth survived him. By a former husband, William Cavendish of Hardwicke Hall [1] was her second son. She was instrumental in establishing the fortunes of the Cavendish family, and in finally building Chatsworth. The library was removed from Hardwicke and placed at Chatsworth. Here the D. MS. probably remained, with other treasures collected by the family, until, in the early years of the nineteenth century, Dr. Nott, describing this volume of verse, calls it the Devonshire MS., *lent from the Duke of Devonshire's library*. Nott's library was sold at his death, and the MS. finally came into the keeping of the British Museum.

[1] He became Earl of Devonshire in 1618. By his mother's death (1608), and his elder brother, Henry Cavendish's death, he inherited great fortunes.

APPENDIX D

(a) *Chaucerian versification* in Pynson's edition of 1526.

1. Whan thát Apríll || wíth his shóures sót(e)
2. The droúght of Márch hath pércèd ye rót(e)
3. And báthëd évery véyn in súche lycóur
4. Of whíche vertúe engéndred ís the flóur.
5. Whan Zépherús eke wíth his sóte bréth(e)
6. Enspýred háth | in évery hólte and héth(e)
7. The ténder cróppes | ánd the yónge són(ne)
8. Háth in the Rám | hálfe his cóurs yrón(ne)
9. And smále fóules máke mélodý(e)
10. That slépen all nýght with ópen éy(e)
11. So prícketh hem náture ín her córagés
12. Than lóngen fólke to gón on pílgrimáges
13. And pálmèrs to séke stráunge strónd(es)
14. The sérven hálowes | cóuthe in sóndry lónd(es)
15. And speciallý | fro évery shýres énd(e)
16. Of Énglànde to Cáunterbúry thy wénd(e)

. . . . .

19. Befýll in that seáson ón a dáy
20. In Súthwèrke at Tábarde ás I láy. . . .

Rules of versification gathered from the extract.

1. Syllable wanting after the cæsura, but Aprill readily becomes trisyllabic.
2. **Pércèd,** pronounced as two strong stresses.
3. 6, 15, slurring on **évery.**
8. **Strong stress after the cæsura.**
10. **slépen all.**
Octosyllabic line with slurring.

11. slurring of verbal "-eth" in *pricketh*.

13, 16, 17. **pálmèrs, Énglànde, Súthwèrke,** with two strong stresses, and cæsura after the *third* syllable. Cf. Trissino's statement, Appendix E.

Variants in Thynne's Edition, 1532.

1. **Whan**] Th. *Whanne*.
3. **veyn . . . lycour**] Th. *vayne . . . lycoure*.
4. **flour**] Th. *floure*.
6. **in**] Th. omits.
11. **corages**] Th. omits *s*; also l. 12.
19. **Befyll in**] Th. *It befel*.
20. **at**] Th. *at yᵉ*.

The rules collected from the above include the chief rules of Wiat's versification, such as slurring of vowels, ll. 8, 15, weak syllables ending in vowel-likes (*i. e.* u, r, l, n), and slurring of verbal ending "-eth" in the body of the verse; the absence of weak stress after the cæsura, and before the strong stress of the second foot; the cæsura after the third syllable, as in "pálmèrs," and the occasional variety of an octosyllabic line.

For trisyllabic feet, in every part of the verse except the last, and other rules of scansion, see the *Study*, pp. 39–50, where the system of versification is thoroughly worked out with parallel examples from Chaucer.

The early use of the trisyllable for the last foot, found in Wiat and *not* copied from Chaucer, was learnt from the fifteenth-century Troilus metre, where it constantly occurred. Wiat appears to have recognized it as a fault, for he does not employ it in his later verse.

(b) *Chaucerian influence.*

The influence of Pynson's *Chaucer* can be traced in the "Caunterbury Tales," the "Troylus and Creseyde," the letter of Dido to Eneas, and "Contra Fortunam," not only in imitation of poems, but in the same phrasing and spelling. The influence of Thynne's edition is to be traced in the "Boethius," the "Testament of Love," the "Astrolabe," the "Troylus and Creseyde,"[1] "Howe Pyte is deed," and "Annelyda & false Arcyte" (see *Study*, Chapter on "Chaucerian Influence").

[1] The "Troylus and Creseyde" is included in Pynson's edition, but Wiat's later poems, especially the Satires and the poems written after 1536, show strong Chaucerian influence at the time when he shows the influence of *Boethius*, which is absent in Pynson's edition.

APPENDIX E

TRISSINO'S INFLUENCE ON WIAT'S VERSIFICATION

The fame of Trissino,[1] a prolific Italian writer, rests chiefly on his work entitled *La Poetica*, published together with his translation of Dante's Latin Treatise on prosody in 1529. All the main examples in the *Poetica* are drawn from Petrarch and Dante; whatever rules these two writers do not support by example are not worth following, in Trissino's estimation. After some search in Trissino's *Poetica* for proofs of definite influence on Wiat's work, I found that the characteristic method of employing two stressed syllables without an intermediate weak syllable for the two first feet, the cæsura after the fifth syllable, the proposed employment of three quatrains in the sonnet, and two kinds of terza-rima, are all sanctioned by Trissino.

1. *Two stressed syllables without intermediate weak syllable.* Speaking of the cæsura, Trissino[2] says, there is "un altra cesura, la quale si fa ne la terza syllaba del verso, essendi la *seconda acuta* (*i. e.* "strong accent") et si dimanda cesura terza come è—

> " Nel mezō || del camin di nostra vita.
> Nel tempō || che rinova i miei sospiri " (fol. xxb).

This illustrates a characteristic rule of Wiat's verse. Cf.—

> Behold love || the longe love ||

[1] Trissino's *foreign* influence up to the present has rested chiefly in his *Sophonisba*, one of the earliest tragedies to be translated and imitated in France.

[2] Wiat had written in this manner before the publication of Trissino; the special interest lies in the fact that it was a definite rule.

2. *The cæsura after the fifth syllable* is given as the first example of cæsura in the *Poetica*, with the following illustration—

Voi ch'ascoltate, in rime sparse il suono (fol. xxb).

The Italian verse, however, has a sixth syllable in the second part of the verse, which balances the line. The method of cutting the verse into two halves is very hard in English, and was later discontinued by Wiat.

3. *Three quatrains in the composition of the sonnet.* Trissino defines the sonnet under octave (*Basa*) and sestet (*Volta*) in the usual manner, namely, two quatrains (two *base*) and two tercets (two *volte*) respectively. He continues : "Ne me è nascoso, che in alcuni antiquissimi autori avanti la eta di Dante si truovino qual che sonetti che hauero *tre base* (*i.e.* "three quatrains") di tre quaternarii : non dimeno giudice che questi cotali base non siano molto da imitare percio che Petrarca e Dante et li altri buoni autori di quella eta mai non usorano.[1]

Now this question of *three quatrains* for the first part of the sonnet instead of two probably led to the idea of employing the third quatrain plus a couplet for the sestet, instead of the two tercets. Wiat had practice with the final couplet, in ottava-rima, and found that whereas the couplet came with ease in English verse, the tercet was hard to manage as a conclusion to the sonnet.

Again, in the *Epitaph to Sir Thomas Gravener*, he employs the actual form described above, namely, three quatrains and the sestet, known in English verse as an extended sonnet, and in Surrey's Elegy on Wiat, he employs the extended sonnet with *eight* quatrains before the final sestet.

4. Trissino gives three forms of terza-rima,[2] that employed

[1] fol. xxxii. [2] fol. lxv.

by Dante and other good writers, and imitated by Wiat in the Penitential Psalms. The second kind is as follows: aba, cbc, dcd. In the Paraphrase "Altho thou se" the rhythm falls under Trissino's second form of terza-rima, according to previous editions of Wiat. For this reason, the rhyme has been considered to break down. Curiously enough, the secondary form, enunciated in the *Poetica*, is obtained by omitting the first line of a tercet.[1] The arrangement hitherto found in Wiat's Psalms is evidently due to a missing line.

By a comparison with the Psalms it is quite clear, however, that more than one line has been omitted; owing to the difficulty of finding a suitable rhyme it was probably left for revision at a later date.

In this edition an omission of two lines is marked.[2]

From the above statement, it is hardly possible to doubt Wiat's knowledge of the *Poetica*, at a time when the influence of Trissino's work in prosody was far-reaching.

The fact that Wiat was definitely following, in certain striking instances, a standard of prosody set up by Trissino gives still greater importance to his work and his achievements in metre.

[1] In the following series, aba, bcb, cdc, ded, efe . . .; if the first line "b" of the second tercet is omitted the series continues cbc, dcd, ede, fe . . . according to the secondary form of Trissino.

[2] The proof that two lines are missing is found in the final quatrain which always completes a poem in terza-rima.

APPENDIX F

SIR THOMAS WIAT AND ANNE BOLEYN

MUCH has been written and conjectured concerning the relations between Wiat and Anne Boleyn. Contemporary gossip and reiterated statements, which are in themselves legendary, have been repeated from time to time, placing them in an ambiguous light. It has resulted, on the one hand, in the repetition of scandalous stories, and, on the other, in assigning Wiat's love poems to Anne Boleyn.

This position may be tracked to three sources—

1. The Wiat Memoirs.
2. Nicolas Harpsfeld's *Pretended Divorce.*
3. A general statement made by the Duke of Suffolk and attached to Wiat's name.

The Wiat Memoirs. Those memoirs relate stories which undoubtedly prove an intimacy between Wiat and Anne about the year 1526, but the actual form of the stories is doubtful, since they were collected and written many years after Wiat's death.

Nicolas Harpsfeld's *Pretended Divorce.* Nicholas Harpsfeld was an unscrupulous man and a partisan of a very violent nature, and wrote for the Roman Catholic party and in defence of Queen Catherine. His opinions and stories are therefore as much to be believed as the views of an opposition party in any political situation of the present day.

The general statement was made by the Duke of Suffolk

in 1536 concerning *a gentleman* of the chamber. Contemporary events proved that this statement did not apply to Wiat.

Wiat's attitude of thought in 1536, and the writing of the First and Second Satires, are in themselves sufficient proof of any connection with the Boleyn affair.

Again, while research amongst State Papers has thrown much light upon the life of the times, no fact has been discovered concerning any relationship between Wiat and Anne Boleyn, while *certain interesting facts* tend to prove that the intimacy was an agreeable one, of short duration, and ceased altogether after 1527.

Certain facts prove that Wiat had little or no intercourse with Anne before 1525–6; he went to France in March 1526, and to Italy early the following year, and in 1528 was sent to Calais until 1532. It is quite clear from the course of events of his life that the anecdote [1] of the King's command to Wiat to break off the intimacy occurred in 1526. Henry's love letters show that he had singled out Anne for attention in that year, and the preparations for the Divorce began in 1526. The events that disprove any serious intimacy between Wiat and Anne before 1525 are, briefly, as follows—

Anne (born *c.* 1503) [2] went to France "as a child," 1514,[3] returned in 1522,[4] and was present at the Christmas revels.[5]

In 1523 the discovery that Anne was deeply in love with Lord Percy frustrated the policy of Cardinal Wolsey and the King in the Ormond case.[6] Anne was sent home tc

[1] The story of the game of bowls is too well known to repeat here.

[2] See Papers by John Round, *Studies in Peerage and Family History*, 1901 ; and *Early Life of Anne Boleyn*, 1886.

[3] *Ibid.*, and *Hist. de la roine Anne du Bouillant.*

[4] State Papers, 1522. [5] *Ibid.* [6] State Papers, and Round.

Hever Castle in disgrace, and does not reappear at Court until 1525. Lord Percy, dismissed from Cardinal Wolsey's household, and handed over to his father the Earl of Northumberland, was summarily contracted to Mary Talbot, a most unhappy marriage. That the attachment was serious on both sides is without doubt. Wiat's presence at Court in 1523 was therefore a most unfavourable opportunity for any intimacy with Anne.

Both are mentioned at the Christmas revels of 1525.[1] This is the earliest date that can be assigned for the friendship.[2] In 1526 Wiat went to France in March with Sir Thomas Cheyne. On his return, the King required him to break off his intimacy with Anne, and by this very fact, and the King's desire to wed her, prove that the friendship had been honourable.

Wiat's poems at this period (1526–7) show disappointment at the loss of friendship, and anger that a lady should "give him leve to go." This attitude fits in with the commands laid upon him. Loyalty to the King, as well as danger to himself, prevented him from attempting any further intercourse.

During the four years at Calais the passing interest for Anne died out, a sure proof that he was not seriously in love, for absence is the strongest proof of real attachment. When real love exists, absence strengthens the bond, and the years deepen the feeling.

Wiat's youthful intimacy with Anne was a kindred feeling and sympathy for one who was vivacious, witty and accomplished like himself. His character deepened during the years of absence, while hers degenerated, and when they

[1] State Papers, 1525.

[2] There are no proofs whatever that a childish friendship existed. Wiat was brought up by his mother at Allington, and went to Cambridge at an early age. His nearest friends were the Cobhams, of Cobham Hall, Kent.

met again, it was as strangers, with no sympathies in common.

The life at Court during the next three years (1533–6) presented a sufficiently sordid aspect to a man of the world, endowed with acute sensibility and with great intellectual and moral qualities such as Wiat possessed. His comments upon Court life in the First Satire, written immediately after his release in 1536, is the surest proof of his moral standpoint, and the little leaning he had towards a low state of morality.[1] Further proof is gathered from the letters to his son in the following year, and the *Defence*, 1541. No man has the power to write convincingly upon a moral standard of life if he does not believe in it or endeavour to act up to it himself, and it is the utter sincerity that convinces us in Wiat's writing.

[1] Bonner's accusation of viciousness is refuted in one of the finest pieces of rhetoric in the language, and the tables completely turned upon the contemptible person of his accuser.

APPENDIX G

EXAMPLES OF WIAT'S PROSE

LETTERS TO HIS SON (E. MS.)

DECLARATION TO THE COUNCIL [1] (Harln. MS.)

[1] The Defence is not included here, because it has no bearing upon the poems. It is reserved for the "Life and Letters of Sir Thomas Wiat."

LETTERS FROM SIR THOMAS WIAT TO HIS SON

No. I[1]

From him out of Spayne to his son then xiv yeres old[2]

FOR as mitch as now ye ar come to sume yeres of vnderstanding, and that you should gather within your self sume frame of honestye, I thought that I should not lese my labour holy if now I did something aduertise you to take the suer fondations and stablisht opinions that leadith to honestye. And here I call not honestye that men comonly cal honestye, or reputatid for riches, for authorite, or some like thing, but that honestye that I dare well say your Granfather (whos soule God pardon) that rather left to me then all the lands he did leaue me; that was wisdome, gentlenes, sobrenes, desire to do good, frendlines to get the loue of manye, and trougth aboue all the rest. A great part to haue al thes things is to desire to haue them: and altho Glorye and honest name are not the verye ende wherfor thes things are to be folowed, yet surly they must nedes folowe them, as light folowth fire, though it wer kindled for warmth.

Out of thes thinges the chiefest and infallible grond is the dread and Reuerens of God, wherapon shal ensue the eschewing of the contraries of thes sayd vertues, that is to say ignorans, vnkindnes, raschnes, desire of harme, vnquiet enmyte, hatred, manye and crafty falshed the verie rote of al shame and dishonestye.

[1] E. fol. 71a.

[2] MS. heading. Letters are written in an Elizabethan hand. The margin is cut away, removing some final letters.

Slightly cropped; the supplied letters are nowhere doubtful.

I say the only dred and reuerens of God that seeth al things is the defens of ye creping in of al thes mischefs into you : and for my part, altho I dare wel say ther is no man that wold his son better then I, yet on my faith I had rathir haue you liueles then subiect to thes vices.

Think and ymagine alwais that you are in presens of some honist man that you know, as Sir Jhon Russel, your fathir in law, your vnkle Parson, or some other such; and ye shal, if at ony time ye find a plesur in naughtye touchis, remember what shame it wer afore thes men to doo naughtily. And sure this imagination shal caus you remember that the plesure of a naughty dead is sone past, and that rebuke, shame and the note therof shal remayne euer. Then if thes things ye take for vayne imaginations, yet remember that it is certayn and no imagination that ye are alwaye in the presens and sight of God; and tho you see Him not, so mitch is that reuerens the more to be had for that He seeth and is not seen.

Men punisch with shame as greatist punischment on erth, ye, greater then death; but His punischment is, first, the with-drawing of His fauour and grase, and, in leuing His hand to rule the sterne, to let the ship runne without guyde to yt owne distruction, and suffreth so the man that He forsaketh to runne hedlong as subiect to al mishaps, and at last with shameful end to euirlasting shame and deth. Ye may see continual examples both of the one sort and of thothir, and the bettir, if ye mark them wel, that your self are come of.

And consider wel your good grandfathir, what things ther wer in him and his end; and they that knew him notid him thus, first and chiefly to haue a great reuerens of God and good opinion of godly things, next that ther was no man more piteful, no man more trew of his word, no man faster to his frend, no man diligenter nor more circumspect, which thing both the Kings his masters notid in him greatly. And if thes things, and specially the grace of God that the feare of God alway kept with him, had not ben, the chansis of thes trobelsome world that he was in had long ago ouirwhelmid him. This preseruid him in prison from the handes of the tirant that could find in his hart to see him rakkid, from two yeres and more prisonment in Scotland in Irons and Stoks, from the danger of sodeyn changes and commotions diuers, til that, wel-belouid of many, hatid of none, in his fair age and good reputation, godly and Christenly he went to Him, that louid him for that he always had Him in reuerens.

And of my self I may be a nere example vnto you of my foly and vnthriftines that hath as I wel deseruid broght me into a thowsand dangers and hazards, enmyties, hatreds, prisonments, despits and indignations; but that God hath of His goodnes chastizid me and not cast me cleane out of His fauour, which thing I can impute to no thing but to the goodnes of my good fathir, that I dare wel say purchasid with continual request of God His grase towards me more then I regardid or considred my self, and a litel part to the smal fear that I had of God in the most of my rage and the litel delite that I had in mischefe. You therfor, if ye be sure and haue God in your sleue, to cal you to His grase at last, ventur hardily by myne example apon naughty vnthriftines in trust of His goodnes, and besides the shame I dare lay ten to one ye shal perisch in the aduentur, for trust not that my wisch or desire of God for you shal stand you in as mitch effect as I think my fathir's did for me, we ar not all accepted of Him.

Beginne therfore betimes, make God and goodnes your fundations. Make your examples of wise and honist men, shote at the mark, be no mokker : mokkes folow them that delite therin. He shal be suer of shame that felith no grefe in othir men's shames. Haue your frends in a reuerens and think vnkindnes to be the greatist offens and lest punishid amongst men, but so mitch the more to be dread, for God is iustiser apon that alone.

Loue wel and agre with your wife, for where is noyse and debate in the hous ther is vnquiet dwelling; and mitch more wher it is in one bed. Frame wel your self to loue and rule wel and honestly your wife as your felow and she shal loue and reuerens you as her hed. Such as you are vnto her, such shal she be to you. Obey and reuerens your fathir in law as you wold me, and remember that long life folowth them that reuerens theyr fathirs and eldirs, and the blissing of God for good agrement betwen the wife and husband is fruyt of many children.

Rede oft this my lettre and it shal be as tho I had oftin writtin to you; and think that I haue herin printid a fatherly affection to you. If I may se that I haue not lost my payne, myne shal be the contentation and yours the profit. And apon condition that you folow my aduertisment, I send you God's blessing and myne, and as wel to come to honestye as to encreas of yeres.

No. 2

Again vnto his son out of Spayne about the same time

I DOUBT not but long ere this time my lettres are come to you. I remember I wrate to you in them that if you read them often it shal be as tho I had written oftin to you. For al that, I can not so content me but stil to cal apon you with my lettres. I wold not for al that that if any thing be wel warnid in thothir, you shold leaue to remember it bicaus of this new, for it is not like with aduertisments as it is with apparel, that with long wering a man castith away when he hath new. Honest techings neuir were, onles they were out of his remembrans that shold kepe and folow them, to the shame and hurt of him self. Think not also that I haue any new or chang of aduertisments to send you, but stil it is one that I wold: I haue nothing to crye and cal apon you for but honestye, honestye. It may be diuersly namid but alway it tendith to one end. And as I wrate to you last, I meane not that honestye that the comen sort callith an honist man. Trust me that honist man is as comen a name as the name of a good felow, that is to say, a dronkerd, a tauernehanter, a riotter, a gamer, a waster. So are among the comen sort al men honist men that are not knowin for manifest naughtye knaues.

Seke not, I pray the, my son, that honesty which aperith and is not in dead. Be wel assured it is no comen thing nor no comen man's iugment to iuge wel of honestye, nor it is no comen thing to come by; but so mitch it is the more goodlye for that it is so rare and strang. Folow not therfor the comen reputation of honestye; if you wil seme honist, be honist, or els seame as you are. Seke not the name without the thing, nor let not the name be the only mark you shote at; that wil folow tho you regard it not, ye, and the more you regard it, the lesse. I meane not by Regard it not, Esteme it not; for wel Ye wot honest name is goodly; but he that huntith only for that is like him that had rathir seame warme then be warme, and edgith a single cote about with a furre. Honist name is to be kept, preseruid and defendid, and not to employ al a man's wit about the studye of that, for it smellith of a glorious and ambitious fole. I say, as I wrote vnto you in my last lettirs, get the thing and the othir must of necessite folow as the shadow folowth the thing that it is of. And euin so mitch is the verye honeste bettir then the name as the thing is bettir then the shadow.

The coming to this poynte that I wold so fayne haue you haue, is to consider a man's owne self, what he is, and wherfor he is. And herin let him think verilye that so goodly a work as man is, for whom al othir things wer wroght, was not wroght but for goodly things. Aftir a man hath gottin a wil and desire to them, is first to auoyd euil and lerne that poynt alone, neuir to doo that, that within your self you find a certain grudging against. No doubt in any thing you doo, if you axe your self or examine the thing in your self afore you do it, you shal find, if it be euil, a repining against it. My son, for our Lord's loue kepe wel that repining; suffer it not to be darkid and corruptid by noughtye example, as tho any thing wer to you excusable bicaus othir men doo the same. That same repining, if it did punisch as he doth iuge, then wer no such iusticer. And of truth so doth it punisch, but not so apparantly. Here, how we deme, it is no smal grefe of a consciens that condemnith it self; but, be wel assurid, aftir this life it is a continual gnawing.

When ther is a custome gottin of auoyding to doo euil, then can a gentle corage be content to be idle and to rest without doing eny thing. Then loo had ye nede to gathir an hepe of good opinions and to get them perfectly as it wer on your fingers ends. Rest not greatly apon the approuing of them; take them as alreadye aprouid, bicaus they wer of honist mens leauings—of them. Of God ther is no question. And it is no smal help to them the good opinion of moral philosophers among whom I wold Senek wer your studye and Epictetus, bicaus it is litel, to be euir in your bosome. Thes things shal lead you to know goodly, which when a man knowth and takith plesure in them he is a best that folowth not them; no, nor he can not but folow them.

But take this for conclusion and some of al, that if God and His grace be not the fundation, nother can ye auoyd euil, nor iuge wel, nor doo any goodly thing. Let Him be fundation of al. Wil thes things, desire them ernestlye, and seke them at His hands, and knolege them to come of Him; and questionles He wil both geue you the vse and plesur in vsing them, and also reward you for them that come of Him; so liberal and good is He.

I wold fayne se that my lettres myght worke to frame you honist. And think that without that I esteme nothing of you, no not that you are my sone; for I reken it no smal deshonistye to my self to haue an vnhonist taught child. But the fault shal not be in me, I shal do the part of a fathir; and if you answer not to that I loke for at your hands, I shal as wel studye with that that I shal leaue to make sum honist man as you.

DECLARATION TO THE COUNCIL

A Declaration made by Sir Thomas Wiatt Knight of his innocence, beinge [imprisoned] vppone the falce accusation of Doctor Bonarde, Bysshope of London, ma[de to] the Councell, the yeare of Our Lorde 15[41].

PLEASE yt your good Lordshipes to vnderstonde I haue knowledge by Mr. Lieuetenant that the Kyng's pleasure is and your commaundement that I shulde wryte and declare suche thynges as haue passed me whylste I was in Themperors curte by worde, wrytinge, communinge, or receauinge with or from any man whearby I knowe my selffe to haue offended or whear by I myght rune in suspecte of offence, namlye in the tyme of that Courte beinge at Nyce and Villa Ffranka.

Fyrste; lyke as I tayke God to recorde, in Whome I trust to be saued and Whose redemtion I forsake yf wyttinglie I lye: so do I humbly in His name besyche you all that in those things that be not fresshe in my memorie no captious aduantage be taken of me, protestinge allwayes that yf I my selffe cane by anye meanes, or your lordshippes or anye other, reduce anye other thynge then I shall touche, or anie other wayes of anie thinge that I shall touche, to my remembraunce syncearely and vncolourably from tyme to tyme to declare the trouthe, in presone or owte. And for my parte I declare affirminglie, at all proffes whearby a Cristian man may be tried, that in my lyf in Cryme towarde the Maieste of the Kinge my master or enie his issue, in dede, worde, wrytinge, or wysshe I neuer offended, I neuer commytted mallyce or offence, or (as I haue presently saide before you) done thinge whearin my thought coulde accuse my conscience. As touchinge worde

H. fol. 5a.
Slightly cropped in parts.
4 1541] H. 15–. Written in the Tower early in 1541.
16 be not] H. *beinge.*

with anye the King's ennimie or treator, in my lyf I remembre not that euer I spake with anie, knowinge hym at that tyme to be a traytor or ennimie, but to Brauncetor at his apprehension in Parres and to Frogmourton at S. Dauis that wolde haue brought me a present of wyne from Pole, which processes I dowte not but it is well in youer Lordshipes' remembraunce.

I had forgott in this place a lyght fellowe, a gunner, that was an Inglysshemane and came owt of Irelande with an Irysshe traytor cawled Iames (I haue forgott his other name and dowte in that also); he coulde schant speake Inglysshe and dronken he was, and on a day I rebuked hym owte of my howse and he soughte to aduertyse me of that Iames comminge agayne, but the thinge was of no valew and I neclected them. And ther was allso a fole, an Iryshe mane, that was lame, maymed in Thempres warres, and there toke hym by the name of Rosarossa bycawse he ware a rede rose on his breste; but there was no substance of those thyngs, but yf ye requere any farther I am reddie to say to yt, tho yt be to non effecte. Writinge I neuer receauid none of anye ther beinge knowne a traytor or beinge suspecte of treasone or none afterwarde prouid a traytor, other than followithe.

Of the Erle of Estesex, beinge then as the Kinges chefe Councellor and after declared a traytor, of Pagettes a lettre beinge inclosed within a lettere of Therel of Estsex directinge an other lettre with the same to Brauncetor; Pates lettres I sent to Therel of Estsex. Of Brauncetor, not yet knowne for a traytor; of Leges, a lettre or too, he beinge in Italie, wheare vnto I aunswerde hym in substance, exhortinge hym to come and see Spayne and retorne into Inglande with me, he then not beinge suspected of anye offence to my knowledge. Of Brauncetor two or three letteres, he beinge at Tower de Himmes in Castell and I at Barcelona, concerninge my monie of the banke. This was twelue monethes before he was discouered for a traytor. Other lettres

18 **ye**] H. *thye*. 21 **the Erle of Estesex**] *i. e.* Cromwell.
25 **Of**] H. omits. 27 **hym**] H. omits.

or wrytings as suche as aboue I neuer remembre that anye came to my handys or thorow my hands vnopened but of the prestes that was my Lorde Lysters Chaplayne, which I opened and after browght them to the Kinge. Communinge with anie declared or knowne then to me a Traytor or Rebell, with sendinge of message, recommendations, aduertysmentes, fauorable tokens or wrytinges or anie suche matter, lett yt be provede and impute yt to me for Treasone. Nor I say not that for that I haue done yt so secreatlie that yt cane not be provede, but as God iudge me I am clere of thought. Receauinge, I am as clere as sendinge, &c. God knowethe what restles tormente yt hathe byne to me sens my hether commynge to examen myselffe, perusinge all my dedes to my remembraunce, whearby a malicious enimye myghte tayke aduantage by evell interpretation. But, as I complayned before your Lordshipes, yt had greued me the suspectes I haue byn in beinge in Spayne, that yt was noysed that I was ronne a-way to the bysshope of Rome; and the Kinges Maieste had so good opinion of me that, as I knowe, at my commynge home theye were punysshed that had sowne that noyse on me. And farther by examination of Mason, the which thinge, with that you name the townes of Nice and Villa Franka, renuethe the suspecte therof, wherof the substaunce and truthe of that I passed there to my remembraunce I shall declare syncerly.

At Thempres arrivall at Villa Francka, which is abowte one myle frome Nice, and wheare is a bott for Gallies, to my gallie came a seruaunte of the Byshope of London * that now is, and Doctor Haynes, aduertysinge me of ther beinge at Nice. I went with my bott withowte delay to them, and, to be shorte, I gatt them at Villa Ffranka righte ouer agaynste my awne as good as the tyme and place wolde suffer, for tho thie wer better lodged at Nice, yet my thought, the Toune beinge full of the Courte of Rome, yt was schante sure nor conueniente, nor so mette for our

26 **the Byshope of London**] *i. e.* Bonner.
* Note in margin, *Doct^{r} bonard.*

communication; thexecution therof nedes not here to be comprehended, yt was then aduertysed of, and bysydys I suppose yt be not thentente of this declaration. I, as God iudge me, lyke as I was contynually imagininge and cumpassinge what waye I myght do best seruice: so restede I not day nor nyght to hunte owte for knowledge of those thinges; I trotted contynually vp and downe that hell throughe heate and stinke from Councelloure to Embassator, from on frende to an other, but the thynges then were ether so secretly handlede or yett not in couerture that I with all myne acquayntance, and myche les theye my colloquies for anie pollice or industrie that I sawe them use, coulde gett anye knowledge. My thoughte, an Emperor, a Ffrenche Kinge, and bysshope of Rome beinge so assemblede, pretendinge an vnion of all the worlde, to be treated by the handes of my maisters mortall ennimie, I beinge present, nether hauinge knowledge of any thynge nor thilk aduertysemente from hens, that I shulde leave no stone unmoued to gett summ intelligens, altho peraduenture my colloques thought that lyttel to be ther charge, butt only to conuerte Themperor by ther lerninge.

Apone this yt chaunced that vppon a day ther was no persone att dynner with vs but we thre and Masone, and the seruaunts beinge from the burde, whether theye were gone for meate or whether I bad them go downe I remembre not, I reherste theffare, and the cure I hade for lacke of knowledge and the necessitie, and demaunded ther opynion: What yf Masone shulde insinuat hym selffe dissimblynge with Pole to sucke sumethynge worthy of knowledge in these great matters? Theye bothe thought yt good, and Masone was content to assaye yt when he shulde se tyme and occasione.

The certayne tyme, how longe I tarried after or how longe I was theare in all, one my trouthe I remembre not, but I thynke I was not there twelue dayes in all afore anye thynge done in this matter.

12, 13 a Frenche kinge, and bysshope] H. transposes *a* and *and*.

To my knowledge my couuerture for my comminge to the Kinge was made vnto me, wherin I had not so myche respecte to the offers that wer made as to the promas and thassurance that bothe thEmperor, Granduela and Cauas made vnto me, that nothinge nether with Bysshope or Kinge shulde be treated and concluded tyll I came agayne yf I came in fiftene or sixtene dayes or that the Kinge dyd sende resolution vppone these affares. This mythought was so gladsome vnto me to wyne to the Kinge, he beinge vnbounde and at libertie, so maynie dayes, with my postinge only and payne in so hyghe matters, that all my pollyces of knowledge and intelligens was cleane forgotten with me; my thought I had ynoughe. The resolution vppone these affares your Lordshippes knowethe, and the successe after shewethe what was mente then. The day passed and my returne, altho I solycited ernestlye my dyspache, the appoyntmente concluded and these Prynces departed.

Tuchynge this deuice of Mason with Pole, this is all that soundethe in anye case to my facte. And lett yt be proued that euer by Mason or anye other I sente hym worde, aduertysemente, or put worde or order in hys mouthe what he shulde saye or do other then I haue declared, and lett yt be imputed treasone vnto me.

The lyke vnto thys I vsed after at Teledo, where I vsed Mr. Ffolemans brother, and an other marchante that had byne spoyled, to seke meanes to enter into Poles lodginge and to sype who resorted thyther and what theye coulde learne, whearby I dyscouered Brauncetors treason, not onlie resortinge to Pole but playnely exhortinge them to forsake the Kinge and follow Pole; whearof I aduertysed, and by that also I knewe of Granduelas beinge there secretly with hym, apone which I gott of Granduela farther knowledge of Poles sutes and demaundys. This I dyd withowte consultation, for I had no colloque with me; but at Pares abowte thapprehension of Brauncetor I vsed Welden and Swerder and that with partysipatione bothe of Mr.

Pate and the Bysshope of Londone to be spies ouer Brauncetor and to put them selues into companie, whearby I euer knewe wheare he became, tyll the ower came that he was apprehended, Weldone beinge in the Chambre with hym. Oure Lorde defende these mene that the thinge that was bothe mente and done in the Kinges seruice shulde be preiudiced by suspecte in this behalffe.

But to returne to the matter of Mason. I mett with Themperor vppone the see afore Marcels, commynge in a bott frome Aquas Mortis, bothe in hasarde of the Mores and naughtie wether by cawse I wolde preuent Themperor and the Frenche Kinges metinge, which shulde be at Aquas Mortes; but I cam to late to breke anye thynge. Now had Themperor byne at Genes, and ther had Masone gotten occasion to entre with Pole, and he tolde me that he coulde sucke nothynge owte of hym for that he semed to suspecte hym. At Venes was I neuer; whilste this was done was I yet in Inglande, and Mason tolde me that he had wrytten to me and Therle of Estesexe what he had done, which lettres never came to my handes, nor almost a yere after to therle of Estsexe handes, as the same Erle tolde me at my comminge home, and farther tolde me how honestlye Masone had declared hym selffe and how well the King toke yt and how good lorde he was to hym, and farther declared vnto me the chaunce that, tho the lettres that Masone wrote to hym came not yet then to his hands, that in serchynge Mason's papers the mynit therof was fownde, and after how the lettre selffe came to his handes; addinge ther vnto thes wordys: "Thei mente at Masone but theie shote at the Wiatt." And I remembre well the aunswere I made was: "Theie strake at me but theie hurte me not, therefore I pray God forgiue them, but I beshrewe there hartes for ther meaninge."

Masone of this all the while neuer wrote vnto me into Spayne

1 Pate] H. *Bate*. 25 mynit] H. *mynist*. 30 beshrewe] H. *besherwe*.

25 mynit] MS. spelling *mynist*. 30 beshrewe] MS. spelling *besherwe*.

but that he was detayned with a quartayne, but I knewe by Granduela that he was detayned by examynation wherin I was suspecte, and further particuler I coulde gett nothynge of hym. And after, as yt may appere by my lettres, I solicited my comminge home for my declaration. Yf these be the matters that may bringe me in to suspecte, me semethe, yf I be not blynded by myne cawse, that the credet that an Imbassadoure hathe or owte to haue myghte well dyscharge as greate stretches as these. Yf in these matters I haue presumede to be trustie more then I was trusted, surely the zele of the Kinges seruice drewe me to yt. And I haue byne alwayes of opinion that the Kinges Maieste ether shulde sende for Imbassadours suche as he trustethe or truste suche as he sendythe.

But all ye, my good Lordes and maisters of the Councell, that hathe and shall in lyke case serue the Kinge, for Chrystes charite waye in this myne innocens as you wolde be demed in your fyrste dayes when you haue charge withowte experience; for yf yt be not by practyse and meanes that an Imbassadoure shulde haue and come to secrets, a prince were as good sende nakede lettres and to receaue nakede lettres as to be at charge for Recidencers. And yf a mane shulde be dreuen to be so scrupulouse to do nothynge withowt warrant, manye occasions of good seruice shulde schape hym.

Tochinge the Bysshope of London and Haynes calumninge in this matter, when yt shall please your Lordshippes to examen me I shall sincerlye declare vnto you the mallice that hathe moued them; and yf I myght be examyner in my owne cawse I knowe theie cane not auoyde there vntruthe in deniall of ther consent in this cawse of Masone. I besyke you humbly be my good lordes and lett not my lyf were awaye here, that paraduenture myght be better spente in some daye's deede for the Kinges

10 **drewe**] H. *drowe*. 22 **manye**] H. *mayne*. 31 **Kynges**] H. *Kyings*.

23 **schape**] i. e. *escape*. 31 **Kinges**] MS. spelling *Kyniges*.

seruice. Our Lorde put in your hartes to do with me as I haue deservyd towarde the King's Maieste.

The King's true faythefull subiecte
and seruaunte and humble orator
T. WIATT.

This withowte correctinge, sendinge,
or ouerseinge.

1, 2 **as I haue deservyd**] repeated in MS.